GROWING DOWN

GROWING DOWN
Theology and Human Nature in the Virtual Age

Jaco J. Hamman

BAYLOR UNIVERSITY PRESS

Cover design and custom illustrations by Hannah Feldmeier

This book has been catalogued by the Library of Congress with the ISBN 978-1-4813-0646-1.

Printed in the United States of America on acid-free paper with a minimum of 30 percent postconsumer waste recycled content.

I dedicate this book to Jami and Michaela.
May it assist you in discovering the art of growing down.

I remember my father, Barry Hertzog Hamman (1921–2014),
who died while I was working on this project.
He loved technology.

CONTENTS

ACKNOWLEDGMENTS

I am grateful for:

- Being a person rooted in family, friendships, and various communities.
- Engineers and visionaries who bring us technologies that enrich and transform our lives.
- Vanderbilt University for granting me teaching leave to research and write this project.
- Students in Vanderbilt Divinity School's Humanity and Technology Seminar.
- The library staff at Vanderbilt University. I am especially indebted to MAT Trotter and Chris Benda.
- Academic conferences and faith communities for allowing me to reflect on and learn about our relationship with technology.

- Carey Newman (editor), Emily Brower (assistant editor), Diane Smith (production and design director), and Baylor University Press. Thank you for believing in this project and providing guidance that enriched its argument.
- The readers and reviewers who will enter into conversation with this book.
- Michelle, my life partner. I receive love, support, and affirmation while you endure early morning alarms, preoccupied moments, and evening weariness.

INTRODUCTION

A great deal of growing is growing downwards . . .
—D. W. Winnicott, "Residential Care as Therapy"[1]

Intuitively we know that something is not right, even if we do not know exactly what is wrong. Or we sense something is wrong, but we do not know why or how to initiate change: a two-year-old fusses to get her parents' attention, and they hand her a tablet wrapped in a brightly colored protective case. On the digital tether their daughter's discontent becomes focused attention as she disappears into her own world. Family friends are gathering to share a meal; the children arrive with phones in hand. Despite encouragement to enjoy each other's company, they continue to be preoccupied with their phones, periodically sharing a screenshot with brief conversation and laughter. Another family is driving to their favorite restaurant. Except for the driver, everyone fingers a phone. The driver gets his fix at stop signs and red lights. No one says a word or notices the street vendor trying to establish eye contact. Upon arrival, they sit down with their phones at their sides. Any conversation remains brief, even staccato, with "Good," "Yes," and "No" forming complete sentences. Would-be lovers sit across from the family. The lovers are anxious about the intimacy that is being formed and find relief in fingering their social media apps; there is no conversation of substance. A student is lonely and bored; he swipes a dating app to find a hook-up. The chase seems to animate him. He has every expectation that he will find a partner this evening.

We know that the technologies we deem smart have changed our interactions with ourselves and with loved ones, friends, coworkers, and even strangers, possibly irreversibly so. Between familial, societal, and technological pressures, we grow up in ways that minimize our relationships and lives. We seem mostly content with how things are developing, even as we sense that things might not be right.

To grow down in a world that promotes and awards growing up is courageous wisdom. Like all wisdom, this wisdom is not easily attained. The forces that beckon children and teenagers to be mini-adults, that propel young and old to reach for a phone or tablet to break a moment of boredom, and that turn everyone into passive consumers to be mined by corporations, are powerful and mediated through screens. Thanks to a searchable Internet, knowledge and answers abound. However, the wisdom needed to become a mature person, to find security in intimate relationships, to have the ability to sustain deep conversation, to build community, and to flourish in life does not come through a screen.

The question that drives this inquiry is the question of being and becoming a person in a technological world. News media, tech blogs, forums, and advertisements remind us that our favorite phone, computer, or smart watch is to be updated with a faster processor delivering longer battery life. Voices discuss the potential and peril of artificial intelligence, which is surely destined to surpass human ingenuity. At technology conventions caring robots are introduced to possibly assist Alzheimer's patients one day. The questions being asked are predominantly technological in nature. Technology, we are led to believe, will take humanity to new heights. *Growing Down* embraces the inevitability of technology in our lives but asks, who is the person using technology?

Human nature, especially since the 1990s, has been greatly influenced by communications technologies: phones, tablets, computers, consoles, and wearables. We find ourselves in a world driven by technological advances but also colored by financial uncertainty and lack of employment. Societies are divided by classism and racism and crippled by homophobia and xenophobia. Nations are wounded by wars and vulnerable to extremism and mass migrations. We are seemingly helpless in the face of global concerns such as climate change, viral pandemics, and poverty. That the world longs for hopeful change is no surprise. Who will rise as change agents? How will they be nurtured and empowered to work across differences and facilitate the well-being of all? Every society needs compassionate, empathic, mature, and wise citizens who embody life-giving values. Because technological advances continually outpace research on technology's effects, having a foundational understanding of human nature to guide our discernment is important. It is comforting to know that the self naturally knows something about growing down, a state of vulnerability and security, of relationship, creativity, and hope.

Infants and young children have many abilities that they tend to lose as they grow up. They constantly seek the face of another person and use their vulnerability to foster interdependence. Their survival depends on building intimacy that fuels care and provision, and they know how to work with caregivers to have their needs met. By doing so children attune themselves to the emotional places the adults around them occupy. They have an active imagination and return to play behavior. All these traits—natural to children born into caring environments—are diminished the moment technology enters a setting or relationship. Adults may lack these basic skills altogether, greatly affecting the ways personal and professional lives are managed. How does this happen? Did things truly go "wrong" or is there a new "right" way to live? What can we do to counter ways of being that diminish human nature while maintaining a relationship with the technology we love? If relational, emotional, and conversational skills were lost along the way, how does one reclaim those skills as an adult?

Gaining an understanding of what it means to be confident and secure, someone with creativity and vitality—being a whole person—is a good place to begin a transformative journey. Friendships can be nurtured, and new skills in self-engagement or being in relationships with others can be acquired. Becoming a parent is often a moment when one can do some rewriting of one's past. Such is the power of welcoming an infant into one's life. Relationships with friends, counselors and mentors, but also life-changing and traumatic experiences can be the invitation for realignment. Illness or education can provide a moratorium of sorts, a suspension of life that allows for the birth of new personal, relational, spiritual, and/or professional identities.

This book explores the formation of a self and the nature, structure, and origins of interpersonal relationships as we increasingly relate to and rely upon communications technologies. Embracing one's humanity in a world driven by technology, financial uncertainty, wars, conflicts, and global concerns takes intentionality, especially for those desiring personal growth and wanting to make a difference in the world. The process of growing down complements and challenges the natural process of growing up, which is accelerating. Grown-downs—those who embrace the journey of growing down—cultivate an imagination that not only asks *why*, and enlivens objects seen and unseen, but also fuels a life of exuberance and creativity. This imagination can bring relief in moments of boredom, awaken play, and ensure that life remains fresh, mysterious, and even adventurous. Grown-downs recognize that mindful living, loving, and working have more potential than speeding ahead and doing what comes naturally with a phone in one's hand. They know that care and compassion are gifts that return with interest when freely bestowed on others. Many grown-ups rarely experience this life first seen in early infancy and childhood. When one grows down like a tree, with roots deeply anchored in secure foundations, seeking the nurture of others comes naturally. Growing down, however, cannot be reduced to a spiritual quest as if it belongs only to the soul. Rather, it demands every aspect of one's being and confronts a culture that rewards persons mature beyond their years, a culture that dangles promises and brings narrowly measured expectations of greatness or success.

Toward an Anthropology Inspired by Winnicott's Object Relations Theory

"Today," French psychoanalyst André Green reminds us, "psychoanalysis looks like a language spoken in many tongues." At professional meetings he experiences "a pretense of tolerance: behind the silence, there is frequently disagreement, disapproval, contempt, if not total misunderstanding."[2] *Growing Down* explores core aspects of human nature by using primarily one spoken tongue with a variety of dialects—British object relations theory—along with psychodynamic psychology. "Object relations can be defined as a designation for the subject's mode of relation to his world; this relation is the entire complex out-come of a particular organization of the personality . . . [It implies] interrelationship . . . involving not only the way the subject constitutes his objects but also the way these objects shape his actions."[3] One's mode of relating to the world, ani-mate and inanimate, is set early (pre-oedipal), not in permanent and deterministic ways, but certainly in persistent ways that can be identified and examined into adulthood. At its core, object relations theory recognizes the internalization of one's primary caregivers as a core human trait. Unlike Sigmund Freud's drive model — built around concepts such as the id, ego, and superego, and libido, eros, and thanatos — object relations theory values one's internal and external relationships.[4]

Dialects within the one language of object relations the-ory, to continue Green's metaphor, were introduced by Mela-nie Klein, D. W. Winnicott, Joan Riviere, W. R. D. Fairbairn, Harry Guntrip, Masud Kahn, Charles Rycroft, Enid Balint, Margaret Mahler, and Margaret Little. *Growing Down* draws extensively on the developmental framework of D. W. Winn-icott (1896–1971), a pediatric psychoanalyst, which is placed in conversation with our love of and reliance on communications technologies. Winnicott, who left no unified theory, is known for his homespun constructs such as "the good enough mother," "primary maternal preoccupation," "transitional phenomena," and "the true and false self." He wrote in a deceptively simple style, appealing to common people. His nontraditional approach to therapy and independent spirit; his idealism, romanticized language, and use of paradox; and his tendency to draw on other analysts' work without recognition received criticism from his peers. Still, analyst James Grotstein declares that "Winnicott, like rare old wine, seems to age nicely," and analysts return to his contributions to understand human nature.[5] The turn to virtual reality has renewed interest in Winnicott's work, especially his thoughts on the intermediate area of experiencing.[6]

Winnicott's emphasis on the role mothers play in establishing the emotional health of an infant and his lack of addressing the father's role opened him up to feminist critique. Psychoanalyst Jessica Benjamin questions Winnicott's infantocentric view of human development and the "ordinary devoted mother" as someone who had no personal need or voice, a mother becoming "preoccupied" with her child almost to the point of being psychotic.[7] Analysts Janice Doane and Devon Hodges, adds to Benjamin's critique of the good enough mother:

> Many feminist advocates of object relations theory believe that [Winnicott] has encouraged a liberating focus on mothers and daughters, women's nurturing capacities, and maternal ways of thinking, all topics that mark a turn away from patriarchal systems. Other feminists [believe] that this quite marketable literature about motherhood is a sign of feminism's embrace of traditional notions of femininity at a time of cultural backlash against women's efforts to expand their domain beyond the home.[8]

Some feminists highlight the thematic overlap between object relations theory and feminism: the importance of relationships, dependence amidst autonomy, and the importance of the mother-infant dyad.[9] Other feminists, however, remain critical of Winnicott, asking: When Winnicott writes about "good enough" mothering, "What views of motherhood does he endorse? What is 'good enough' mothering? Good enough according to whom? How are standards of maternal propriety established and sustained?"[10]

Growing Down does not narrowly focus on the role of mother, but on the holding environment parents or primary caregivers create for infants and children. This environment, as would be true for an infant, is relational, social, dialectical, cultural, and historical. Environments that are loving and caring, with much face-to-face engagement and touch, are proven to be conducive to healthy infant development vis-à-vis settings where children are rarely engaged, touched, or loved. This book provides a view of human nature in the glow of screens as the main clause—elements not immune to critique from psychoanalysis' "many tongues."

Because Winnicott is closely identified with the Wesleyan and Anglican traditions and because he identified religion as one location of creative living and of cultural experience, elements of a Judeo-Christian anthropology can be found in Growing Down.[11] Moreover, I am a pastoral theologian partaking in the "the art of making space for others to grow."[12] Pastoral theologians weave a tapestry using threads of different psychologies, sacred texts, theories of religion, and approaches to culture.[13] Religions are often lived experiences and spiritual practices, but they include theological reflection and draw on the wisdom within Scripture and other sacred texts. This wisdom anticipates conversations, habits, and practices around our handheld devices that lead to human flourishing. Growing Down thus moves toward a Christian anthropology and critical analysis of our relationship with technology as described in the subtitles of each chapter. Elements of a Winnicottian psychodynamic anthropology are explicit, whereas a Christian (or religious) anthropology remains implicit, even as pastoral theological reflection and biblical hermeneutics permeate the book. A Christian anthropology desiring to speak into culture and society needs to reckon with the wisdom offered from the diverse disciplines informing us on our human nature or else it will become irrelevant to all but a few like-minded individuals. Growing Down welcomes a constructive theological exploration of humanity's relationship with technology, but does not offer such a theology.[14]

The Discernment of Meaning

Growing Down seeks to inform a conversation for those interested in human nature, especially those who are curious about the meaning of the personal rituals and habits we have formed around technologies with small screens. Discerning meaning is inherent to the psychoanalytic project and to living a life of mindfulness and intentionality.

A boy was referred to Winnicott because his parents felt he was obsessed with string.[15] The boy would join tables and chairs together with string and once tied a rope around his sister's neck, alarming his parents. Having listened to the parents and their history of parenting, Winnicott played a collaborative game with the boy. The boy communicated to Winnicott that he feared separation and tying things together was his way of denying that fear. It so happened that during the first few years of his life, the boy was separated from his mother on a number of occasions. Winnicott reminded the mother that, as a phone connects people, the boy used string to seek connection with her, but also with his father.

Winnicott did not impart blame, but encouraged the mother to talk with her son about this fear and his need for secure relationships. Initially the mother found the advice silly, yet she had the conversation with her son. After the conversation, the boy's need to tie things together with string greatly diminished, returning a few times around anxious moments. With his parents addressing his need for security, the boy's use of string receded even in those moments. String, this case reminds us, is a form of communication that extends to other forms of communication. It is a mirror or an extension of the boy's inner life and has symbolic meaning even as it keeps things from falling apart or from getting lost.

Mindful that everyday behaviors have meaning, this project originated from asking specific questions: What are the personal meanings of the communications technologies we rely on? What does one's relationship with a phone communicate about oneself, one's inner and outer worlds? What is the attraction to enter into virtual worlds? What visions of human nature does technology project or instill? Questions of meaning, value, and purpose have to be explored. Honoring humanity's complex nature, we understand that discerning meaning is deeply personal and always relational, and it requires wisdom. A quick answer will not suffice.

On Growing Down

The process of growing down is rich and takes intentionality. It is an arduous journey toward a second birth of sorts, one best informed by religion, philosophy, psychology, sociology, and other disciplines. Growing up, especially when done too fast, leads to the lack of core aspects of being the person one hopes to be, a person who will participate constructively and justly in society. The references to growing down also carry an explicit invitation: growing down is the reclamation of core aspects of oneself in relationship and becoming a responseable, ethical, and caring person.

Winnicott, writing that "[a] great deal of growing is growing downwards . . . [to] become small enough to get through the little hole called dying," brings the challenge of learning how to be dependent again, to be vulnerable enough to be held, and to grow secure enough to face the biggest unknown, death.[16] One needs to learn how to let go of visions of omnipotence—I can create my own future—and independence—I do not need other people—to not only live, but die well. Letting go of a sense of omnipotence and independence in the face of uncertainty is a sign of maturity. Winnicott named death a small hole. Life, of course, is filled with small holes, too.

W. E. B. Du Bois, renowned African American philosopher and social activist, names growing down as a key task of being a student and a university in a speech he gave at Fisk University in 1933. "[The education] of youth in a changing world is a puzzling problem," he states. "Instead of the university growing down and seeking to comprehend in its curriculum the life and experience, the thought and expression of lower classes, it almost invariably tended to grow up and narrow itself to a sublimated elite of mankind."[17] Du Bois' argument is this: students and teachers who do not wrestle with slavery, racism, and poverty but who come to university to join the wealthy, the powerful, and the elite—to climb the social ladder—are on a fatal path. Universities, Du Bois asserts, do growing up well. He argues for applied knowledge, knowledge that addresses racism and poverty and that challenges wealth or power, for applied knowledge is like a plant without roots.[18] "Narrow" selves know loneliness and maintain a world where the rich become richer and the poor poorer. Such selves cannot liberate themselves or others. Students and graduates with applied knowledge, Du Bois envisioned, would work toward societal integrity. Little may have changed since 1933 as society creates and rewards selves groomed since childhood and now in virtual spaces to experience success and join the elite. When one does not live up to society's expectations, one is easily overlooked and forgotten. Contemporary education continues the grooming process identified by Du Bois. Students arrive as packaged selves wrapped up in parental and societal expectations.[19]

Psychologist James Hillman also informs a focus on growing down. In *The Soul's Code: In Search of Character and Calling*, he writes, "Descent takes a while. We grow down, and we need a long life to get on our feet."[20] When persons ascend too fast and anxiety and loneliness sets in, Hillman sees them taking a "downer." They climb an imaginary societal or economic ladder, like Jacob's angels, a ladder most often given to them by parents, teachers, other authorities, and popular culture.[21] We want to know that we are on track, that the promise we carry and the promises we received will come true. For Hillman, personal well-being and spiritual and emotional maturity are not found by moving up or even by growing up, but actually in the paradox of descending, by growing down. He draws on Greek thought, which encouraged growing down to Hades, and on Carl Jung, who wrote that "in every adult there lurks a child—an eternal child, something that is becoming, is never completed, and calls for unceasing care, attention, and education. That is the part of the human personality which wants to develop and become whole."[22] Hillman is correct in saying that growing down is the only path to take, but taking one's whole being on the journey— and not just one's soul—changes everything.

Multiple Intelligences for a Technological Age

In the following chapters, the psychodynamic thought of Winnicott is placed in a specific framework that posits certain intelligences needed to thrive and feel alive. Six intelligences are identified:

Self Intelligence: The wisdom that neither *act* (doing something) nor *being* (passively waiting, resting) defines the embodied self as it longs for security, identity, and transformation.

Relational Intelligence: Growing in the art of being in authentic, loving, caring, and ethical relationships with persons and easygoing, balanced relationships with things.

Transitional Intelligence: The ability to traverse three worlds: the inner-subjective, the outer-objective, and the potential space in-between, mindful of the unique contributions each world brings to the Other, the Divine, culture, and nature.

Reparative Intelligence: The courage of discovering the truth of one's childhood and life, seeking restoration for oneself, and facilitating the restoration of persons, relationships, communities, and nature with compassion, care, and empathy.

Playground Intelligence: The capacity to rely on play behavior to build a sense of self, to deepen relationships, and to move effortlessly between inner and outer worlds.

Technological Intelligence: The art to discern the impact of technology on oneself as well as one's relationships with the self, the O/other, culture, and nature while engaging and being able to evaluate digital and virtual content and objects.

These intelligences anticipate a range of abilities shaped by one's environment even as the abilities shape the environment in turn. Their origins can be traced to early infancy, but they inform life until one reaches the small hole of death. Discovering the meaning of these intelligences is a responsibility of discernment no one can escape without significant personal and professional cost.

To grow down implies becoming an authentic human being with all the complexity human nature represents and the challenges and opportunities life brings. Not every person matures into a grown-down. Many find safety in abstractions and in thinking their feelings, whereas others can engage emotion with empathy and compassion. Some persons remain interpersonally awkward or exploitative, unable to play or collaborate with others or burdened by loneliness while living lives of constant reactivity, void of any creative responsiveness. Others do not partake constructively in a world in need of a fresh look at global and ecological crises. Those who started their grown-up life in early childhood rarely feel alive as they strain under the emotional and relational burdens they carry. Powerful forces propel them toward success, consumption, and insatiable ideals, but they find that the ladder they climb is unending.

The journey of growing down that starts shortly after birth quickens at times, as mentioned. *Growing Down* seeks to accelerate this journey, for the path is an invitation with promises that deliver. It is for real people, especially ones frequently entering virtual worlds who know that because technology is "neither good nor bad; nor [. . .] neutral," one's use of technology demands discernment.[23]

1

SELF INTELLIGENCE
Toward a Theology of Being an "I Am"

Don't ask yourself what the world needs. Ask yourself what makes
you come alive and then go do that. Because what the world needs
is people who have come alive.
— Howard Thurman, personal advice to Gil Bailie[1]

There is "[something] both attractive and repulsive about
that saying [I am]," writes biblical scholar Michael Willett
Newheart.[2] He makes this statement thinking of God telling
Moses, "I am who I am" and Jesus drawing on those words
with his "I am the bread of life" statement. Theologically, being
an "I am" reflects the image of the Creator. Tradition histori-
cally interpreted the "I am" in terms of independence, individualism, and being a rational being, but increasingly theology sees
a self in terms of mutuality, responsiveness, and having a sense
of purpose and meaning—a sense of vocation. God's and Jesus'
"I am" statements are but two of many memorable statements:
"I am Spartacus!"; "I think therefore I am" (René Descartes);

"I am only one, but still I am one" (Helen Keller); "Ich bin ein Berliner" (President John F. Kennedy); "I'm a woman in progress" (Oprah), "I am whatever you say I am" (Eminem); "I'm good thinking outside the box" (will.i.am); "I am aware of all the insecurities I have" (Taylor Swift); and, "I text, therefore I am" (found on Google). To say "I am" reflects agency, self-confidence, and personal purpose. It can also reflect uncertainty, insecurity, confusion, and anxiety. Invariably one's "I am" communicates.

To be a self or an "I am" is arguably the biggest nonphysical need one has. It surpasses one's identity, though the two are intricately linked. The self is increasingly being scripted — one is urged to live according to another's narrative — and one's identity is becoming virtual and under threat of being hacked. One's sense of self is exposed when it is under threat, when it is confused, or when one posts brief snapshots of oneself online. "Selfie" as the *Oxford Dictionary*'s word of 2013 and the hashtag *#Iam*, are two examples of the need to be and to express a self. When tragedy hits or societal questioning reminds us of systemic injustice, "I am" hashtags are tweeted to express public outcry and lament, whether *#JeSuisCharlie* or *#Icantbreathe*.

Howard Gardner first put us onto intelligences.[3] His intelligences are linguistic, logical-mathematical, spatial, bodily kinesthetic, musical, interpersonal, intrapersonal, and naturalist. It was psychologist and journalist Daniel Goleman's "emotional intelligence" (EQ), however, that went beyond classrooms into boardrooms and other professional places.[4] For Goleman, EQ describes self-awareness, self-management, motivation, empathy, and social skills. Persons with a high EQ can reason about and perceive emotion in themselves and in others and can use emotions to enhance thought, behavior, and discernment. *Growing Down* identifies Self Intelligence, being smart about the self, as foundational to EQ, even if the two intelligences overlap in interest. Self Intelligence is the wisdom that neither act (doing something) nor being (passively waiting or resting) defines the embodied self as it longs for security, identity, and transformation.

Despite the essential nature of the self, defining it is a vexing problem. The question, "What is a person/self?" demands knowledge beyond an answer, and even then, knowledge falls short. William James (1842–1910), an influential philosopher and psychologist, saw the self as "*the sum total of all that a man CAN call his,* not only his body and his psychic powers, but his clothes and his house, his wife and children." For James, the self includes one's possessions, reputation, and even one's bank account. Other physical objects, such as one's childhood home or birth country, also become extensions of the self. James' self has interiority and includes the internalized images of oneself, parents, loved ones, strangers, and God. These images are alive—one can talk to oneself or a beloved departed—and cannot be erased, though one can change one's relationship with these internalized objects. When possessions "wax and prosper, he feels triumphant; if they dwindle and die away, he feels cast down," James writes, "not in the same degree for each thing, but in much the same way for all."[5] James was one of the first psychologists to explore the fact that persons are extended selves where both "me" and "mine" form the "I am." Today, the sum total of who a person is includes a phone, a laptop, a computer, and numerous online and virtual identities. When one is disconnected from these technologies, the fear and anxiety that one might be missing out on something increases.

The self has many parts, some biological and others not, some internal and others external, all shaped over years within relationships and through experiences, but always inseparable from the physical body. Grown-downs embrace this complex self as they unlock personal and relational potential. It did so for psychologist Carl Jung. Jung dreamed he was in an unfamiliar two-story house, which he knew represented his self.[6] He was in the upper story with old furniture and precious paintings. When he recognized that the lower level is unfamiliar to him, he descended one floor. The floor on this level was dark and older, dating from the fifteenth century, with medieval furnishings. He discovered a stairway to a cellar. He descended into what looked like a Roman building. His interest was intense, and when he pulled on a ring, a stone slab moved to reveal yet another stairway leading down. Down he went to discover a cave with a dust floor cut out of rock. Jung saw pottery and some bones, as if a historic, primitive culture lived there. When he noticed two human skulls, he promptly woke from his dream.

The dream, Jung says, was an invitation to discover the depths of his self and became pivotal in developing his psychology. It also indicated a core aspect of growing down, which is discovering the complex parts and dynamics from which the self is built, layers of sorts with fault lines that allow what is deep to surface at times. This chapter invites discovering the self in seven interrelated, psychodynamic ways informed by object relations theory. These aspects bespeak the propensity of Winnicott's thought to draw on the obvious, to resist dichotomous thinking, and to partake in the psychoanalytic tradition. Specifically, the chapter explores the self's need for a holding environment, the self as a psyche-soma, the self as neither male nor female, the self as true *and* false, the sexual self, the self believing in itself, and the self's constant desire to be transformed.

The Self Needs to Be Held

Cesaria Evora, the queen of Cape Verdean music, has a distinct, soulful voice. The *morna* music found in taverns on her island is intimate, unhurried, and inviting. Her voice awakens *sodade* (or *saudade*), a longing difficult to name. This longing is appropriate for raw moments such as birth or death. Anticipating the birth of their firstborn, a young couple chose Evora's voice to greet their newborn. Evora fills the hospital suite where the blinds have been drawn to protect against the intrusion of light and to create the right ambiance. The infant apparently loves her welcome, taking the breast readily and sleeping, well, like a baby. In the adjacent room, another couple welcomes its newest member. NASCAR races over the television screen and through the room. People come and go with the pace of a pit crew. The baby cries — a lot. A third baby was born prematurely and was rushed to a neonatal unit where concerned parents and nurses gather. Tubes feed and lights give warmth. The baby's tiny hand grasps a pinkie finger when it is offered. The first few weeks after the baby's birth are spent under lights and in contexts of concern. A fourth baby is given up for adoption to a loving family by a mother unable to care for her. There is a good likelihood that the forces of relinquishment and adoption will remain intimate companions on this baby's journey toward being a grown-down. Knowing one's birth narrative and the experiences that surrounded early childhood can inform and validate one's sense of self.

Any loving, caring adult can provide a welcoming environment to an infant. The holding environment, a metaphor Winnicott introduced to describe both a relationship and a setting, speaks not only to a mother and her baby, but to all relationships that welcomed that baby.[7] Winnicott's mothers, feminist scholars showed us, is often romanticized and idealized, rarely tired or fatigued or frustrated, despite Winnicott using good enough language to describe motherhood and identifying eighteen reasons why mothers hate their babies.[8] Still, the metaphor of holding informs parenting, the therapeutic practice, and life in general. In her book *Holding and Psychoanalysis: A Relational Perspective*, Joyce Anne Slochower highlights the paradoxical nature of nurture, that parents experience deep ambivalence even as they create a holding environment for their infant. She reminds us that all persons, young and old, need to be held.[9] As a setting of mutuality, holding creates the illusion of attunement through the acceptance and reception of feeling states. Attunement is an illusion, Slochower reminds us, because true attunement is not possible. Still, holding awakens a sense of safety and nurture, whether for the infant held by a parent, a person held in a psychotherapeutic setting, or a person held in friendship. A holding environment is a setting that allows one to merely be (without doing much), because need is met and meaning is discovered (and not given). Here, touch eclipses sight as through touch one is perceived. The holding environment is important, for it provides a sense of safety, protecting against emotional and physical impingements and dangers.

Adults need holding to feel loved or when life's circumstances remove a sense of safety and belonging, when a reparative experience is needed or during liminal moments. Liminal moments bring us in direct contact with the living God. Increasingly, we find ourselves held by virtual spaces, a tendency that is explored in these pages.

The attraction to enter virtual spaces is not just that these spaces connect persons, stimulate minds, make collaboration possible, are fun, or save one from boredom, even though they do these things rather well. Virtual spaces mirror the holding environment that welcomes a child into the world. As a new mother has a near-constant presence to her infant, so too virtual spaces are ever present and, in that sense, reliable. Touch is pertinent as one reaches for a phone, a screen, or the trackpad on a laptop. Virtual spaces allow for personal identity, communication, recognition, relationship and mutuality, excitement, and restoration—dynamics first experienced in the holding environment of early childhood. In many ways, virtual spaces allow for more freedom than one finds in nonvirtual holding environments. Still, virtual spaces hold the same promise and peril as other holding environments. As primary environments disappoint and injure, which they inevitably do, so too do virtual spaces. The gift and danger of virtual technologies are not that they provide us with a new experience, but rather that they allow us to re-experience intimacy with ourselves, others, and the environment. We create this intimacy on demand by merely picking up a phone or tablet, drawing on a sense of omnipotence not unlike infants who have not yet discovered there is a not-me beyond the me. As strange as it might sound, by holding a phone, one experiences something experienced before. In a world where "Who am I?" is never separate from the forces of production and commodification, expectations dictate and uncertainty reigns. "What will I produce, how much money will I make, and who will make money off me?" is not a life-giving paradigm to live by.

As a container of warmth, care, and reliability, holding allows one to grow down and discover self-holding, the ability to feel without judgment or confusion or passing anxiety along to others. Being held implies intimacy, and Winnicott describes the act in terms of an infant having a "sort of intercourse with the environment at the time the birth arrives."[10] The desire for such intimacy remains throughout life and is a core aspect of being a self.

The Self Is a Psyche-Soma

The self is naturally placed in the body. Because we have been created from the dust of the stars, however, our relationship with the body has been ambivalent. We will easily deny the body for the sake of the soul, the mind, or increasingly, for virtuality. Religions often partake in such denial. Psychodynamic theorists and clinicians are arguably more interested in the body than the mind. This interest should not be confused with culture's pre-occupation with the body, whether it is the thin body, the black body, the gendered body, or the body that needs to be kept alive at all costs. Popular culture brings the paradox of us being more embodied than ever, yet we have lost our relationship with our bodies. Self Intelligence recognizes that the only place one truly indwells is the *soma*–one's body.

While being held in infancy, a baby discovers ways to feel at one with his or her body. When tensions come to the baby and the internal and external holding inevitably fail, those tensions often enter the body as a symptom. Sometimes the mind takes control, resulting in the body losing the ability to feel. In extreme situations one can dissociate from one's body, at which point the ability to participate in everyday life ceases. With the mind taking control, thinking one's feelings is common, even if the body harbors painful memories. Psychosomatic symptoms and a rational approach to affective worlds inhibit personal, relational, and professional flourishing. Symptoms are a burden, and having no affect removes the possibility of feeling real. As fingerprints and footprints remain in dust, the body catalogues its experiences, which requires no language or consciousness, to surprise us later. The surprise can come as an eating disturbance (often hunger) or a migraine or menstrual ache; as allergies and asthma; as rashes, hemorrhoids, and gastrointestinal difficulties; or as stammering, ticks, bodily movements, and fatigue. The creativity of the body is endless, as every person has a preferred way to embody tension. This dynamic shows the body's intricate relation to the *psyche*, that part of the self that imaginatively places feelings in the body and its functions.[11]

As canaries in mines warned miners long ago against potential toxic gasses, so too do symptoms warn against a self whose coping mechanisms are insufficient, a self about to be compromised. A self with mature defenses such as humor, anticipation, and altruism rarely experiences psychosomatic symptoms. Still, psychosomatic symptoms are signs of hope, the hope being that the necessary emotional and relational connections will be made to no longer need the symptom. To know the self is to know how the psyche places feelings in the body and to explore the sounds the body makes, the smells it discharges, the twitches it has, the weight it holds or needs to gain, and the cravings it has.[12] Winnicott tells of a little boy who had stomachaches: "I often get asked to see children who have pains that have not yet been localized. This boy had not yet decided where to have the pain, but it had something to do with his inside. Actually he himself had not yet decided even to have the pain, but he had something. This something was to do with mother's having just had a baby. He believed he had a baby inside. It must be a boy baby. He did not want to lose the baby, would prefer to keep it inside."[13] Unlike this boy, who yet has to decide to have the pain and where to locate it, adults readily have localized pain.

Therapist Nitza Yarom's *Psychic Threats and Somatic Shelters* explores the human tendency that "whatever threatens us to feel, think, and remember is easily and unconsciously channeled into our bodily practice."[14] Yarom, who is in private practice in Tel-Aviv, reminds us that gaining an interest in the intimate relationship between one's body, its symptoms, and the personal experiences one has or had is central to vital living. Children, she writes, can "learn to identify distress in terms of pain (in the stomach or the head) or somatic difficulties (in breathing and other somatic difficulties) and in terms of pain killers and other medications for those problems . . ."[15] Psychic shelters, as Yarom refers to symptoms, are witnessed by loved ones, friends, colleagues, teachers, and mentors. Like the proverbial elephant in the room, however, they remain mostly unaddressed.

Yarom introduces her readers to Sean, whose parents divorced, making him into the man of the house as a teenager. With his mother starting a career and his father a new family, Sean changed from a good boy into an impulsive teenager. He developed facial and shoulder tics and profuse sweating, gained considerable weight, and had difficulty breathing. Yarom writes, "The tics and the fatness that Sean develops at the beginning of his adolescent development . . . serve as a 'second skin'—a psychodynamic defense, which assists him in transforming from his mother's 'good boy' . . . into a budding young man who searches his own way without due support. . . . He 'sweats' in growing up."[16] All these symptoms negatively affected his social life. He started skipping school and got in trouble. The narrative he lived by, however, was, "Everything is under control."[17] In working with Yarom, Sean discovered that he communicated through his body. Empowered to not only name his emotions, but to feel them, Sean is closing the gap that developed between his psyche and his soma. As seen with Sean, a psychosomatic symptom often contains elements of the tension it holds. He could not "sweat" life and now sweats. What goes against one's grain can cause a migraine; what cannot be stomached presents itself as acid reflux; and the emotional relationship that smothers can bring on asthma.

Yarom also discusses Monique, who came from a family where her father indulged her with food while her mother was constantly dieting.[18] The mixed messages from her holding environment led to anorexia as a teenager, which she overcame. At the time she sought the services of Yarom, Monique used recreational drugs and added frequent sexual encounters to her practices. With men, she felt submissive and lost, but physically desired. They took her emotionally to similar "bad places" that she once visited as an anorexic. After dispassionate sex, she felt sad and filled with despair; she sometimes had asthma attacks.

Monique identified a connection between her father's lack of attention and her seeking evasive and unstable men. She felt her father wanted a boy instead, and as a result, as she matured into a young woman, her anorexia set in. With Yarom, Monique explored the emotional significance of her asthma, her need for immediate sexual satisfaction, and her relationship with food. Monique learned that she can hold her loneliness and found that her hunger was returning. She was grieving, too, for losing a symptom is like losing an old friend.

What happens to the symptoms the body carries as we increasingly engage with technology and seek virtual experiences? Of course, the illusion can be there that the ways we engage with technology have nothing to do with our bodies. Or maybe we believe that after thousands of years of somatizing, we suddenly stopped doing so in the technological age. It is not necessary to definitively answer the question raised or solve the problem of somatization in a technological age. Self Intelligence complicates matters even as it provides visions of human nature. It is naïve to think that we stop somatizing only because we hold phones and tablets in our hands. Rather, the opposite can be expected. The constant exposure to the curated lives of others, the anxiety and fearmongering that drive news media, and even the blue light being emitted from our screens all come home to one's body. Playing with a symptom one's body shelters, whether depression, anxiety, or insomnia, is courageous. Asking how the symptom might be related to the rituals and practices one has with technology or to experiences had in digital spaces may lead to new personal insights. Our growing relationship with technology does not naturally encourage deeper knowledge about being a psyche-soma, about being an embodied person.

Self Intelligence invites saying "I am my body." It affirms persons as fearfully and wonderfully made, as the psalmist states.

The Self Is Male/Female

Before it was shown that binaries, such as male and female, black and white, or rich and poor, most often sustain power and privilege in ways that do not serve personhood or societal living, psychoanalysts argued for the integration of opposites and the embrace of paradox. Sigmund Freud, for instance, argued that humans are *polymorphous perverse* — "perverse" here not being a judgment, but an identification of the diverse ways one finds sexual pleasure. For Freud we are bisexual, with culture calling forth one heterosexual orientation in adolescents. Jung, in turn, drawing on Greek thought, gave us insights into the *anima* (the unconscious inner feminine element in men; the spirit that gives life and embraces affection) and the *animus* (the unconscious male element in women; that which fuels logic and creativity and facilitates procreation, but also seeks control and power), the results of internalizing parental images (or *imagos*).[19] Psychodynamic theory accepts the fact that every person carries significant opposites seeking integration in his or her person. As such, this conversation about being bisexual (Freud) and the anthropomorphic archetypes of the unconscious mind (Jung) is different from contemporary conversation about gender and identity as social constructs. Whether one is male, female or transgendered; or heterosexual, homosexual, or bisexual, the integrative task of psychoanalytic and psychodynamic theory remains.

Winnicott followed Freud and especially Jung by stating that every person is male/female. Rather than translating his contribution into a modern idiom, we will keep his rather sexist language. "We have to allow for both a male and female element in boys and men and girls and women," Winnicott writes.[20] His contribution does not directly speak to the societal views of being male, female, or transgendered (gender), nor does it speak directly to the desire for male or female sexual objects (hetero-, homo-, or bisexuality). For every person, the male/

female element remains, challenging a world where masculinity is often valued over femininity and where words such as "male" and "female" have specific cultural meanings. With one's male and female elements a person is a "we" and an "us," not merely an "I" and a "me."

The female element speaks to *being* (inward existence as distinguished from outward focus), identifying, joining and being at one with, and resting. A feminine way of being, analyst and theologian Ann Ulanov writes, is "a way of knowing and doing that emphasized continuity over contradiction, being in the midst of experience over abstractions from it and generalizations about it, a subject-relations theory rather than an object-relations theory, connection and interconnected mutuality over hierarchy where one sex and one mode of discourse is privileged over the other."[21] The female element in each person allows us to cohere around a core self that can be shared with another person and the outer world. It opens the possibility to relate deeply with other subjects, birthed in a mother or primary caregiver who related first. Formed preverbally, the female element often speaks through the body before it speaks with words.

The male element is formed after the female element is established. It refers to actively relating—*doing*—or being passively related to, to acting and claiming a Me separate from the Not-me. Reflecting on the male and female elements, Ulanov writes, "Instead of enjoying identity with the object through the female element of being, the male element accents separateness of I and other." The male element can identify with the Other, but does not become the Other, as the female element would do. After initial identification with an object, the male element allows us to stand back with a critical distance, to notice differences, to compare and contrast. "Instinctual energy infuses [this differentiation] so that we want to finish our project, secure our loved one, realize our insight into action, elaborate our ideas, pushing to some kind of climax. We want to do and be and be done with."[22]

A person needs both elements to feel alive and to thrive in life. In relationships, for instance, men need to be able to establish connection and interconnected mutuality over hierarchy, which are ways of being brought forward by their female element. Likewise, women need to distinguish themselves from their partner by building a personal identity, which relies on their male element. A poorly developed self often experiences envy and rage. Until we develop other language besides *male* and *female*, these descriptors may remain problematic, but the opposite elements of personhood remain: One *does* life with authority, conviction, and separateness while being receptive to truth and mystery moving in and through one's way of being, able to enter into a community and seek moments of solitude. As it separates, differentiates, and distinguishes and identifies the Other, the one element knows exactly what it wants. The other element in turn opens one to experiencing something new and fresh, to visions and to surprise, awe, and wonder. The one element wishes—it knows what it wants; the other element hopes—it anticipates an unknown but benevolent future. Unable to wish and hope, life becomes dull and open to despair.

Virtual spaces, unsurprisingly, either serve one (the male) element or the other (the female). Playing games, especially violent ones, or tweeting, posting profile updates and blogposts, receiving texts, commenting or "liking" posts, or browsing profiles on Tinder—an app that facilitates personal hook-ups—suggests one way of being. Watching a movie, listening to an audiobook or music, browsing the creativity of others on Instagram, or fingering updates and feeds on Facebook or Pinterest suggests another. Posting online to be recognized by others, however, is like the behavior of an infant who has to earn the bottle or breast, who needs to smile first to be loved. There is little rest or passive waiting with a receptive attitude even if one goes online to relax or ward off a moment of boredom. This strengthens the doing element over the being element in one's being at significant personal, relational, and professional cost.

Both the male or doing element and the female or being element are important. Imagine a professional setting: The male element puts one out there and takes risk and even control. But soon those actions lead to disconnection, power, dominance, and aggression. Without the female element reining in the male element, creativity and teamwork, the patient assessment of options, and the portrayal of vulnerability, compassion, care, or a nonviolent approach to work and life will be absent. Few will succeed as professionals leading only with their male element. To grow down as a male/female in a world that actively fuels hypermasculinity (aggressively making things happen) while the importance of gender identity is at an all-time high is difficult. Still, it is a task that awaits every person. Likewise, nurturing one's female element and allowing care, empathy, and the capacity to be to determine one's actions and thought is equally important. Life provides enclaves, such as intimate relationships, religious experiences, and the arts, where the balance between one's male and female elements is not only respected, but cultivated. If this balance is disturbed, especially in childhood, the false self steps forward, reactive to the emotional and relational demands of its holding environment.

The Self Is True and False

Every infant faces this dilemma: How can I be authentic if I am so dependent? It is a primary task of every child to find ways to manage the moods of mother, father, another caregiver, or a sibling. This task leaves everyone stuck between being compliant and reactive to outside demands and trying to claim authenticity

and spontaneity. How one navigates this tension greatly determines one's quality of life. As suggested, the tension is birthed
early in life when one is first held. Imagine a mother ready to
bathe her baby, who is cranky. The mother, who does not feel
like engaging a "difficult child," coaxes her son with smiles,
songs, and tickles. The boy, only a few months old, feels the
tension in his mother and "restores" her by becoming compliant
to her "wish" for a cooperative child. He stops crying, and she
praises her son. Something moved him to turn into a little angel,
teaching him that to get praise as a good son, he needs to provide others what they need. Or, imagine a father giving food to
his eighteen-month-old daughter. She wants to eat all by herself.
He brings the spoon to her mouth, but she pushes it away. She
wants to claim her entitlement to food and freedom but notices
her father's growing frustration and insecurity as he enters a
role unfamiliar to him. Moments away from her father claiming
control over her in anger, she drops her hand and lets her father
feed her. To receive food and possibly survive her father's anger,
she restored her father's role as caregiver. Some part of her
moved her to acquiesce to her father's growing frustration and
insecurity, a part that could foresee possible neglect or physical
harm. Both youngsters find themselves in a lose-lose situation.
If they remain defiant, they risk losing a parent, at least emotionally. They also put themselves in danger of physical harm
or neglect. If they comply, living for the Other, they risk losing
themselves; rather than feeling like an "I," they feel like an "it."

These situations are not unique: variations of them play out
for adults too, whether in personal, relational, or professional
settings. Monique knew the wishes of her father and Sean of
his mother. Reading the politics of one's work setting, one plays
along. "Liking" someone's Facebook page when one really does
not is common. Living with a self that cannot read social contexts
or a self that is always spontaneous and free-flowing inevitably

brings tension and fuels conflict. Reading situations makes attunement and care possible, which is a blessing for individuals and society, but sacrificing authenticity and spontaneity diminishes the feeling of being real. Polonius, the concerned and wise father in Shakespeare's *Hamlet*, gives his son Laertes this advice: "This above all: to thine own self be true, and it must follow, as the night the day, thou canst not then be false to any man."[23] In health, one has a false self that knows compliance and a true self that carries little awareness of emotional and relational expectations, political protocol, and social etiquette.

Winnicott theorized the concept of a false self, a self born in the misattunement between a caregiver and an infant. As already suggested, these moments take many forms: when an infant is hungry and food does not miraculously appear as the infant believed it would, the false self soothes by bringing a thumb to the mouth; finding the process of falling asleep scary, the false self comforts an infant to sleep by using a blanket held tightly; experiencing little emotional warmth, a child learns that smiling profusely brings some attention and personal and relational security, even from depressed caregivers; pleasing an alcoholic or angry parent minimizes angry volatility; and compensating for abusive or absent parents by caring for younger siblings gives purpose and a sense of authority. In these moments of misattunement, known to all in some form, the false self steps forward as a caretaker self, protecting the self from harm. This self knows that if one is spontaneous and carefree, possibly calling out the absurdity and failure of the holding environment, the risk that a relationship can become stressed or that someone can be neglected or hurt increases. The defensive nature of the false self has a positive quality: it protects the infant by hiding the true self, and it creates a space where the infant can survive. As an adult, one uses the false self to be mannered and polite, to follow protocol and custom, to read social cues. Persons whose false self is poorly developed have a difficult time navigating their social, relational, and professional lives.

The false self sets itself up as being real, and one can become very successful on the basis of a false self alone, especially if the false self lays claim to the intellect. Academic success may be prized or might become the safe escape. However, in "living relationships, work relationships and friendships . . . the False Self begins to fail. In situations in which what is expected is a whole person, The False Self has some essential lacking."[24] When a partner asks for intimacy and vulnerability, the false self finds ways to create distance. Partners, family, and friends want to discover a person's passions, hopes, and fears, but they instead receive the words and thoughts that belong to someone else. Sometimes all people see is the stare of the logo on the back of a device. In moments of conflict, staying connected is important, but lashing out in self-protection, withdrawing in silence, or activating the symptoms of the psyche-soma can occur.

The true self brings spontaneity and creativity with a sense of omnipotence thrown into the mix. Initially, good enough caregivers buy into an infant's sense of omnipotence: the baby cries (and envisions a breast or bottle to still the hunger) and immediately the bottle appears, leaving the baby with the perception that he created the breast, that she created the bottle. Of course, the breast or bottle was there all along and someone presented the food, but infants do not know that initially. The sense of omnipotence we carry comes from the true self. It is the true self that fuels creativity and instills the feeling of being alive, whereas the false self instills mere existence. The true self can be impulsive whereas the false self is reactive. At all times, one has to work hard to show the true self, for the false self hides its counterpoint. Sometimes alcohol and recreational drugs are used to weaken the defenses of the false self and allow the true self to show itself.

Because no one is held without disappointment, the true self can be shy to show itself, but in moments of creativity, spontaneity, and adaptability or during the use of symbols, the true self can be recognized. Whereas the false self leaves one with a sense that something is lacking, the true self fulfills as it generates what one needs. The false self remains under obligation when the true self can relax and enjoy. Still, an unfiltered true self can alienate others because one's friends or colleagues may not be ready to receive the intensity of such raw authenticity. Sometimes the personal self-disclosure of the true self is inappropriate because the true self does not follow moral or ethical codes. When yet another politician or celebrity posts pictures of his or her anatomy online, when someone tweets or posts without careful discernment, when a young man in college assaults his partner, the false self failed to step in. Without the true self, one cannot be real; without the false self, the true self cannot be.

Our communications technologies allow ample opportunities for the false self and the true self to enter into virtual spaces. The false self, the self that is reactive to outside demands, is activated with every notification that says, pay attention to me, now! Sensitive to the communications it receives from online sources and mindful that only certain answers are valued, the false self presents itself as if it is a whole person. Likewise, should one converse with others with a phone in hand or a laptop open on the table, especially in moments where it is expected that one should show up as a whole person—someone whose true and false selves discern carefully which part will be shown, when and how—others will likely experience the false self only or the inappropriate showing of the true self. Because the majority of popular virtual spaces are commodified, online worlds are interested in the compliant false self as well as the true self that will act without discernment. As will be discussed in chapter 6 ("Technological Intelligence"), sites and apps are developed with this in mind. The false self gives people what they want and nurtures a defensive stance from which a person can experience little or no personal passion. The true self, likely to disregard process, deadlines, rules, and expectations, fuels poorly made choices, tension-filled situations, conflict, and even boundary violations.

Inevitably, one has to come home to oneself. Either one comes home to a false self of appearances that disallows the existence of the true self and fuels a reactive and defensive life, an impulsive and creative true self that struggles with relational intimacy and social practices, or an integrated false *and* true self that is keenly aware how one needs both elements to feel real. Three choices, three different lives. Where one locates oneself will determine much. Winnicott warns that it might be joy for the true self to remain hidden, but it is a tragedy when it is not found.

The Self Is Sexual

The self (as a psyche-soma) is sexual. This is an obvious statement, but it is not always evident in a world where genital sexuality rules. Awareness that one is sexual comes as early as the fifth or sixth month of life as the erotic moves from the mouth to the hand and other-than-me objects.[25] Sexuality refers to "love in its sensual, erotic, possessive, desiring, attaching, affectionate, and devotional sense."[26] Self Intelligence assumes awareness that sexuality is central to being human and that sexual energies flow between persons and between persons and objects. When those energies flow prematurely, not at all, or across boundaries, selves are wounded and relationships suffer.

The sexual act that leads to a birth is also the act that remains present in one's fantasy, even into adulthood. Witnessing a primal scene is traumatic for a child, yet "The primal scene (parents together sexually) is the basis of individual stability since it makes possible the dream of taking the place of one partner. . . . Seeing the parents together makes the dream of their separation, or the death of one of them, tolerable."[27] By imagining one's parents having sex, as embarrassing as it is for children of all ages, one can imagine oneself in the same position. It opens the possibility to be a partner to someone else, which implies the risk of loss. The advertising world, mass media, and especially the porn industry, with its exploitation of female sexuality, relies on persons young and old remaining curious about persons being together sexually. The sexual self is the voyeur self, but it speaks to much more than having sex or looking at sexual images. It also holds the paradoxes of individuality while losing oneself in unity, of togetherness and separation (inherent in the self as male/female), of submitting and surrendering, and of life and death. Our voyeur self, recognized in terrifying stories such as the rape of Tamar in the Bible (2 Samuel 13) shows us that our sexual self has not changed much, if any, over the past few thousand years.

The sexual self seeks to find itself in the other person, a process that is located in the space between the self and someone else. "In the adult erotic relationship, vital aggressive love/ hate, the cuddling which is aggressive-transgressive, [and the] affectionate mutilation of the body [tell us the Other exists]."[28] When these acts of loving go too far or not far enough, the relationship suffers and selves hurt. In some instances, a partner's body can become a toy to play with and not a gift discovered in the space between subjectivity and objectivity. Sex reduced to genitalia, which the false self will allow and the true self will exploit, collapses the space between partners, leaving both with desire and needs unmet. In the hookup culture of Tinder and other social apps, the risk of these dynamics are high. The sexual self longs for lasting, loving relationships and a holding environment, experiences that fleeting moments brought about by social media only hint at.

Remaining in the space between partners where each can find and discover the other unleashes a playful vitality filled with imaginative and physical potential. In this space one can regress yet remain mature, trust that one's partner is reliable, and imagine perfect love while knowing that such a state does not exist. This sexuality carries a rich vocabulary—the language of love found in poems, songs, and novels. Genital sexuality, however, seeing orgasm as a primary goal, is most often described in four-letter words where the other-than-me is aggressively controlled and possessed. A focus on genitals and orgasm, which denies full-body experiences, is contained in fantasying that may lead to a return to orality (oral sex) and anality (anal sex), but the individual remains isolated, absorbing energy but not contributing to personal, relational, or societal living.[29] Pornography thrives on fantasy, as the face of the Other is seen as an object ready to satisfy, for the object is also a possession. When sexuality remains focused on genitals, it is not only a sign of immaturity, it is also a defense against being a sexual psyche-soma.

"[Persons] who use sex to defend themselves from sexuality have significant problems with the sense of self," analysts Mario Bertolini and Francesca Neri write as they reflect on "sex as a defense against sexuality."[30] They write about a twenty-one-year-old who had an active and intense sex life since age seventeen but was unable to maintain intimacy. Entering a family business successfully, he went to great lengths to communicate being a professional and a person deserving respect, yet he felt empty inside. Despite being selective when choosing partners, he was unable to sustain a stable, long-term relationship, something he both feared and longed for. Emotionally, he could not be in the same room with the person he had sex with. After orgasm he left immediately, sometimes running himself physically into exhaustion. "His need for love and to feel loved is not satisfied by his attempts to discharge it by going through the motions of having sex."[31] Rather, the act of sex, though filled with promise, threatens and suffocates. He abandoned this partner as his family abandoned him.

The young man lost an infant brother to death prior to his birth and received that brother's name. After birth, his aunts raised him because his mother could not bear caring for him as an infant. He returned home after he passed the age of his deceased brother to be met by a depressed mother. Still, he idealized his mother and his childhood. "Through his flights," Bertolini and Neri write, "he sought the advantage of denial, discharging in the activity of his muscles the hate he felt for the women to whom, through his seduction of them, he was in reality submitting himself, through his compulsion to relive his primitive primary relationships."[32] He submitted without interest or passion. Fearing loss, he left before loss can occur. By leaving and running, he escaped from loss as well as confrontation and conflict, only to return like a moth to the flame. Unable to feel that he was someone's child, the young man felt useless and carried a sense of futility. He could not surrender to a partner even if surrendering is the invitation of the sex act. Rather, he claimed omnipotent control over his relationships and excitement never became pleasure.

The sexual self is a creative self, drawing on fantasy and curiosity to create love, care, protection, and intimacy. The false self can use creativity defensively to seduce, feed voyeuristic tendencies, and ward off psychic pain. The false self knows how to keep others at a distance. When used in life-giving ways, the creativity originating from the true self instills a sense of meaning, joy, and excitement. *Growing Down* accepts the lifelong task of integrating being sexual and having sexual relations. Because being sexual exists prior to any activity, the integration is never a given. The false self can resort to sex as a defense against the anxiety that the mere thought of having sexual relations brings. The true self can seek pleasure in sex without recognizing that one's whole being participates in the sex act and is asked for in relationships. Being a whole person is an achievement, and seeking relations with another whole person is a gift.

The Self Needs to Believe

The self believes in two ways: It has the capacity to believe in itself and can be trusting, reliable, confident, and grown-down; and the self believes in God, country, money, power, sex, and other objects. The two forms of belief are related, but distinct. The two ways of believing are seen in the difference between keeping an internal image alive versus needing the constant presence of an external object. When believing in oneself, one's inner world can hold external worlds, whereas external worlds are believed to hold an internal world. As an attribute, the self believing in itself is personal and has a qualitative nature, whereas "belief in" is public, cultural, communal, and quantifiable. The self's belief anticipates openness and flexibility, whereas belief in is frequently rigid, seeking clarity and certainty. Belief in oneself is an expression of self-love and self-esteem, whereas belief in an object often compels one to love others and recognize their worth. Where the former speaks to feeling alive, the latter anticipates the giving and receiving of life. The self's belief in itself and believing in an object are two sides of the same coin. However, believing in the self—to be trusting, reliable, confident and able to grow down—comes first.[33]

Self Intelligence not only recognizes the difference between believing in oneself and believing in an object, but it also holds the tension that these two forms of belief induce as they relate to each other. All cultures and all people believe in, the result of what has been called an incredible need. Self Intelligence's primary focus is not the objects of belief. Rather, it assumes there will be objects that the self believes in. The journey to maturity includes a desire to learn more about belief in objects—God, Mystery, the Cosmos—and often reflects a deep personal commitment. The catalyst of believing in, however, is one's capacity to believe in oneself.

The self believing in itself implies reclaiming an inner security that allows one to commit oneself wholeheartedly to a relationship or a cause. It is best seen in a self with esteem, confidence, positive regard, worth, assurance, and a basic sense that one is trustworthy. Small children loved and held in good enough ways naturally believe in themselves. With outstretched arms they yell, "To infinity and beyond!" As they grow up the brokenness of reality touches their lives and their belief in themselves slowly fades. Soon they relate to themselves through the lenses of shame or insecurity. Generally speaking, girls and children growing up in poverty experience this in more pronounced ways compared to boys and children of wealth. When belief in oneself has faded, narcissism, egocentricity, selfishness, antisocial behavior and/or even delinquency are found, all of which point to an insecure self that seeks exaggerated self-appraisal. The self then presents with a sense of entitlement or seeks ways to force the environment to become significant. Whereas a poorly developed belief in oneself makes one feel small and present as large, a secure self feels large but may present as small. A secure self can risk humility, grace, and, at times, self-effacing meekness. Those we perceive as wise role models often project this mature self. A secure self is less anxious. Growing down, which requires being held, an integrated psyche-soma, a nurtured male/female element, and an integrated true and false self, anticipates the self believing in itself.

With inner security one can risk solitude and need not protect oneself against the anxiety that idle time and boredom bring by fingering a phone and going online. One definitely has little desire to force one's way in life or to split reality into good-bad or other binaries, which is a natural defense. Furthermore, a believing self can celebrate the gifts of others without experiencing envy. One can risk not knowing and can imagine authorities and truths as fallible and in need of interpretation and contextualization. With responsiveness to one's emotions and the emotions of others, somatic reactivity has no function. Others witness this personal belief and know intuitively that their selves can be nurtured if they enter into a relationship with a self that believes in itself.

The Self Seeks Transformation

The self continually seeks experiences to change affect, thought, and action—moments that will transform it. This search is a basic human trait as recognized in an archetypal story such as the Garden of Eden. Eve had a desire to be like God and to know good and evil; this led her to believe that eating a fruit would meet her need. Today's economy is built on this same dynamic, as the advertising industry promises a new self if one buys a specific product. The transformation of the self is best recognized in how parents engage infants. Merely a couple of months old, an infant searches the face of her mother or father who smiles with love and warmth, igniting a smile on her face. Another time the infant searches for a loving face, but finds mother or father preoccupied by his or her phone. In the absence of a smile and warm eyes, the infant's face shows no energy as she holds on to her blanket or searches for her pacifier. And then there are moments where the infant looks and sees the sad or troubled face of mother or father. The corners of her mouth turn down as if they are too heavy to hold up. After a few more years, the toddler will help mother or father smile. Psychologist Daniel Stern took a series of photographs referred to as "still face studies" that show the powerful dynamics between a caregiver and an infant in these situations.

Psychoanalyst Christopher Bollas describes what plays out in these moments by looking at the foundational relationship between an infant and a parental figure in *The Shadow of the Object*. Bollas identifies parents, caregivers, and toys, as well as aesthetic experiences, as transformational objects, as entities that are "experientially identified by the infant with processes that alter self experience."[34] For babies, their mother or primary caregiver is the first agent who changed their self experience. Later, other caregivers, a soft toy, language, teachers, and counselors join the parents and caregivers in this role. Whereas children *possess* a soft toy and *acquire* language skills, Bollas observes that adults *pursue* relationships and experiences that will change and transform the self. That adults pursue is important, for it provides another psychodynamic explanation for why technology is so readily embraced, not only by children, but by adults too.

Bollas looks at the search to transform one's inner world as a hopeful act. As with hope, where something in the future is relied upon to change the present, the pursuit of a transformational object or experience manifests the future. When the hope sets in and transformation occurs, one deepens one's relationship with that object and becomes subjectively attached to it. Part of the hope is the longing that some reparation of wounds received earlier in life will occur, even if one has no conscious memory of those wounds. It is the hope for transformation that takes one to aesthetic or cultural experiences, whether reading books, listening to music, or attending the theater or the movies. It is as if the artist is remembering the self formed in a life-giving holding environment and now creates the possibility for a restorative experience. The hope for transformation and alteration of one's sense of self also takes us to our hobbies or to special interest groups, even the community one finds at a CrossFit box. The hope for an integrated self and restoration and for feeling real is stronger than the need for knowledge, talent, or success. Rather, these latter traits and accomplishments are exposed for their futility if one has not grown down to a position where one can feel alive and be a whole person to others.

The desire to be transformed, as is clear with Eve, does not always take one on life-giving paths. Shortly after taking the fruit, Eve and her partner, in the shame of their nakedness went into hiding. They discovered that life downstream from Eden was difficult and full of peril. Archetypal stories often have these swinging changes. One constantly runs the risk of being transformed in ways that do not lead to integration, restoration, realness, or spontaneity. Placing oneself at a center for abused women and children or doing a chaplaincy program informs the self in one direction, whereas consumption, the excessive use of food, alcohol, sex, or risky behavior takes one elsewhere. Even in destructive choices the kernel of hope to be transformed can be seen. Bollas states that when one seeks "negative aesthetic experiences," by which he means experiences that transform in life-depriving ways, one often repeats earlier experiences where the holding environment failed.[35] The hope is always that a restorative metamorphosis of the self will occur, but when this does not happen, despair replaces the initial hope.

Today a primary choice to alter self-experience is through using communications technologies and by entering virtual spaces. The pursuit of the transformational object and self-altering experiences provides another reason why technology holds such attraction and why entering virtual spaces happens without much discernment. In a screen and the content it portrays, one sees (or hopes for) the promise to be transformed, and it longs for a world once known by the true self. The relief found online promises to counter the emotional distress, relational tension, or somatic symptoms the body may have, but without lasting success. The rush and release one finds online mirrors the smile once received as an infant. As a person in infancy handled a spoon or pacifier, a phone is now grasped, the self ever aware of the phone's presence or absence. It is irony that an infant's primary focus is eight to ten inches from a parental face, a distance slightly shorter than an adult facing a handheld screen. Psychologists identify phantom vibration syndrome, or "ringxiety," to describe the tactile hallucination that one's phone received a notification, upon which one promptly checks in with one's device only to discover no notice arrived. Sometimes one's muscles will twinge, creating the sensation of a vibration. Such is the power of handheld technologies as transformational objects.

That Bollas sees adults surrendering to their transformational object is no surprise. He introduces Peter, a twenty-eight-year-old with a disheveled look, a sad expression, a sardonic sense of humor, considerable loneliness, and an intelligence and education that others use and he cannot enjoy. Since his last breakup, he is mostly alone. After work he slumps in front of the television, eats a prepackaged meal, masturbates, and then ruminates about a future as he bemoans the good luck of others in the face of his bad luck. Peter lived in a time prior to computers and virtual technologies. One imagines a contemporary Peter gaming and staying online into the morning hours. Peter was referred to Bollas to deal with depression, which was fueled by a personal sadness and loneliness. Peter's mother idolized her firstborn as if he was a mythical object. In this context, where being someone else was more valued than being himself, Peter's false self became emboldened as his true self waned. He visits with his mother weekly, something he detests in himself, as she loves to maintain the myth of his potential. She never seems to notice that Peter has little sense of self and is struggling, telling him that things will change soon. Peter's mother sees him coming into wealth and being happy and famous. The language that Peter learned was silence followed by sighs, groans, and physical symptoms. Bollas does not tell how Peter's journey ends, but Peter's desire for transformation took him into a relationship with Bollas, a relationship with potential. There is a core to the self that continually seeks places and moments of promise.

Toward a Vision of Health

Michael Newheart states that his *I am* often feels small and insecure, that he longs for self-confidence, a sense of self-possession, and a grasp of who he is.[36] To be alive and go through the motions of life is one thing; to feel alive with a sense that one is thriving and contributing to the world is something else. Feeling overwhelmed, confused, exhausted, anxious, uncertain about the future, or exploited and stuck are everyday experiences for many. In a world of economic uncertainty, political stalemates, and religious militancy, such emotions can be expected. Growing a self today elevates the importance of a process that, though natural, needs intentionality and guidance or it risks derailment. The self gathers various parts to become one. Growing up takes this process for granted, whereas growing down sees it as a process best done with intentionality. Informed by a Christian anthropology, this chapter went beyond seeing the self in terms of independence, individualism, and being rational and deepened our understanding of mutuality, responsiveness, and having a sense of purpose and meaning. The *imago Dei* received additional traits, whether it is being male/female, true or false, or always seeking transformation.

The self can also be viewed through the lens of health. One definition of a healthy self is being six at the age of six. The vast majority of children born after World War II were too mature for their age. Being a child means being eight or nine at the age of six, or going on fifteen at the age of twelve, emotionally and relationally always ahead of one's chronological age.[37] Society birthed latchkey kids, brat packs, and children who could be home alone, outsmarting dimwitted adults and doing quite well without any adult supervision. Such premature articulation of the self, however, comes at a personal cost and creates an emboldened and inflated false self. Then there are those, much fewer in number, who are emotionally and relationally thirteen at the age of sixteen or eighteen at the age of twenty-three. Delayed articulation of the self is a modern concern. Health as being six at the age of six relies on neurological, cognitive, emotional, relational, and spiritual maturity that come with time and through physical maturational processes that cannot be rushed. Under smiles and compliments of "She is so mature for her age," nobody noticed a young girl compromising core aspects of herself. Now she struggles to find her voice. Encouraged to "be a big boy," a young boy learned early not to show emotion and vulnerability. Now his anger lurks and cannot speak, but it surprises with its volcanic power and ferocity. Children who grow up too fast are compromised, burdened by the sense of responsibility their experiences brought. These children feel special, but they find the gaps between possibility and actuality or between choice and accountability overwhelming.

Technology fuels an accelerated self where today's children are many years ahead of their chronological and emotional age due to early exposure to market exploitation and adult content. Whether through advertising, television shows, virtual games, societal role models, or the ways the media world tries to make children into consumers, children receive message upon message that being a mini-adult is not only desired, but also rewarded. To be an age-appropriate child or teenager today is being part of a definite minority and is not possible without resisting the dominant cultural messages. The cost to the person so mature for her or his age, however, may be more than any person can afford. Because outside forces cannot accelerate emotional and relational maturity, which depends on emotional and relational development, neurological maturation to think abstractly, and more, the self is always compromised if it is too mature for its age.

Delayed selves, emotionally and relationally younger than their chronological age, find that the world never stops to allow them to get back on board. Left behind, they can become lost in attempts at transformation. They often underfunction, resisting doing the personal emotional, relational, vocational, and financial work that will ensure a self that feels alive. Underfunctioners typically find themselves in emotional distress (anxiety and/or depression) with addictive behaviors, relational tension, vocational insecurity, and financial debt. They rarely reach the potential they hold and others see in them. When a person who was fourteen at the age of ten meets a person who was ten at the age of fourteen, it can be a match made in heaven.

This chapter highlighted seven core aspects within a psychodynamic understanding of the self: one's need for a holding environment, being a psyche-soma, being male/female, having a true and a false self, being a sexual self, believing in oneself, and transforming the human desire. These traits, among others, fuel vitality. To come alive, as African American philosopher Howard Thurman states, is not only the biggest gift one can give oneself, it is also the gift the world needs. Feeling alive is nearly impossible, however, if one is held in ways that fuel anxiety and reactivity, if physical symptoms imprison the body, or if personal insecurities hold one back. It might not always be these aspects that weigh one down, but rather the ways one learned to defend against them in infancy. With cognitive defenses the self can devour data, find things merely interesting when an affective or relational response would be more appropriate, and live with the fantasy that knowing more leads to personal and relational well-being. Chemical defenses such as alcohol or recreational drugs can become addictions. Emotional defenses, such as offering a loud, extroverted persona, or relational defenses, such as hooking up and having shallow relationships, assure a safe distance between the self and others. These defenses are like Eve's fruit: they may taste good, but they do not deliver on their promises of transformation made.

Winnicott's wisdom that "A word like 'self' naturally knows more than we do; it uses us, and can command us," gains significance as our extended selves incorporate communications technologies into who we are.[38] The self not only knows much, it tells much. The ability to interpret what it says is a foundational intelligence needed to flourish in a technologically driven world.

2

RELATIONAL INTELLIGENCE
Toward a Theology of "Being With"

> To know how to sustain an ongoing human relationship means
> to know what it means to be an "I" and a "me," to know that I am
> an "other" to you and that, likewise, you are an "I" to yourself
> and an "other" to me.
>
> —Seyla Benhabib, *Situating the Self*[1]

Being alone, it is written, is not suitable. Seeing this, one creation story says, God formed Eve, and the need to be in a relationship was confirmed. Walking in the cool evening breeze, as if loneliness was unbearable for God too, God sought Adam and Eve. One discovers here a relational God and persons made into that image. From the moment of conception until the moment of death, the need for relationship remains. Our communications technologies rely on this need, though meeting the need is not as easy as opening a social media app. One reason for this is that being in a relationship requires both sameness and difference to coexist. The desire to be independent and authentic—an I am—is not possible without recognizing the same need in the Other. Stated differently, the desire for individuality and uniqueness is challenged by the need for belonging and identification with a larger group or cause. At all times the need for security is challenged by the risk of loving. It takes a grown-down to recognize and hold the paradoxes of being in relationship.

Because *being with* comes naturally, being in relationships rarely receives conscious attention unless it becomes problematic. It may be impossible to be truly alone, even in moments such as birth and death. In the depths of loneliness, conversation with one's internalized relationships continues. Self Intelligence, with its awareness of the complex nature of the self, supports Relational Intelligence. Still, achieving the art of being in relationships is never guaranteed. It is ironic and possibly worrisome that addressing this primary need remains part of the informal curriculum of life, that it does not receive more explicit and intentional attention. From pre-kindergarten to college and beyond, everyone can benefit from Relationship 101 classes, as each stage of the life cycle brings new relational challenges. Because entering, establishing, and maintaining relationships are vulnerable to experiences past and present as well as to cultural forces, one's relationships require full attention. Life happens and relationships are established, but being mindful about the building blocks of life can make a difference.

Whereas Descartes' "I think, therefore I am" led to competitive individualism especially in the West, the African self and communal living are built around another belief: "I am because we are," the essence of the philosophy of *ubuntu*.[2] Two proverbs illuminate the difference: "A rolling stone gathers no moss," and "My friends who love me grow on me like moss." The latter proverb is from Southern Africa—the cradle of humanity—and describes the nature of an interconnected humanity. Constructs mirroring the *ubuntu* philosophy and the self's need to be held are found in much of the Global South and the majority of the world. Moss has medicinal qualities that assist healing, prevent infections, and insulate against cold. Within the proverbs are two views on relationships and two different selves, one hurried and disconnected, the other with a sense of place and belonging. Rolling stones are always busy, on the brink of being overwhelmed, and short on time and intimacy. Individualism does not support intimacy nor a willingness to communicate the vulnerability and openness needed to thrive personally and relationally. Intimacy—whether with lovers, family, friends, colleagues, or strangers—informs one's relationships. Friends-as-moss seek face time; they eat and celebrate life together; they carry each other in times of joy and sorrow; they are hospitable and gracious; they recognize and shape each other. Stones are just stones. Bigger ones crush smaller ones into sand, and when really big, stones become protruding rocks and islands. The ability to be intimate originates from one's first good enough holding environment.

In a technologically driven world, the promise of relationships is enticing. Sherry Turkle, an analytically informed researcher at the Massachusetts Institute of Technology, has been a student of the human-technology relationship for more than three decades. In her *Alone Together: Why We Expect More from Technology and Less from Each Other*, she does not hide her concern for "technologies of relationship" that offer themselves as "[architects] of our intimacies." "We are lonely but fearful of intimacy," Turkle writes. "Digital connections . . . may offer the illusion of companionship without the demands of friendship. Living a networked life allows one to hide from others even as we are tethered to each other. We'd rather text than talk."[3] Technology is reshaping the landscape of our relational and emotional lives as communication becomes public and the meaning of face-to-face is rewritten. These changes, however, should not be confused with the need to be in relationships, a need that has defined human nature for many thousands of years. Intimacy still longs for privacy and losing itself in someone's eyes. Turkle is skeptical that technology can meet a person's deepest needs.

Technology makes new ways of relating possible — increasingly digital and/or virtual — necessitating being smart about relating to others. This chapter addresses a specific kind of wisdom: Relational Intelligence is growing in the art of being in authentic, loving, caring, and ethical relationships with persons and easygoing, balanced relationships with things. It is an intelligence that begins with at least two faces, one of a caring adult and the other of an infant, but thrives in fantasy even as relationships awaken powerful feelings, some in flirtation. It is an intelligence that can protect fidelity and manage the frustration relationships inevitably cause.

Faces

Faces are a shared form of uniqueness, as they signify particularity and commonality. Relational Intelligence begins with a face and is recognized in the ability to maintain eye contact. In the Judeo-Christian tradition, our facial existence is traced to an in-your-face God. This might scare some, but being in a relationship with an in-your-face God is grace, for it speaks of a responsive and compassionate God longing for relationship. God's face, we are reminded, shines upon us and constantly turns toward humanity.[4] "Christianity," theologian David Ford writes, "is characterized by the simplicity and complexity of facing: being faced by God, embodied in the face of Christ; turning to face Jesus Christ in faith; being members of a community of the face; seeing the face of God reflected in creation and especially in each human face, with all the faces in our heart related to the presence of the face of Christ; having an ethic of gentleness . . . to each face; . . . and having a vision of transformation before the face of Christ."[5]

God is like a mother, always searching for the eyes of her child. In her *Bonds of Love*, feminist psychoanalyst Jessica Benjamin describes where recognition and relationship begin. "A mother cradles her newborn, gazes into her eyes, and says in the high-pitched voice universal to adults communicating with infants: 'I believe she knows me. You do know me, don't you? Yes you do?' Another mother asks her newborn: 'Hey stranger, are you really the one I carried around inside of me? Do you know me?'"[6] Both mother and infant draw on mirror neurons that make this experience of togetherness possible. Mirror neurons allow perception to follow action and vice versa, making imitation possible. The baby's disproportionately large eyes assist in triggering the mirror neurons of adults facing the infant. This mutual recognition between mother and infant "is so central to human existence as to often escape notice; or, rather, it appears to us in so many guises that it is seldom grasped as one overarching concept. There are a number of near-synonyms for the mutual recognition facing can bring: 'affirm, validate, acknowledge, know, accept, understand, empathize, take in, tolerate, appreciate, see, identify with, find familiar . . . love.'"[7] These are the building blocks of Relational Intelligence.

As one face communicates "I am, I do," and another face affirms, "You are, you have done," selves are formed and relationships are built.[8] These moments of mutuality cannot be imposed or achieved by submitting to another's power, or denying or repressing the Other's individuality. Rather, mutuality implies a central paradox: to establish an independent identity, one needs to recognize the independence of another. Holding the paradox leads to moments of intersubjectivity, moments where one knows that another exists, feels, and thinks.

When a baby looks at her mother, she sees herself. Such is the power of mutuality.[9] Before a physical mirror captivates an infant's imagination, there are the faces of mother and father or of loving family members and friends. Apperception sets in, and one sees oneself by being seen. "When I look I am seen, so I exist. I can now afford to look and see. I now look creatively and what I apperceive I also perceive. In fact I take care not to see what is not there to be seen (unless I am tired)."[10] One's ability to enter into a relationship depends on the experience of having been seen.

With mutuality one discovers oneself anew and feels real on the bedrock of emotional security and personal significance. If mutuality is consistently absent, the false self steps in as the caretaker self to keep up the appearance of connection. Life without mutuality is certainly possible, but it is compromised. One will seek ways to insert oneself into the vision of others, unaware that this is an attempt to meet a deep need. Journalist Clive Thompson, reflecting on this compromised self, presents the following tweet: "I need to be noticed so badly that I can't pay attention to you except inasmuch as it calls attention to me. I know for you it's the same."[11] In 140 characters a self is captured. The creativity people use to be seen is often impressive and receives millions of views online, earns them an invitation onto a reality television show, or awakens the response of an authority figure—ways of seeing that rarely foster a sense of mutuality. More important than receiving wisdom from someone is being seen in life-giving ways. Of course, receiving wisdom and being seen often coincide. Relationships typically thrive when partners, family members, friends, colleagues, supervisors, or even strangers are recognized, when mutuality is cultivated. Without turning one's face toward one's partner, without making and keeping eye contact, and without sustained interaction and communication, any attempt at intimacy is likely to fail. As one face turns to another, love, care, wisdom, and grace follow. Rolling stones just move too fast for this to happen.

As stated above, much facing of others takes place online. Building the sustained relationships needed for personal gratification, however, is the exception and not the rule, as one friend is easily interchanged with another. Taking a selfie and posting it online or browsing someone's pictures or wall satisfies the same needs of recognition and belonging that compels one into face-to-face relationships. Social media in particular relies on the need for and power of a human face. Social media companies use facial recognition software to build biometric databases of users to match images and make suggestions to other users. Through faces they can offer customized advertisements. Research affirms the effectiveness of virtual faces to inform identity formation in teens and young adults, for good and ill.[12] The same research indicates virtual relationships cannot replace face-to-face encounters.

The face with its gaze, so central to mutuality, carries ethical responsibility. This responsibility is explored by philosopher Emmanuel Levinas, who sees being someone as inseparable from recognizing the Other.[13] Whereas Winnicott sees relationships as the defining aspect of human nature, Levinas sees relationality as an event, meaning that being someone does not naturally translate into knowing how to be in an ethical relationship. "Inward existence," Levinas writes, "does not consist in receiving the recognition of the Other, but in offering him one's being. . . . To be in oneself is to express oneself, that is, already to serve the Other."[14] To truly be someone, Levinas argues, is to be someone good. Levinas moves beyond merely recognizing the Other as he argues for doing good to the Other. This offering of goodness to the Other is seen in simple acts of kindness, compassion, hospitality, civility, and politeness. Ethics (what one *ought* to do) thus precedes ontology (who one *is*), and therefore, the ethical responsibility the other person brings is not a choice to make in freedom, but an obligation one cannot escape. Living ethically, Levinas reminds us, has a payoff: it leads to enjoyment (or *jouissance*), a state similar to feeling alive and real.

One lives face-to-face and no other life is possible. Levinas is especially concerned with the gaze that does not awaken mutuality but rather operates in a "privileged" way.[15] Here two faces do not gently touch, but one becomes a force that grasps and creates gaps in one's being (see chap. 4, "Reparative Intelligence"). The force of Levinas' argument for ethical relationships speaks powerfully to online and virtual worlds, in two primary ways. First, the "Eurocentric, masculine, hegemonic notions of power, privilege, and inequality" often found in virtual worlds are reinforced.[16] When a gaze becomes a stare that penetrates or a hand that grasps, as when voyeuristic and pornographic desires are satisfied, or the Other is annihilated with words, persons and communities are diminished. In the intersectionality of power, privilege, and patriarchy found online, the need for an ethical response beckons. The need for ethical relationships, however, also speaks against the online gaze that never recognizes the Other. A person looks or sees, but does not recognize. Social media, allowing one to have many friends, easily permits looking and seeing, even creating the impression of closeness, without recognition. Achieving Relational Intelligence implies discerning gender, class, race, sexual orientation, and difference. It reminds us that seeing and being seen easily become corrupted. Rather, one is called to recognize how someone's otherness mirrors one's own difference. In the mirror one sees one's neighbor; in one's neighbor, one sees the in-your-face God offering relationship deeper than friendship.

Despite a proclivity to be mirrored, faces raise anxiety, especially if the face is foreign. Anxiety, in turn, often splits reality, leading to seeing life or an experience in terms of good or bad, right or wrong, us or them. Starkly demarcated choices provide some sense of security. Locating the source of one's anxiety, which can be emotional, sexual, relational, or even financial, in someone else is another common defense: projection. When someone identifies with a projection, the flow of anxiety is complete. Whether one relates in person or posts online, Relational Intelligence expects knowing the issues or experiences that fill one with anxiety, being aware of the ways one protects oneself when anxious or insecure, and finding mature ways to address and protect the self and others from anxiety.

Fantasy

One's relationships are not only face-to-face or virtual. Rather, relationships originate in fantasy as the inner relates to the outer. To know fully and be fully known speak to emotional, relational, and spiritual needs. These needs cannot be met if one relates through fantasy. In psychodynamic thought, fantasy describes the ways subjectivity assigns meaning and purpose to others and experience. All relationships are shaped by *projective mechanisms* (finding some of oneself in the Other) and *identifications* (finding some of the Other in oneself). These mechanisms prevent authentic living and a sense of mutuality. Faces do not awaken any ethical response as the sacredness of the Other is not recognized. A life without experiencing the joy of authentic relationships is possible. Still, every person longs to relate with a "Thou," not an "It," as Jewish theologian Martin Buber writes.[17] As Buber, quoting Rabbi Menachem Mendel, notes elsewhere, "[If] I am I because I am I, and you are you because you are you, then I am I, and you are you. But if I am I because you are you, and you are you because I am I, then I am not I and you are not you."[18]

Relating through fantasy is a primary dynamic for infants who cannot initially distinguish between the Me and the

Not-me, between what belongs to the infant and what belongs
to the environment. The paradox is that the infant creates in fantasy what is present all along. Imagine two babies nursed by a
breast or bottle. One baby is feeding himself, for he has not separated his Me from the Not-me. For the other baby, mother or
father or an other-than-me person is feeding her, for such separation occurred. Good-enough parents and caregivers know not
to blow apart the paradox fantasy introduces, as is seen when a
young child gives life to a soft toy. Did the child create the toy
or was it given to the child? No caring adult reminds a child
that a beloved teddy bear filled with warmth and comfort is just
stuffed fabric! Without a sense of the Not-me, all that is left is
primary narcissism where the Me rules, driven by a sense of
omnipotence: I am the world and the world is me. For some, this
primary narcissism continues beyond infancy and becomes sec-
ondary narcissism, a condition describing a personality disorder
and a compromised self. Infants, then, rely initially on subjective
fantasy filters to relate to the world.[19]

Meeting someone outside the area of projective mechanisms
or beyond one's omnipotent control requires *destroying* any elements of fantasy fused to that person. Preconceived notions
about others, especially those marginal to one's life, prohibit
or color authentic face-to-face encounters. To call for further
destruction in a violent world can sound foolish, but destruction in this psychodynamic context is inherently life giving.
Whereas destruction in fantasy is a hopeful act of seeing and
being seen—of mutuality—interpersonal anger, aggression,
and hostility lead to despair. Good enough relational maturity
implies accepting the work of destruction and dismantling preconceived notions of others and systems. Surviving the destruction of someone trying to find one anew is grace. It often takes
someone who looks one in the eye, sharing that one's words or
actions cause hurt and distance. When fantasies are destroyed,

persons and relationships come alive and hope is found. Physical destruction, also driven by the need to be seen, in turn leads to annihilated selves, despair, grief, and hopelessness. Ironically, we use the destruction-survival dynamic within our relationships to discover the uniqueness of another person or group of persons. Fantasy seeks control and creates persons according to one's prejudices, turning the Other into an It. Reaching toward Relational Intelligence implies recognizing the personal autonomy and sacred integrity of the other person—a Thou.

Experiencing destruction in fantasy can be hurtful to others, as finding a flesh-and-blood person beyond fantasies and projections does not come easily. Whether a loved one, a friend, or a stranger, the Other needs to survive the peeling back of layer after layer of fantasy placed over him or her. One might say awkward things, project additional material, or become afraid of the deepening intimacy and emotionally distance oneself. Destroying internal representations should not be confused with exploiting the Other or even with acts of physical violence. Physical violence, as a sign of despair, rarely leads to seeing the self and the Other anew. When the recipient of hostile projections retaliates, often with matched anger, aggression, or physical violence, any process of finding each other stops.

It is normal that months or even years into a relationship one recognizes that a partner is not the partner imagined, but someone else, someone uniquely alive. Parents know that their children are always trying to figure out who mother or father is and remain responsive (and not reactive) to the destruction-survival cycle. Not all adults survive the attempts of destruction by a child (or another person). In despair the adults become reactive, often with hostility matching the destruction. A sad moment is amplified when one is in the process of destroying the representations one has of someone and that person accidentally dies. The illusion that the death was caused by one's thoughts—tapping into infantile omnipotence—is powerful. With the process of finding each other thwarted, the remaining subjective projections can become fused with guilt and grief.

The ability to internalize relationships, whether with persons or objects, some whole and others just (body) parts, and to enliven them with fantasy is normal. This human symbiotic dynamic is addressed in Barbara Johnson's *Persons and Things*. For Johnson, humanness is mired in an inability to treat persons as persons on the one side while personifying things on the other. Accepting the realities of human desire and physical materiality, Johnson shows how language is used to turn persons into objects and to bring objects to life. Building upon Buber, Johnson sees persons being addressed as persons and as things: "A person who neither addresses nor is addressed is functioning as a *thing* in the same way that being an *object* of discussion rather than a subject of discussion transforms everything into a thing."[20] Johnson reminds us that personhood and thinghood are deeply woven together by speech. The uncomfortable truth is that it is not possible to know the Other without objectifying the Other. This objectification, always in need of destruction, relies on Relational Intelligence's ethical quality. The process of destroying in fantasy while surviving in reality is the only way to live into the paradox of turning persons into things and things into persons.

In a section called "The Thingliness of Persons" Johnson discusses Winnicott's psychodynamic theory of enlivening dead objects, such as a soft toy, with meaning (see chap. 3, "Transitional Intelligence"). She also addresses the dynamic of placing persons outside the area of one's subjective experience, a dynamic Winnicott calls "object usage"; usage here does not mean exploitation or taking advantage of, but rather discovering the Other anew after the destruction of one's personal fantasies. "For most people the ultimate compliment is to be found and used," Winnicott writes.[21] Relationships determined by fantasies lead to "object relating," which assures a breakdown in mutuality. Johnson sees language as central to the destruction-survival dynamic in authentic relationships. She faults Winnicott for his tendency to use exaggerated language. The paradox inherent in human relationships as the inner relates to the outer and discovering the Other, who might be known, however, resonates with her. Johnson concludes, "Perhaps a synonym for 'using people' would be, paradoxically, 'trusting people' . . ."[22] Trust after destruction in fantasy is the paradoxical wisdom of Relational Intelligence.

As one grows down, one learns not only how to destroy in fantasy, but also how to survive someone else's destruction of his or her fantasies. Believing in persons and objects that survive empowers authenticity and independence. Because attempts at omnipotent control of the Other or anger, hostility, and annihilation in reality are acts of despair, one has little choice other than pursuing this difficult achievement destroying in fantasy. The world knows the despair of interpersonal violence, hostility, and war. To be an agent of hope and to experience hope oneself, embracing the work of destroying in fantasy any preconceived notions held of persons, groups, and systems is essential.

Feelings

Relationships awaken powerful feelings. From feeling anxious to accepted, betrayed to blessed, cautious to curious, distant to driven, empty to ecstatic, or from feeling afraid to feeling zany, emotional life is rich and varied. *Growing Down* distinguishes feelings from emotion and affect. *Feelings* are the *personal* expression of emotions, those spontaneous, perceptual appraisals that govern one's life. As personal expressions, feelings are engendered in a male/female self. Feelings always remain true to their etymological roots: from the sixteenth-century French *esmouvoir*, meaning "to stir up, to cause civil unrest." *Emotions* are more *universal*, describing interpretive schemata (such as anger or shame) "that any kind of people in the world might (or might not) make use of to give meaning and shape to their somatic and affective feelings."[23] Feelings and emotions are also distinguished from affect. "Emotions are . . . short-lasting, but potentially intense, and *affect* is defined as long-lasting and not as intense."[24]

Primary feelings, such as fear, happiness, disgust, sadness, surprise, and anger, appear within the first eight to nine months after birth. By thirty months, an infant portrays self-awareness vis-à-vis feelings and experiences more complex emotions, such as embarrassment and envy. By age three, children experience all the feelings adults experience. Naming feelings is important, but so too is being able to provide a home for them. As the discussion on being a psyche-soma indicates, feelings often come home in unwanted ways. Being effusive and allowing the free flow of feeling from self to others will wreak havoc on one's relationships and professional life. Being devoid of any feelings, however, as if persons are minds that only offer thoughts, or bottling feelings up, is equally disastrous. Grown-downs know that their feeling world is central to their relational life, as feelings are signals to apprehend what is happening.

Learning to deny, control, or hold onto feelings occurs early in life. This intrapersonal and interpersonal skill is related to *being alone in the presence of others*. Within a good enough holding environment, infants and young children can take risks to feel and emote, for they intuitively know that those who love them are stronger than any feelings experienced. Play in particular is one place where feelings from exuberance to aggression can be recognized. It is through play that one learns how to feel, how not to get flustered, and how to realize that the presence of mother or father or someone else can reduce fear. The reassurance found in a caregiver allows for play to continue. Later, the near-constant physical presence of a parent is no longer needed, but closing one's eyes when watching a scary movie diminishes the fear. Later still, feelings are brought to awareness and contained, leaving one alone with others present.

Embracing the paradox of being alone in the presence of others implies being comfortable relating to one's self and knowing when it is appropriate to enter into two- and multi-body relationships.[25] Even iconic figures, like King David of David and Goliath fame, lacked this capacity. Imagine David as he enters his last years as king of Israel. He is standing on his palace roof and sees a naked, beautiful woman. Erotic desire fills his whole being. Rather than telling himself to get off the roof, or at least to lose his gaze or go to Nathan (his prophet friend), David continues to watch her, and he ventures onto a risky but exciting path with various conspiracies to get Bathsheba. The rewards are short lived. As he succeeds, David initiates both his downfall and the painful disintegration of his family. Why did David allow his erotic desire to drive his choices and actions? Why did he remain unresponsive, only experiencing anger, at the news that his daughter Tamar was raped? Surely he was a man who felt deeply, as his psalms attest! Nations and God recognized his military and leadership skills, but he ends his life in relational conflict and familial chaos. All persons can identify with the experience of having feelings too weighty to carry alone. How one responds in those moments reflects on the development of Relational Intelligence.

Whether one relates face-to-face or virtually, one relates to others according to the relationship one has with one's feelings. If withdrawal into loneliness in reaction to feelings, not feeling at all, or passing feelings unfiltered to others are one's only choices, flourishing personally, relationally, and professionally is near impossible. Sometimes withdrawal is important, especially when heated moments should cool down, but it cannot be one's only action. Enriching or developing the self requires numerous affect-laden relationships, some internalized, some face-to-face, and yet others increasingly virtual. "It is only when alone (that is to say, in the presence of someone) that the infant can discover his own personal life," Winnicott writes.[26] For adults, this truth remains, for adults too need someone present, someone available who can empower them to risk feeling and seeking personal experience. Partners, family members, friends, mentors, counselors, and spiritual directors are the folks who empower in such ways. In these relationships feeling alive is nurtured.

Relationships remember and have a sense of time. Feelings, however, do not know time. This is one reason for time's inability to heal. This is a gift and a burden. Any feelings tied to events past or forthcoming can carry immediacy, as feelings bridge time and distance. Due to feelings' odd relationship with time, they are best approached as here-and-now and not as there-and-then. Recognizing, naming, and addressing the feelings experienced or being witnessed is the best way to give feelings time. Addressing the immediacy of feelings carries relational possibility, while focusing on any past event ("You said . . ." or "You did . . .") or foreseeing the future ("You will . . .") takes a relationship into quicksand. Focusing on feelings in the present moment moderates feeling and creates space for a new relationship with one's past and future. Grown-downs know they cannot change the past nor control the future, but they do have a say in how they engage events past and present.

In his *Feeling Matters*, analyst Michael Eigen explores the centrality of feeling in relational life, including in the relationship between him and his clients. "As long as feelings are second-class citizens in the public dialogue, people will remain second-class citizens," he warns.[27] He laments that in a consumerist and technological world, personal experience, which drives feeling, is reduced to sound bites or economic and political strategy. This both excites and dulls feeling. There seems to be no time to reflect on feelings and experience, Eigen laments. Because feelings are complicated and uneasy, most grown-ups have learned to move past them with rapid pace or ignore feelings all together, especially if the self is wounded.

"We carry around an annihilated self," Eigen writes. This wounded self shows up in one's feelings. He shares his own wounded self, when, as a five-year-old, he was made to look at his naked Aunt Bertha as she sought assurances for her insecurities on the eve of her wedding. Sometimes, Eigen relates, his wounded self meets the wounded self in one of his clients, and both selves shudder. "My hope is," Eigen continues, "that making room for the annihilated self will enable us to be less destructive. We often injure, even destroy each other, in order to reach the realness of our annihilated beings. How much destructiveness aims at 'showing' how destroyed we feel. Therapy is one place to try to contact the annihilated self without destroying ourselves. Speaking, sensing, and imagining is a less costly method of discovery than giving in to the compulsion to destroy."[28] Therapy is one of the last places where feeling worlds are explored with no haste.

The journey of growing down is not without peril. Sometimes it requires giving up a feeling or two, as if losing an old friend. But giving up something is never easy, especially if it is something that served in an empowering way or as an intimate companion. We are reminded that most people do not resist change, but they resist loss. What if a feeling is the link that keeps a relationship going? Affirming that the exploration of feelings is difficult, Eigen sees even therapists like himself "flail along in semi-blundering fashion" when facing a feeling.[29] Far from being a hopeless view or the result of incompetence, Eigen's admission of possible missteps when engaging feelings honors the complexity of emotional life, especially in the context of a society that shuns feelings unless it can be commodified. The complexities, nuances, and possibilities of exploring feelings within a safe, reliable relationship are filled with hope and possibility.

Frustration

It is grace to have relationships that can survive relational life as faces frustrate and relationships rupture. Family and friends provide such a protective context, working as the moss that guards against the blows and the cold of life. It is in these relationships where one is most likely to destroy fantasies held of those loved or encountered. Deep relational ties have the stability and the strength to withstand the tensions that projections and their dismantling bring. In Western society, it is primarily family and friends who have such durability. In other parts of the world—as is seen in Africa's *ubuntu* philosophy—society can have durability too. One needs family and friendships that function not only as a backdrop, but as bedrock.

Frustration: One wants to be noticed, but there is no one to reciprocate; there is a face, but the gaze lands elsewhere; someone does look, but not in a way appreciated. Because perfect attunement is impossible, "[most people] have never seen from the outside, or played a part in, the simple reality of two people understanding each other, respecting each other, feeling no rivalry toward each other but feeling straightforward affection for each other, finding pleasure in giving and receiving mutually, and having a stable trust in each other."[30] In his *Mental Pain and the Cure of Souls*, British analyst Harry Guntrip explores what happens when the basic need for self-realization in and by means of relationships of mutuality is frustrated. "Our fundamental need, the need that defines and characterizes our nature as human beings, is the need to relate to ourselves . . . and significantly to other human beings," Guntrip writes.[31] Fear, anxiety, despair, hostility, or even anger can set in when one is about to lose a relationship that fulfills (a good-object relationship) or if one is stuck with relationships that withhold, abuse, or persecute (bad-object relationships). One's need to be in a relationship is so strong that one would rather cling to a bad-object relationship than have no relationship whatsoever. For Guntrip mental pain is living with relational needs unmet, living a life of perpetual anxiety.

Guntrip draws upon the importance of internalized relationships. All persons have at least three kinds of internalized relationships that actively seek external relationships that will mirror them. First, one has internalized relationships that meet emotional and relational needs. A person has many such relationships, also with spiritual entities. They are kind and gracious, loving and supportive, even if they inform boundary-keeping. Second, there are internalized relationships that excite and tantalize, yet do not meet one's need: here we relate to desirable deserters. Desires are stirred, but are unaddressed, fueling frustration, anger, and hostility. Frustrated, one moves to the next desirable deserter that has promises dangling like carrots. Here, emphasis is placed on one's internalized relationships that persecute and then withhold—the hated denier—which return as the inner critic, a destructive attacker. The hated denier reminds one of the mistakes made and how one falls short, that others will discover oneself as the fraud the self believes it is.[32] Any relationship can change form and function, and a loving or exciting relationship can become a persecuting voice. It takes all but a crisis to turn God from a loving friend into a distant, aloof old man with a white beard.

The face one sees, whether it is the face of a loved one or the face of a stranger, can be seen through the eyes of that part that is loving and compassionate, the part that knows desirable deserters, or the part intimate with the hateful denier. The first part is able to enter into a mutually enriching relationship. The second excites but remains unreachable, and the third criticizes and finds fault. Whereas the hated denier is most often heard as an *internal* voice, the criticism can be projected onto others. When we project this denier onto others, we criticize easily, communicate in angry and hostile ways, and find pleasure in being a troll. Desirable deserters are often pursued. Online voyeurism and pornography easily fill this role. Deniers fuel guilt, anxiety, and fear, whereas the deserters fuel desire, risk, and excitement. When these parts of the self function unconsciously in the background guiding relationships, one feels neither authentic nor vital, even as the parts entice and persecute, leaving one wanting. Substitute gratifications wrapped in relationships bring either excitement (hooking up, pornography, and violent video games can fill this role) or relief from tension (symptoms as the body absorbs the anxiety, eating, drinking, or mindlessly surfing the Internet). Searching for substitute gratifications can become a way of living or defending against authentic relationships and the precarious risk mutuality brings.

Whether the need is deep intimacy, passionate desire, or raw vulnerability, personal need is rarely met in relationships lacking mutuality. Relational Intelligence knows what to do with the inevitable frustration that sets in when one enters into a relationship. It resists the easy temptation of allowing the unconscious to address the self's needs, which it will readily do through either excitement or criticism. Unmet recognition, love, touch, and intimacy show how easily relational life can frustrate. Personal expectations, no doubt, are high, and when not met, they frustrate and are the point where relationships fail. Every relationship frustrates, and everyone has unaddressed needs. Addressing those needs beyond behaviors and attitudes of possessiveness, compulsion, aggression, or short-term gratification reflects relational maturity.

Flirtation and Fidelity

People flirt, either with themselves or with others, by utilizing words, success, ideas, risk, madness, and even death, unless a sexualized culture has replaced the ability to flirt with hooking up and having sex. To flirt is to inject energy into one's life and relationships. To never flirt would be a sign of inner deadness and a sad reality. When one flirts, one revisits an early form of being in a relationship when, as an infant and child, one utilized seductive techniques to gain the attention of parents and other adults. For adults, flirtation longs for prior times and is an attempt to reopen and rework one's life. Flirtation can be restorative if it mirrors a new relationship with oneself, a new belief of sorts, or a desire for a restored erotic capacity.

In *On Flirtation*, British analyst Adam Phillips defines flirtation as "the art of making ambivalence into a game, the ironic art of making it a pleasure."[33] For Phillips, the word and act create an atmosphere of uncertainty and surprise, as one never knows how the beginning of a story will unfold. By weaving together innocence and experience as well as intent and opportunity, flirtation cultivates wishes and gives life even as it seduces. It makes a pleasure of instability and erotizes one's life by turning doubt and suspicion into suspense and passion. Drawing on psychodynamic theory, Phillips locates the origins of flirtation in early relational life, where infants discover the illusion of omnipotence (I can fulfill my own need) and the disillusionment that follows (I need others to have my needs met).[34]

Flirtation is an escape and can behave "as if . . ." and avoids reliability and commitment. Unlike relationships of duration—family relationships and friendships—flirtation is short-lived and impossible to sustain; it keeps an open future. For those who cannot commit, flirtation can be a hidden game of taking chances on illicit possibility. It places one halfway between sexual intimacy and caring love, between feeling trapped in a relationship and being understood. With its sexual overtones and leaning toward secrecy, flirtation can lead to infidelity as one breaks covenants with oneself or someone else.

Grown-downs know there is more to flirting with another person than just flirting. Flirtation fulfills the need to see and to be seen. It acts as a regulator, managing personal need for relationships or the desire for intimacy and filling the gaps of anxiety that can set in between faces and frustration. Flirtation uses words, smiles, and sight as touch as it soothes and stimulates. People return to flirtation because it delivers and promises excitement, vitality, and a sense of feeling real. Flirtation also addresses the needs to be creative, to test reality, to play and have pleasure (see chap. 5, "Playground Intelligence"), and to surrender. Especially flirting with ideas—imagining oneself different from who one is at the moment, in a different vocation or relationship—can meet many needs. Online identities and virtual worlds, especially comment sections and forums, provide ample opportunity for flirting with oneself and others.

Like much in life, flirtation can also be used defensively because it avoids commitment and long-term intimacy. Rather than loving relatedness, one seeks fleeting moments of connection or lust. Flirtation can also protect against the fear of fusion or rejection, personal uncertainty and disintegration, and even the loss of self. Through flirting one can protect against the feeling that the intimate other is experienced as persecutory or smothering. It also protects against fear of one's own destructive impulses when loving and hating are split and not integrated into the self. When flirtation feels mutual, it can be authentic; when aloof and distant, it is defensive.

Because flirtation lacks the bedrock of a holding environment, it is not only fleeting, but it can become risky, unfaithful, or even unethical. Flirting can turn someone into a thing, an object to be used for one's own pleasure. The risk increases if one is not aware how emotional, relational, spiritual, and sexual energies flow between persons and between persons and objects. Having fidelity and being faithful to one's own values and the covenants one made to a partner, family, friends, a community, and colleagues are inherent to the security found in life-giving relationships. Being loyal to dysfunctional relationships or a painful past should be questioned. Sometimes, however, such loyalty can keep a person safe from greater harm. Online relationships not only provide opportunity for flirtation and relationship-building, but also for moments of infidelity. Research shows that online infidelity is rationalized differently compared to being unfaithful face-to-face and that many relational break-ups begin with online infidelity.[35] The effects on one's relationships and professional self when virtual infidelity is exposed are equally destructive.

Relationships All the Way Down

The opening quote to this chapter from Turkish-born ethicist and political theorist Seyla Benhabib indicates that Self Intelligence—the nature of one's "I am"—and Relational Intelligence—how one enters into and sustain relationships—are intricately related. Psychodynamic theory and contemporary ethics converge on the importance of relationships with ethical integrity. Benhabib's *Situating the Self*, with its intersubjective, relational, and embodied self and interactive, contextual, and language-dependent understanding of rationality, provides additional visions of being a grown-down. The self is not a thing, she asserts, but a person with "a life's tale," a story.[36] Her project explores "the concrete other [which] requires us to view each and every rational being as an individual with a concrete history, identity and affective-emotional situation,"[37] the concrete other reminds us that moral living, the good life, is impossible without a relationship with the Other, a just life. In this complementary or "reciprocal recognition, [. . .] the capacity for reversing perspective and the development of the capacity to assume the moral point of view are intricately linked. . . . We seek to comprehend the needs of the Other, his or her motivations, what she searches for, and what s/he desires."[38]

Postmodernism's and the West's radical individualism is challenged as the concrete self finds identity in stories and actions woven into the concrete other. Whereas moral autonomy—to do or believe what one wants and find identity in one's actions, a contemporary mindset—fuels economic, political, and relational injustices, relationship with the concrete Other promises affirmation of humanity in general and human individuality in particular. Religion and theology, tied to eternal truths as they often are, fear postmodernism and its close ally, secularism. Grown-downs know that there is no "slippery slope" if one has Relational Intelligence. Relationships are never relative; they are situated and concrete, and have place, meaning, historicity, and culture because persons—and not the idea of persons—are involved. Benhabib reminds us that relationships require self-reflexivity, intentionality, and accountability. The face one sees, the face that responds, and the face one refuses to see and avoid all remain.

Comprehending one's own or another's story begins with the art of sustaining conversations. In her *Reclaiming Conversation: The Power of Talk in a Digital Age*, Sherry Turkle laments the loss of conversations with oneself, with friends and family, and with fellow educators and coworkers. "We have embarked on a voyage of forgetting," Turkle writes. "*At a first, we speak through machines* and forget how essential face-to-face conversation is to our relationships, our creativity, and our capacity for empathy. *At a second, we take a further step and speak not just through machines, but to machines*. This is a turning point." We face a moment of reckoning in our human nature, Turkle concludes. "It is an opportunity to reaffirm what makes us most human."[39]

Practicing facing—with oneself, with others, with God and nature—until one's last breath is taken makes life worth living.

3

TRANSITIONAL INTELLIGENCE
Toward a Theology of Illusion

There is . . . the third part of the life of a human being, a part that
we cannot ignore . . . an intermediate area of *experiencing*, to which
inner reality and external life both contribute.
— D. W. Winnicott, "Transitional Objects
and Transitional Phenomena"[1]

Linus has his blanket, Calvin has Hobbes, the French have
their *doudous*, and most infants have a thumb, a pacifier,
a soft toy, or a blanket. These possessions soothe and initiate
living in three distinct but interconnected worlds: the inner or
subjective world, the outer or objective world, and the world
in-between. Most children have a powerful, creative imagination to animate teddy bears, blankets, and pacifiers and effortlessly move between inner and outer worlds. Typically, these
objects from childhood go into limbo with age, when new spaces
for creative living, including art, culture and religion, emerge.
When one's imagination cannot flow from blankets and *doudous*

into culture, one's growth is stunted. Through a psychodynamic lens, there is a strong tie between the objects one first possessed, how one engages with culture, one's belief in God, and seeking a fulfilling life.

The human tendency to enliven objects has a long history. Because the imaginative search for meaning inspired our ancestors to portray other worlds on cave walls, enter into trance-inducing dances around fires, make offerings to gods on mountaintops and in temples, or listen to worlds created by storytellers, immersive worlds to which inner lives and external realities both contribute are valued and sought after. These transitional worlds, neither subjective nor objective, are essential: they hide and reveal meaning; they ignite fear or awaken hope; they impart vitality and anxiety or bring peace; they gather or scatter; and they provide rest from inner torment or outer pressures. For persons of all ages, the ability to enter immersive worlds is a sign of good health.

For religious persons and theologians, worlds that are neither objective nor subjective are powerful realities. Elisha, a prophet, frustrated the king of Aram more than 2,500 years ago. He told the Aramean king's secrets to the king of Israel.[2] Enraged, the king of Aram sent his army to capture Elisha, striking fear into Elisha's young servant boy. Alerted to the presence of the Arameans, Elisha prayed, for prayer is one way to enter transitional worlds. The eyes of the servant opened, and he saw large numbers of horses and chariots—all made from fire—surrounding the Arameans. It is as if the scene came from a game on Xbox or PlayStation! As the servant's eyes opened, the Arameans went blind. Elisha came to their rescue by leading them into the Israelite camp, where Israel found its enemy within reach. "Shall I kill them, my father? Shall I kill them?" the king of Israel asked. He could barely hide his excitement. Like the king of Aram, this king—who goes unnamed in the narrative, which shows how little importance he had—had never seen armies of fire. "No, do not kill them; give them food and water and let them go," Elisha replied. And so the two enemies feasted, after which the Arameans abruptly left. The narrative ends by saying the Arameans stopped raiding Israel. Transitional realities have much potential, then and now. Worlds both ancient and modern were built around power that encouraged killing, Those who can embrace the illusionistic world, however, feed, feast, and know peace.

Transitional Intelligence describes the ability to traverse three worlds—the inner-subjective, the outer-objective, and the potential space in-between—mindful of the unique contributions that each world brings to the self, the Other, the Divine, and culture. In the spaces created by Transitional Intelligence one can live without sacrifice of self or the need to flatter others with imitation or compliance. As the chapters on Self Intelligence and Relational Intelligence indicated, one's inner world constantly engages with the outer world and assigns meaning to it. By assigning meaning to it, one co-creates the outer world and is even able to liberate it. At the same time, one lives in response and reaction to an outer world that seeks to control one through signs that demand compliance. The space between these worlds is in turn filled with symbols, creativity, and potential. Transitional Intelligence embraces the dialectical process where subjective fantasy and outer reality inform, preserve, and negate each other but also seek integration, which never occurs. Symbols retain a healthy tension with signs and notifications, even if the latter are becoming regular, larger, brighter, and louder.

Objects and Spaces

Sigmund Freud described the oral fixation of babies who put a hand or a thumb in their mouth shortly after their birth. Much is happening as an infant portrays oral excitement, most notably self-regulation and discovery. In the months and years ahead, the thumb is complemented with other objects that are often soft and warm to the touch. Words and sounds, whether infant babbling or nursery rhymes and songs, play a similar soothing role. These moments are not only the beginnings of what are referred to as "transitional objects and transitional phenomena," which represent an area of experience *between* the infant and her thumb or between a toddler and his teddy bear, but they are also the beginning of their entrance into internalized relationships.[3] Objects and spaces anticipate a paradox: the infant does not create the object, which symbolically represents the breast or the bottle; it was given by a loving parent or caregiver and might have been there all along, yet the creative imagination of the infant assigns new meaning to the object as if the infant created it.

Beyond a self that is aware and has parts that remain unconscious, one has transitional experiences that indicate a place between *subjectivity* (Me) and *objectivity* (the Not-me world). This in-between space is central to culture and religion, for something is happening *between* a reader and a book, *between* a listener and music, *between* a celebrant and communion bread, or *between* a person and the Divine. When one is engrossed in play behavior, reads novels or poetry, watches movies, or listens to a good speaker, one is readily pulled into a similar intermediate area of experiencing. A person unable to enter this space faces boredom, prizes the objective world, or gets lost in subjectivity others cannot understand. Transitional objects and phenomena thus speak to a third part of life beyond signs and notifications, a part playing a central role in making life worth living.

The area between subjectivity and objectivity is filled with potential. In this space things happen and preferably go unchallenged. Calvin's parents do expose Hobbes as a toy, possibly made in China from various forms of plastic and other fabric, for in the potential space *illusion* reigns. "Illusion," with etymological roots that suggest intense or serious play (Lat., *ludere*), refers to transcendent thought or entities created by the imagination. Illusion assigns meaning and enlivens what is already there. Whereas Freud looked down on religious illusion, psychodynamic theory values illusion as a sign of health, whether it finds a home in art, culture, or religion. In illusion one surrenders control to the object and enters into a significant relationship with it. *Fantasy* (the mechanism through which meaning and purpose are assigned to experience, an attempt of the inner world to control the outer), *hallucination* (sensory experiences with no stimulus present or a conjuring of what is not there), and *delusions* (having false beliefs) are distinguished from illusion. Fantasy, hallucination, and delusions do affect one's life and relationships, but illusion is the master of creative living.

Objects like Linus' blanket and Hobbes have specific qualities: They are paradoxical in nature. Did Calvin create Hobbes or was Hobbes given to Calvin? Are they inanimate or alive? Objects are owned as a prized possession. They cannot be given and cannot be changed by someone else. They are affectionately loved, snuggled and excitedly dropped, mouthed or thrown, and even hated and dragged. The objects give life as they exude love, warmth, and acceptance. In time, one can lose one's attachment to a specific object as it goes into limbo. This loss is not really mourned or missed as one's attention flows to other relational, creative, and cultural experiences.[4]

Psychodynamically and relationally, objects of faith function like transitional objects. Does a person find God/Jesus or does God/Jesus find a person? God is certainly not a product of one's inner world, and no one has access to an objective God "out there" or "in here." Somewhere between a self and what tradition offers, God is thus unique to every person even if there is overlap with tradition or with communities of faith. Although some might argue that God is the first mover, the question of how persons and God find each other contains the paradox of spaces and objects: what is there all along is found or created. Religion often forgets that God is a possession that remains mostly untouched by critical historical methods of understanding or other hermeneutical approaches unless experience invites a person to discover God. The attempt to remove or change a person's God brings anxiety similar to a child's when her family leaves her "blanky" at home when going on vacation or when it is washed and now smells foreign. Followers of religion can be violent and for some God is a vengeful tyrant—the product of inner fantasies and our projections—yet God, ultimately, exudes love, warmth, and acceptance.

Grown-ups seem to prefer the objective world, for that is where they believe they need to succeed. They can follow signs, react to notifications, and deem embracing religion or surrendering to a community childish, infantile, or foolish. Grown-downs, however, know differently and live and thrive in three worlds: The inner-subjective world, the outer-objective world, and the world in-between. The subjective world is the world one knows the least about even though it is the most intimate. Dreaming, a nightly activity and a window to one's inner world, is difficult to communicate or to decipher. The objective world is the one known best, as the criteria for success are clear: education, independence, wealth, power, privilege, and social advancement, as in W. E. B. Du Bois' argument described in the opening chapter. Increasingly, virtual worlds are coopted by the objective world, where imaginary entities merely reflect the world of signs and notifications. The intermediate area of experiencing describes a third, in-between world, one that, though natural for children, now takes intentionality to enter. Entering this space is a natural, grown-down choice, especially if one's inner and outer worlds are in need of transformation.

In his *The Play of the Imagination: Towards a Psychoanalysis of Culture*, Dutch psychologist Paul Pruyser reflects on this tripartite view of reality. Pruyser explores how imagination is used in various contexts, such as the sciences and religion. He rejects a binary world where subjectivity and objectivity are the only choices, arguing for a third world built around illusion.[5] Pruyser has a critical conversation with philosopher Ludwig Feuerbach, who said, "The imagination is the original organ of religion."[6] For Feuerbach, religion is anthropology; for Pruyser, religion is illusion-processing, which is filled with mystery that leaves one dumbfounded. It also holds transcendence, which traverses the space-time frame. Children who can find delight in "God" and "dog" being palindromes embrace mystery and transcendence in ways grown-ups question.

Vital living requires illusion-processing, a skill that can be acquired but is vulnerable to stress or impingements from the outer world. Anxiety diminishes illusion-processing, as one withdraws into one's inner world or flees to the certainty of perceived reality. Culture provides spaces for illusion-processing, as it invites one into a third world created by the arts, books, music, cinema, religion, and crafts. Pruyser's three worlds are the autistic world, a private, inner world whose essence is difficult to convey due to its subjective nature (and distinct from "autism"); the realistic world, that public space open to inspection and verification; and the illusionistic world, a unique world that contains elements of both the autistic and realistic worlds. The three worlds are distinct:[7]

The inner world	The transitional world	The outer world
Being childlike	Being grown-down	Being grown-up
Unconscious fantasy	Intentional imagination	Sense perception
Dreaming	Playing	Working
Depression, dread, and ecstasy	Awe, hope, and joy	Power, anger/fear, and success
God-like thinking	Audacious thinking	Reality testing
Visions	Images, legends, and myths	Facts
Free associations	Inspired connections	Rational connections
Indescribable images	Evocative images	Imitative images
Personal events	Imaginative, illusionary events	Actual events
Private needs	Relational and cultural needs	Tangible needs
Symptoms	Symbols	Signs and notifications
No productivity and abstruse individuality	Creativity	Production
Internalized object	Transitional object	External object

The inner, the in-between, and the outer worlds, woven together from around twelve months of age, indicate not only the transitional quality of human nature, but also an intelligence one needs to (re)claim. One cannot escape the inner and the outer worlds, for good or ill. With intentionality and mindfulness one can enter into the potential space and become a citizen of a third (psychodynamic) world.

Life is best lived as a displaced but grounded person, living between the inner and outer worlds. Within the transitional space, questions of what is real, if real means something objective and unmediated (but accessible through sense perception), become obsolete. Realness is that which is woven together from three worlds. When an experience within the transitional space becomes more real than anything perceived by sense perception, one has to acknowledge the power of in-between, illusionistic worlds. This paradox is especially seen in symbols, which invite one to imagine oneself as being part of ever larger worlds.

Symbols

The world that exists between the inner and the outer, between subjectivity and objectivity, is also the space between the symbol and the symbolized. "To distinguish symbol and symbolized is to distinguish one's thought from that which one is thinking about, one's feeling from that which one is responding to."[8] Symbols help us understand our past as they guide the present to the future. They invite one to be an interpreter of culture and the inherited tradition. Grown-downs interpret and creatively engage with what is received, neither from a stance of immediate acceptance nor from reactionary over-againstness. Tradition is best accepted on the basis of inventiveness, for one finds personal truth in what tradition or culture provides. The process of engaging symbols is a challenge in a world that is relentless in providing signs and notifications that demand action or offer promises while commodifying persons in the process. Not all contexts accept the inherent negotiation that is required from living in three worlds. Some contexts, especially hierarchical ones, prefer signs over symbols as illness prefers symptoms.

Symbols, whether religious or not, are always in need of discovery. When symbols are created in or remain in the inner world, however, they rarely communicate. Rather, they may be seen only in symptoms. Per definition, the symbolic sets in when meaning is attached to what is already there. When symbols remain in the outer world, they lose their transformative power, which is inherent to the transitional space. Stuck in the outer world, symbols are diminished to signs without much power and with meaning apparent to all. A personal relationship that interprets symbols keeps the truths from becoming extraneous. Grown-downs seek the meaning of symbols, knowing that personal relationships determine the meaning. This search is a challenge in a technological world that flourishes on signs.

Due to their transitional and liminal nature, symbols bridge here and there, before and after, and the familiar and the unfamiliar while leaving one tongue-tied in a confrontation with meaning. Whether one witnesses birth or death, faces good or evil, feels guilt's burden or forgiveness' freedom, experiences awe and wonder, or encounters transcendence and mystery, transitional moments are inherent to life. The length of the bridge spanning the symbol and the symbolized and the ability to remain on the liminal moment's horizon are determined by one's Transitional Intelligence. When transitional intellgence is poorly developed, a person is likely to lean toward signs with a clear meaning, even if most of those signs are offered by large corporations with financial aims. If one creates the sign oneself and it represents one's inner world, few might find meaning in what one offers. When a person is "spatially" challenged, rarely residing in the transitional space or unable to move between the inner and outer worlds, one can expect a collapse of the symbolic. The art of bridging worlds is a skill not every person grows into.

Mature adults desiring to partake in society need Transitional Intelligence to discover the symbolic meanings within life and culture. A life without symbols, where *this* points to *that*, might be exciting and even successful, but ultimately without life-giving energy and possibly even meaningless. It is in the cultural field where new experiences can lead to the discovery of truths and wisdom, where symbols transcend signs. As one allows symbols to bridge one's inner and outer world, resting in the potential space in-between, the symbols become sources of meaning-making. Transitional Intelligence makes one aware of the constant psychical movement across the inner world, the outer world, and the world in-between.

The Divine is arguably the biggest of all symbols, even though a world that has come of age often renders God a sign void of immanence or transcendence. God, like all transitional objects, draws on the subjective, the objective, and the world in-between, but God resides in the latter. This is not a theological statement, but a psychodynamic one that addresses one's relationship with the Divine. Faith moves between the outer and the inner worlds to meet God in the transitional space. In this space, God waits upon discovery. In her book *The Birth of the Living God: A Psychoanalytic Study*, Ana-Maria Rizzuto explores the transitional nature of God and how personal or private relationships with God are formed: "God, psychologically speaking, is an illusory transitional object . . . God . . . is located *simultaneously* 'outside, inside and at the border' . . . God 'is not a hallucination.'"[9] Rizzuto sees God *functioning* much like Hobbes and Linus' blanket. "God is a special type of object representation created by the child in that psychic space where transitional objects—whether toys, blankets, or mental representations—are provided with their powerfully real illusory lives," she writes.[10] One does not "create" God, Rizzuto argues, either by hallucination or omnipotent grandiosity. Neither does one have objective, direct access to God, even if tradition believes it can offer such a God. Located in the in-between world, one person's God can overlap with the Gods of others, for their Gods too are created from the inner and the outer worlds. Some overlap is needed to inform and sustain a sense of togetherness or community. What makes God a "special" transitional object is that, unlike a blanket or a teddy bear, God is handed down from generation to generation and does not go into limbo. A person outgrowing God might be spending too much time in the objective and subjective worlds. Limit experiences ensure that mystery is never forgotten and also not under one's magical control. God's faithfulness is experienced in that God is "always there for love, cold disdain, mistreatment, fear, hatred, or any other human emotion that lends the object of God its usefulness."[11]

Rizzuto's research on God representations shows how representations are woven together in the transitional space. "In the course of development," she writes, "each individual produces an idiosyncratic and highly personalized representation of God derived from his object relations, his evolving self-representations, and his environmental systems of belief. Once formed, that complex representation cannot be made to disappear; it can only be repressed, transformed, or used."[12] She tells of twenty-seven-year-old Bernadine, who saw God as good, but critical of her and always withholding. She would rid herself of God if she did not believe in God's existence and power.[13] Rizzuto met Bernadine when she was hospitalized for depression, anxiety, back pain, and attempted suicide. Growing up as the oldest of seven children born to teenage parents, Bernadine was overwhelmed by responsibility, as her parents were unable to meet her need to be held and nurtured. Her mother was mostly rejecting, reminding Bernadine of the pain she caused her at birth and that Bernadine was a demanding baby. Her father was emotionally hungry and found in work an escape from home. Both her parents were overwhelmed, angry, and unhappy, as emotional, relational, and financial resources were scarce. Bernadine wanted to be the ideal daughter and tried to be nice, only to fall short of standards projected onto her, projections she readily identified with. School too proved to be a terrible experience, and she got herself in trouble throughout high school in failed attempts to be recognized.

Despite her parents being agnostic, Bernadine and her siblings were sent to Catholic church, where God was mostly good. The trauma at home was somewhat buffered by a loving paternal grandmother and a kitten. Traumatically, Bernadine's father killed the kitten by accident. God's goodness did impress, but because she rarely experienced goodness, Bernadine could not really connect with God. Now an adult, she feels worthless, often searching for a relationship that would recognize and validate her. Bernadine believes she does not deserve a relationship with a loving and compassionate God. Those around Bernadine, including God, fail to instill a feeling of worth in her. Unable to hold ambivalence, she oscillates between hope and rejection, love and rage, always longing for recognition. If only she was not such a worthless, inadequate person, she would be loved.

In Bernadine's transitional space, God, her desirable deserter, is someone with whom to communicate in private, and like the sun, he gives "a bright, clean, warm feeling." The devil, personifying (all Bernadine's) badness, also lives in her transitional space. Bernadine, isolated and alienated, has little use for or contact with others. There is touch without recognition, presence without warmth, rules without love, and power without grace as she is tormented but also held by her image of God. God wants her to be another person. Rizzuto shows how Bernadine constructed her God from childhood experiences, the outer world, and elements of her inner life, especially her feelings of being worthless. Should Bernadine engage in the work of growing down, she will have to confront a God that depletes her sense of worth. "Bernadine Fisher's psychic life has remained as it was when she was a small child," Rizzuto writes. "She has continued searching for the approval of [her parents]. . . . God, as a representation, has had no better luck with her. He too must respond [to her need for validation]. Until now he has failed."[14] Hope remains for Bernadine, for the self longs to leave life-depriving places and relationships. Her symbolic world longs for relief.

To believe in and have faith, one has to make believe by meeting the Divine in the intermediate area of experiencing.

Creativity and Culture

"Come at the world creatively, create the world; it is only what one creates that has meaning for you." Winnicott writes.[15] Creativity is not brilliance, genius, or even intellect, but it identifies the unique way one approaches the world. Creativity is the act of finding meaning through controlled illusion. Very few persons, if any, do not have the capacity for creative living, a capacity that is greatly determined by how one is held in infancy and foundational to one's cultural experience. "Cultural experience starts as play and leads to the whole area of [humanity's] inheritance, including the arts, the myths of history, the slow march of philosophical thought and the mystery of mathematics and of group management and of religion."[16] It is a healthy person who can traverse the three worlds and contribute to inherited tradition, for living creatively implies engaging culture and tradition.

The inherited tradition is central to any experience of culture, as creativity assigns new meaning to what already exists. A life of cultural plagiarism, where one merely accepts what is received, is a life devoid of creativity and the interplay between what is handed down and what is discovered. Likewise, a life of autistic self-centeredness comes at a cost of intimacy and belonging. Culture is a location grown-downs frequent. The transitional space is filled with transactions shaped by creative apperception. One needs to create over and over again to feel alive. In surprise, discovery, originality, and humor, life is discovered as worth living. Should a person's creative living be foreclosed by depression, anxiety, or desperate attempts at survival, doubt that life is worth living sets in. Theologian Martin Buber once said that mindfulness and art supplement each other as if they were two electric poles between which a spark jumps. The spark is creativity and, when found, it infuses life with vitality.

Meditating on the meaning of a life's journey, for example, releases symbolic and transformational power and highlights personal truth. With refreshed senses, a keen mind, and a soaring spirit, one can traverse the inner world and the outer while finding purpose in the transitional space. This movement (or oscillation) within the transitional world, where the outer world informs the inner world, which in turn interacts with the outer world, transforms a self, allowing one to partake fully in society and culture. This movement describes everyday creativity. Oscillation is present when one listens to music, gets pulled in by a novel or a poem, is captivated by a film, or surrenders in meditation to a spiritual practice such as prayer. Entering such transitional spaces takes commitment as well as protection against the impingements from the outer world—increasingly coming to us through technology—and a willingness to be transformed.

Living creatively, psychoanalyst Elizabeth Presa writes as she reflects on the importance of art, is "sustaining a 'healthy' state of 'madness': the body and soul's revolt against compliance and normality."[17] She reminds us that "madness"—from the Latin *insanus* (insane, outrageous, excessive, extravagant)— and "health"—from the Old English *haelen* (to heal) and *halig* (holy, sacred)—come together in the act of creativity as holy madness. Whereas the outer world places monetary, moral, or even spiritual value on objects and products, creativity arouses personal meaning. Value determined by others leaves one wanting, whereas creating and finding personal meaning promises fulfillment and fuels a sense of curiosity.

Opportunities for creative living and contributing to culture have increased as technology has become a dominant presence in personal ways of being. It is estimated that every two days the two-plus billion people online create as much intellectual, narrative, and pictorial content as humanity did from the dawn of civilization until 2003, about five exabytes of information![18]

YouTube, Pinterest, Instagram, Wikipedia, online games, blogs, and similar creative and collaborative sites are places where everyday creativity thrives. Research shows that not only do video producers have a tacit knowledge of what viewers want to see, but that viewers can assess a producer's openness to experience and creativity (understood as a combination of narrative content and aesthetics).[19] Virtual spaces can inform either the inner world with its subjective orientation, the external world with productivity and signs, or the in-between world where rich symbolism invites a person on a life-giving journey.

We are attracted to the in-between world because the creativity inherent in Transitional Intelligence instills a sense of aliveness and freedom. This creativity is far removed from the compulsive use of technology or the false belief that multitasking increases productivity. Like the false self trying to present itself as a whole person, multitasking in settings where others anticipate one will be present draws attention without recognition. Behind a steering wheel, multitasking, which places oneself and others at risk, reflects a personal ruthlessness one has yet dealt with. Creativity is not only the antidote to multitasking (see chap. 6, "Technological Intelligence"), but it is also the answer to boredom.

Boredom

Grown-downs welcome boredom because boredom is the gateway to creative living. With screens readily available and new apps released daily, persons young and old rarely experience boredom. In *On Kissing, Tickling, and Being Bored*, Adam Phillips defines boredom as "that state of suspended anticipation in which things are started and nothing begins, the mood of diffuse restlessness which contains that most absurd and paradoxical wish, the wish for desire."[20] Boredom is being listless and restless, seeking experience while lacking interest in a drawn-out experience of time. Boredom reminds us that each thing has its time. It is an interruption of sorts, happening after something ends and before something begins. By asking, "Are we there yet?" and, "What shall we do now?" children confess they are on the brink of boredom or that boredom has already overwhelmed them, and the tension is unbearable. Children can reach boredom, either with the ride itself, with themselves, or with a boring object, in no time.

Philosopher Martin Heidegger reminds us that boredom is an essential or profound feeling and has a subjective and objective quality.[21] Heidegger sees boredom as the concealed destination of the scientific era and distinguishes being bored *by* (as a subjective experience) from being bored *with* (where boredom is seen as a quality of an object). He describes boredom as time becoming long or too slow (from the German *langeweile*), "being held in limbo," and "being held out into the Nothing."[22] Without time passing, boredom cannot set in. Psychodynamic theory joins Heidegger in seeing value in boredom as an inner mood of quiescence when waiting for an experience.

The capacity for boredom originates in an infant learning how to be alone in the presence of others, which speaks to being comfortable with a one-body relationship and knowing when it is appropriate to enter into two- and multi-body relationships. Boys and men tend to score higher on boredom scales than girls and women, regardless of culture, a fact ascribed to boys receiving easy attention from caregivers because of culture's masculine bias. Phillips reminds us that boredom and frustration are partners. In boredom, a child becomes frustrated by a lack of preoccupation: "Neither hopeless nor expectant, neither intent nor resigned, the child is in a dull helplessness of possibility and dismay."[23]

When adults hear, "Are we there yet?" or, "What shall we do now?" they often hear it as a command, as if they somehow failed at providing something interesting for a child or need to solve a problem. In part the lack of provision is true, for behind the question children long for mutuality, for face-to-face recognition, and for transformational experiences. "How often, in fact, the child's boredom is met by that most perplexing form of disapproval, the adult's wish to distract him—as though the adults have decided that the child's life must be, or be seen to be, endlessly interesting."[24] Today, parents and teachers have been replaced by technology, which readily offers distractions. The giving of an interesting life, however, prohibits the discovering thereof. With a phone in hand or while staring at a tablet, life passes by. In boredom, time seemingly suspends itself as it waits on creative living. For children and adults, boredom is a blessed burden if one can allow oneself to stay with it and in it. Grownups rarely have patience for boredom, whether with themselves or with others.

Phillips describes an articulate eleven-year-old whose false self would not allow him to be bored. From an early age he learned how to be good according to parental demands. He lived with the expectation that he would have many interests, "of the respectable, unembarrassing sort, nothing that would make him feel awkward or strong." His false self protected him from boredom and kept his true self at bay. The false self's protection and the capacity to hold anticipation begins in early infancy when objects to grasp are within reach, and the infant either takes hold of the object after a moment of hesitation or does not find it at all. For the boy the cost of an overly developed false self came in the form of loneliness, an inability to make friends, misery, and uncertainty as to who he was. "When I'm bored," the boy tells Phillips, "I don't know myself." The boy never learned how to hold his mood, nor has he learned how to make use of adults in nonimpinging ways. When boredom brings uncertainty and frustration, the boy prematurely flees elsewhere. He cannot try things out, or even fail, because his parents provided distractions that ensured success. According to Phillips, most adults experience boredom as "unexplaining, inarticulate; certainly not pathological but nevertheless somehow unacceptable."[25] Boredom is something that needs to be removed, for the lack of desire is unbearable.

Boredom is the invitation to and a gateway to creative living. In itself boredom carries little potential, for boredom never enters the transitional space; it merely anticipates. With imagination one never has to be bored. Children often rely on adults and increasingly on technology to relieve them from boredom. Technology has banished boredom at a cost rarely reckoned. Those who have known technology since birth and who handle it often may not even know what boredom is. Technology killed idle time and, in the process, eradicated boredom. Advertisements and algorithms offer exactly what one desires — something distracting or titillating, if not stimulating. When a moment of hesitation arrives as boredom approaches, a phone or tablet is grabbed, a screen is fingered or watched, and images from the outer world flow inward. Eyes transfixed by screens and minds jumping from one site or app to the next have replaced daydreaming and mind wandering. The false self sighs, convinced of a job well done, as the true self retreats in silence. Transitional Intelligence includes the ability to be bored and denies false solutions to the inherent tensions of boredom. Boredom without creativity, if fused with leisure time, is positively linked to addictions, overeating and increased consumption, drunk driving, excessive gaming and gambling, aggression, increased sexual activity, feelings of meaninglessness or despondency, reduced vitality, and higher levels of mortality.[26]

Fleeing from boredom discloses the poverty of one's creative imagination and heightened narcissism with a concomitant sense of omnipotence. It takes creativity to know what to do with one's time, to have realistic goals, to not procrastinate, or to guard against foreclosing the anticipation boredom brings. Boredom gives way to the ability to create internal representations and to maintain a sense of self that is neither compliant to outside demands nor wrapped in a false sense of omnipotence. When a child discovers she can hold the anticipation, internalized images or toys come alive. Later, the child can stand in front of a clean canvas and wait for an image to appear, stare at a blank page waiting for a poem to reveal itself, wait for an elevator or at a red light without reaching for a phone, or experience solitude. For persons of faith, waiting upon the Sacred to speak into their lives demands not collapsing the boredom into busy thinking or activity. Meditative and contemplative practices are structured exercises in boredom as one patiently waits upon wisdom or revelation. Maybe one always waits upon the Sacred. One has to have some belief in oneself, some trust that the waiting will deliver and something good will come, to risk the boredom that leads to solitude.

Grown-downs, embracing boredom, resist a harried life, for such a life is never creative. In waiting lies the promise of discovery and vitality. It takes courage to wait and not know exactly who will arrive or what will appear. By linking memory (past, present, and future), perception, and desire, boredom offers the core ingredients of a creative life. It allows one to see the world unfiltered and allows one to surrender to the transformational object, which alters self-experience (see chap. 1, "Self Intelligence"). Phillips concludes his reflections on boredom by saying that boredom makes tolerable the impossible experience of waiting for something without knowing what it could be. "For the adult, it seems, boredom needs to be the more permanent suspended animation of desire. Adulthood, one could say, is when it begins to occur that you may not be leading a charmed life."[27] This view is kinder than Søren Kierkegaard's, who saw boredom as the root of all evil because in boredom, one refuses to be oneself.[28] Kierkegaard was correct in identifying having a higher cause as an antidote to boredom and also in seeing boredom as having the capacity to initiate motion. But he was wrong in seeing boredom as evil and a refusal to be oneself. In the absence of distraction, potential hides. Seeking to escape boredom can lead to losing the self and foreclosing a creative life filled with meaning and purpose. When an adult follows boredom all the way down to childhood, boredom lost can be found.

Toward Polyphony

No one is ever freed from negotiating the inner and the outer. It takes Transitional Intelligence to master this art. Dietrich Bonhoeffer, the German theologian who loved music, wrote poetry, and imagined religion in a world come of age, died too soon at the hands of Hitler's Nazi troops in 1945. In *Letters and Papers from Prison*, Bonhoeffer describes *polyphonic* living, a musical metaphor describing creative living. Writing to his friend Eberhard Bethge, Bonhoeffer reminds Bethge that one's erotic loving and living are countered by the love of the Divine. Human love and God's love together form "the polyphony of life . . . [God's love provides] a *cantus firmus* to which the other melodies of life provide the counterpoint," Bonhoeffer states.[29] Polyphony is a style of composition "in which a primary and unchanging melody (the *cantus firmus*) is progressively joined by the counterpoint melodies which superficially oppose it but, taken as a whole, form a powerful harmonic whole."[30]

In the polyphony of life Bonhoeffer comforts fellow prisoners as bombs make them anxious and as he anticipates his own death. Like Elisha's servant boy who lost his fear, Bonhoeffer witnesses the multidimensionality of a life that discovered meaning in the potential space between security and insecurity, between chaos and that which remains constant, between the inner and the outer, and between a present and absent God. In a follow-up letter to Bethge, Bonhoeffers admits that the image of polyphony still pursues him: "I couldn't help thinking that pain and joy are also part of life's polyphony, and that they can exist independently side by side."[31] It requires Transitional Intelligence and the space in-between to harmonize pain and joy, distress and peace, and even evil and the Divine into a polyphonous whole.

Transitional Intelligence promises feeling alive and anticipates a place of living where one can thrive. This place transcends location and circumstance. It is an intelligence that describes a person asking unanswerable questions, seeking experiences that give life and deepen meaning, and discovering truths that are handed down. For those unable to appreciate the polyphony of life or who find living in three worlds oppressive or even stifling, Transitional Intelligence reflects madness. "[We] are poor indeed if we are only sane," Winnicott writes.[32]

4

REPARATIVE INTELLIGENCE
Toward a Theology of Care

The "I'm sorry" text is a missed opportunity.
— Sherry Turkle, *Reclaiming Conversation*[1]

Measured for empathy, today's college students show a decline of 40 percent compared to their peers thirty years ago. Research by the University of Michigan measured the "empathy concern" of college students between 1979 and 2009 and discovered this significant decline. "Having empathy is an important factor in the motivation and ability to inhibit harmful behaviors because imagining the potential harm that one might cause deters antisocial behaviors," the researchers write.[2] "[We] speculate that one likely contributor to declining empathy is the rising prominence of personal technology and media use in everyday life. Clearly, these changes have fundamentally affected the lives of everyone who has access to them. With so much time spent interacting with others online rather than in reality, interpersonal dynamics such as empathy might certainly be altered."[3] The researchers' speculation is more than a mere probability.

Psychodynamically, empathy speaks to one's capacity for concern and one's ability to engage in acts of reparation. If we are made from the dust of the earth, as one Christian narrative says, the fingerprints and footprints from all who touched us, whether in moments of love or moments of violence and trauma, show. As stated earlier, the self catalogues its experiences (see chap. 1, "Self Intelligence"). Every person is thus in need of reparation, which goes beyond Christianity's emphasis on salvation. Although reparation does not exclude salvation, salvation most often excludes reparation. Whereas salvation can be pronounced, reparation demands personal and relational work. Persons on the path of restoration, who are not burdened by the wounds of trauma and neglect, can risk care. Care is a risk because one does not know in advance how another will respond. Still, with emotional, relational, and spiritual energies to invest in others as empathy, care, and concern, those who know reparation can be a healing presence to themselves, others, and nature. How does one develop a sense of care and of moral engagement? How does caring and wounding take place in a technological world? Are we becoming less caring as we engage with handheld technologies more deeply?

In *The Capacity for Care: Gender and Ethical Subjectivity*, Wendy Hollway explores how "respect for difference and care across [gender and other] differences are achieved."[4] Drawing on British object relations theory, she locates care in unconscious dynamics, emotional and psychic conflicts, the intersubjectivity formed between two people, and interplays of body and mind. "Babies are not born with a capacity to care but they do need care," Hollway writes. Infants do have "a capacity to communicate their internal states, and by extension their needs, to someone, usually an adult, on whom they depend absolutely for physical survival, psychological security, and viability."[5] Vulnerable to caregivers, not all children have their emotional and other needs met.

Some children are gifted intellectually, but all children are gifted in surviving holding environments that inevitably failed them. In these relationships love and hate were not balanced, and perfect attunement proved impossible. We carry the gifts of defense and survival mechanisms that hide the wounds received from those we love and those who did not care. Being gifted beckons the work of reparation, growing into a person whose wounds no longer dictate one's personal and professional lives. Without reparation, the wounds continue to hurt despite the passing of time. Most often the wounds are kept frozen and hidden so as not to be felt or revealed. We witness each other's wounds, whether in somatic illnesses, attitudes, and behaviors or in an inability to sustain relationships. The hurt one carries is projected onto others or makes us prickly and porcupine-like. Sometimes numbness, oversensitivity, fragility, or defensiveness characterizes the wounded, or a person seeks compensation elsewhere so as not to feel the pain. Others grow into being aloof, stoic, depressed, or grandiose. With experiences of pain and trauma kept frozen, the self has little emotional, relational, and spiritual energy left to share with others.

Adults who were gifted children may be successful in the eyes of the world and able to keep things together, but they often lack interpersonal vitality or the ability to sustain intimate relationships. Sadly, some gifted children become perpetrators and wound others through emotional distancing, shaming, causing loss, raging, or engaging in other abusive and exploitative behaviors. Repeating the wounds and traumas one received is a risk every gifted-child-now-grown-up faces. It is no surprise that gifted parents parent gifted children. The process of growing down anticipates moving toward one's wounds and revisiting the truth of one's childhood and life. It also invites one into the presence of a person or persons where one can be held again, for in such relationships the promise of reparation can unfold and the caretaking of the false self can be surrendered. Healing one's wounds takes courage, which comes easier if surrounded by caring people. The reward of reparation is not just personal; it also frees one to participate more fully in the reparation of others and the world.

In *The Drama of the Gifted Child*, Polish-born Swiss psychologist Alice Miller explores some of the wounds a child experiences in moments of misattunement, unreachable expectations, and abuse. These wounds leave young and old with feelings of emptiness, abandonment, depression, guilt, or shame, as well as the possibility of generally feeling helpless and overwhelmed. The wounded are often depressed. "[To] become whole," Miller writes, "we must try, in a long process, to discover our own personal truth [about our childhood], a truth that may cause pain before giving us a new sphere of freedom."[6] Miller's giftedness is not intellectual giftedness, but it may include it. Rather, it originates in the defenses that protect against hurt: self-denial, intellectual wisdom, grandiosity, acute emotional perception in others, various forms of performance and perfectionism, or even antisocial behavior. The gifted "have all developed the art of not experiencing feelings, for a child can experience her feelings only when there is somebody there who accepts her fully, understands her, and supports her."[7] Without reparation a gifted child becomes a diminished adult, for the cost of survival is giving away aspects of the true self and allowing the false self to grow. "We can repair ourselves and gain our lost integrity by choosing to look more closely at the knowledge that is stored inside our bodies and bringing the knowledge closer to our awareness. *Most people do exactly the opposite.*"[8] Miller warns that denying or running away from one's wounds is natural when moving toward and embracing personal wounds promises restoration. The process of growing down anticipates revisiting one's wounds and reclaiming the innocence and vitality once experienced in childhood.

Reparative Intelligence is the courage of discovering the truth of one's childhood and life, seeking restoration for oneself, and facilitating the restoration of persons, relationships, communities, and nature with compassion, care, and empathy. Restoration is not a return to wholeness, an unreachable goal; rather, it is a way of living with vitality and with a sense of feeling alive while being able to recall traumatic events. Whereas a desire for wholeness reflects infant grandiosity, restoration includes seeing reality for what it is: broken. Restoration is finding meaning in one's history and discovering and integrating a new story for the self, one that includes one's past. Reparative Intelligence inevitably takes us toward caring and compassionate faces: friends, guides, teachers, mentors, and counselors. It beckons a compassionate God who promised, "I will repay you for the years the locusts have eaten."[9] "[What] has broken relationally must be repaired relationally," analyst Donald Kalsched reminds us.[10] Healing relationships are most often face-to-face, reliable, trustful, respectful, and honest, communicating empathy and understanding and holding whatever feelings arise. In these relationships one can be oneself with no need to be compliant, whether to the internal script of the false self or to external demands.

Online worlds often portray the wounds people carry and induce. One place we witness this is in comments posted online. In *Reading the Comments: Likers, Haters, and Manipulators at the Bottom of the Web*, Joseph Reagle explores the complex nature of online comments, a reality that has become ubiquitous. A video or photo uploaded with the caption "Am I ugly?" will unleash a torrent of disparaging comments. Reagle wonders if the person posting the comment receives the validation sought, because criticism stings more than a kind word protects. "Comment can be used to express hate or support," Reagle surmises, "but I sense that the deluge of hate leaves a much stronger impression than even the kindest expressions of encouragement."[11] There is an inescapable gender dimension too, with much misogyny, sexism, and homophobia found online. That many hateful comments are no longer offered under the guise of anonymity is a concern and reflects changes in human nature, Reagle states.

Reparative Intelligence is central to a flourishing humanity, for it denies cycles of wounding and invites realness and authenticity. It takes one toward one's loving and hating, supports growing in care and concern, and encourages participation in acts of reparation. Not every person grows down into the wisdom of Reparative Intelligence.

Love and Hate

Grown-downs love deeply and passionately and can hate with equal intensity. Love is a "sense [or state] of *responsiveness*, which is unwearying, tolerant and even appreciative, insighted and alert."[12] One finds such love in the Divine, who is "gracious and compassionate, slow to anger and abounding in love, who relents from sending calamity" (Joel 2:13). Hate is reactivity to emotional, relational, and personal need not met; it is a demand for love. Whereas love nurtures, hate always self-frustrates even as it empowers. With Reparative Intelligence, one can own one's loving and hating, knowing that passionate energies always flow to the self and others. Whereas the language of love is readily embraced, the language of hate is strong, especially in a violent world. Still, humans are ruthless and aggressive: they hate. Hate befriended, however, can turn to frustration being contained and the Other being discovered.

Growing Down's psychodynamic understanding of love and hate is different from a philosophical, ethical, or theological evaluation. From a psychodynamic perspective, the human capacity for love and responsive companionship grew out of an infant's needs for nurture, dependence, and self-preservation. When the need for nurture is frustrated, hate sets in. Here, human love finds correlates in those mammals that nurture their young for a prolonged period, such as baboons, elephants, dolphins, and whales, mammals in which a bond of love can be recognized between mothers and their young. Loving and hating are the first experiences in an infant's holding environment and are thus closely tied to parents and primary caregivers. If by age three, a child experiences all the emotions adults experience, personal patterns around loving and hating are set early.

Ian Suttie, a Scottish psychiatrist who argued for sociability and anticipated psychologies built around relationships, is arguably the first theorist to identify loving and hating as central to the pre-oedipal child, to infants born "in a state of nurtural dependency [with] the whole instinct of self-preservation."[13] In *The Origins of Love and Hate*, published in 1935 shortly after his untimely death, Suttie rejects notions that love originates from a divine source (religion), that love is a reaction of fear of the father or purely sexual instincts (Sigmund Freud), or that love is a "chemical change in the germ plasma" (biology).[14] Love originates in a prolonged and sheltered immaturity as the infant retains a primary companionship to have his or her physical and emotional needs met. When these needs are not met, it produces hate (e.g., rage and terror) as a defense against isolation, loneliness, and, ultimately, death. Furthermore, love unmet can convert into despair, unworthiness, guilt, shame, or even a sense of loss and grief. Suttie identifies play as being central to assisting the infant in having his or her emotional and relational needs met as an infant is weaned and grows in independence (see chap. 5, "Playground Intelligence"). In time, sibling relationships, friendships, community, and society become substitutes for the first love with mother or other primary caregivers.

The need for love ensures that person-based relationships are stronger than relationships focusing on things or issues. "For all our language, cultural achievements and our family life, our love need is still seeking new techniques of social relationship," Suttie wrote in 1935.[15] He would support modern technologies that build relationships, foster community, and allow for additional choices in having one's love needs (e.g., touch, recognition, belonging, safety, or emotional and physical nurture) met. The fact that persons get anxious when not connected with their devices, Suttie might argue, indicates that love needs are not met through technology, for when an infant's love needs are met, even imperfectly, as is always the case, the infant grows in independence away from mother, father, and her primary caregivers. We are growing more attached to technology, a contemporary form of regression. Because frustration sets in when love needs are not met, the same technologies we use to build relationship and community become the mechanisms by which persons unleash hate into the world. Research indicates that anxious people not only engage with technology more readily, but that they also tend to drift more toward violent video games, which can provide an outlet for the hate they carry.[16] It should be no surprise that violent video games are the best-selling genre in an ever-expanding world of gaming. This growth exposes North American society's orientation and ambivalence toward hatred and violence. In the 2011 US Supreme Court case *Brown vs. Entertainment Merchants Association*, the question was raised whether violent material and images should be regulated in the same way as sexual images and content. The court said no because violent games are protected by free speech.[17]

If love is a state of *responsiveness* birthed in one's need for nurturance, hate is *reactiveness*, a discomfort or a frustration, even an appetite awakened when love needs are not met. "[*Love*] *threatened* becomes anxious, that is to say partly transformed into *anxiety*. So far as it is *denied* it is transformed into *hate*, while external interference (supplanting) switches it into *jealousy*."[18] Psychodynamically, the purpose of hate is not to destroy, and aggression is not merely an attempt to alleviate frustration. Whereas an infant uses aggression to distinguish the Me from the Not-me, hate is a call for love and an attempt to induce responsiveness from one's holding environment. As an attempt to have personal needs met, hating persons we love has a relational edge and leaves emotional residue that hatred aimed at anonymous and faceless persons or enemies does not. We do not expect anonymous commentators in cyberspace or elsewhere to love us and provide a holding environment for us even if comments from others are readily sought in a Web 2.0 world. Holding environments inevitably demand face-to-face encounters. Undirected and objectless love and hate that does not *recognize* the Other ultimately frustrates, and one typically moves on to the next recipient of one's hate until one's needs are met. Because hate is not an optimal way to seek satisfaction for one's needs, it always self-frustrates and leaves one deprived. Reparative Intelligence empowers one to seek life-giving ways to meet physical, personal, and relational needs. It fosters a caring and empathic attitude toward oneself, others, and the world.

To Have Concern

Loving and hating are not the only narratives by which one lives. Care and having concern for others are powerful narratives too. "Concern refers to the fact that the individual *cares*, or *minds*, and both feels and accepts responsibility."[19] Not every person develops concern, and not every person with this ability has it to the same extent. Growth in one's concern is a sign of health and is the result of integrating loving and hating into a process that starts in infancy and continues into adulthood. Having concern includes being mindful that one's actions affect oneself and others and that hating is not a constructive way to meet one's own or someone else's love needs.

All of relational and social life, as well as playing and working, depends upon individuals being concerned. Concern describes a natural sense of guilt and is the foundation of human moral development. Feeling guilty when one hurts another person is a sign of maturity. This sense of (healthy) guilt is relieved through acts of reparation. Guilt feelings, which are those feelings that undermine one's well-being and are seemingly resistant to being willed or prayed away, reflect the lack of integration of loving and hating one's person or holding paradox.

Established early in life, a personal sense of morality predates any moral code society or religion instills.[20] An infant with a sense of omnipotence — I am the world and the world is me — is ruthless and shows no concern. She bites her mother's nipple or pokes a finger in her eye, as mother is not yet a Not-me and thus does not exist. Other times the infant pulls the hair of the person that holds her without any indication that she is hurting the person holding her. Of course, in both instances hurt is inflicted and the adults may even hate the infant for a moment. In health, one grows toward a sense that the Other exists, and one begins to feel responsible. Out of such acts of aggression the Other is distinguished; one loves more and hates less. Sadly, many persons remain ruthless and show little awareness that their actions affect themselves and others. They hurt themselves physically, emotionally, relationally, spiritually, and economically; say hurtful things to those they love or those they have never met; text while driving and put lives at risk; answer e-mails in settings where personal presence is required; and they impinge, abuse, bully, or troll. With the technology we have at hand, our ruthlessness has been redefined. As Reagle reminds us, online forums, comment sections, and other virtual spaces expose the hate many persons freely unleash on others.[21] Sherry Turkle writes on "the cruelty of strangers" seen in online worlds: "If you share something intimate with a stranger, you invest in that person's opinion. Anonymity does not protect us from emotional investment. . . . We build technologies that leave us vulnerable in new ways."[22] Technology, with its brief and anonymous forms of communication, exposes the lack of concern we have. When one seeks to meet personal need in ways that will disappoint, hate and ruthlessness are awakened.

The psychodynamic origins of care and concern or empathy are found in the life stage when an infant moves from a one-body relationship (there is only me) to two- or multi-body relationships (there is me and others) and when an infant's sense of omnipotence diminishes. Around the fifth month, an infant begins to distinguish the Me from the Not-me and a natural sense of guilt sets in as the infant discovers the Other through acts of aggression—reaching out to others by causing hurt. The infant's guilt stems from a sense that something was taken from a caregiver (the milk or food ingested) and now the caregiver has a hole in him or her. The infant may also feel guilty for the physical hurt caused when a nipple was bitten, for the infant notices the wince on mother's face. There might also be guilt for keeping parents and caregivers awake at night. This aggression, which has no intention to hurt, does however hurt if one is on the receiving end. When an infant bites her mother and the mother does not retaliate by immediately weaning her daughter to a bottle, an infant can discover that the mother exists as another person, a Not-me. The infant learns how to hold back aggressive impulses and finds ways to restore mother if mother is hurt in the process of feeding.

Concern is thus the awareness of the infant that she caused some damage, that she has to hold the discomfort this awareness brings, and that she can extend an act of reparation to her mother. Acts of reparation first appear as spontaneous gestures around the fifth month. Acts include feeding without biting, offering a smile, holding a gaze, going to sleep without fussing, having a bowel movement, or touching lovingly and allowing some cuddling. Hollway tells of a mother driving with her young children who could not stop fighting on the back seat. Exhausted, the mother confessed, "I slammed on the brakes and started banging the steering wheel and shouting at them to go away and shut up, and leave me alone. Then someone started stroking me and Carl [the two-year-old] said 'it's alright Mummy, it's alright.' "[23] There are complex interactions between infants and children and their caregivers.

With maturation, acts of reparation can be seen in the admission of guilt and having remorse; being nice after being naughty; staying close to mother or father or giving them a silent hug; obeying house rules; wanting to withdraw emotionally, but staying connected; apologizing and asking for forgiveness; not pressing send on a hurtful text, e-mail or post, or not being totally annihilated when receiving such communication; and partaking in society and culture in positive ways, which include religious activities and communities. For the religious, it is a comfort to believe in a God at whom one can be angry without living in fear of being struck by lightning, or to trust in a Savior who survives physical destruction. When skilled in the act of reparation, one can remain in relationships that in their passion can become unwieldy, even with elements of hate. Discovering creative ways to offer spontaneous gestures to others makes life worth living.

With concern the infant can distinguish between the parent who is flesh and blood — Winnicott identified the "environment mother" — and the parent who is alive in the infant's imagination — the "object mother" — as an internalized relationship.[24] It is the environment mother who needs to survive the aggression while her infant continues a relationship with the object mother. The new relationship with the object mother leads to a less ruthless, quieter relationship with the mother who offers her breast or a bottle. Only at this point of development can the infant assume responsibility. "The word 'concern' [describes] in a positive way a phenomenon that is covered in a negative way by the word 'guilt.' . . . Concern implies further integration, and further growth, and relates in a positive way to an individual's sense of responsibility, especially in respect of relationships into which the instinctual drives have entered."[25]

Thriving relationships and communities depend on communicating care or concern and engaging in acts of reparation. Sadly, many grown-ups lack the integration of this core human trait. They either did not have the opportunity to offer reparation themselves and experienced their hate and aggression by annihilating the Other, or they were exposed to the ruthlessness of someone and the reparation never came, or they have given up on the continual work that Reparative Intelligence demands. In extreme situations, the lack of concern can be so pronounced that a person may lack empathy altogether. Even then, the true self's hope that reparation will prevail remains.

Concern grows in relationships that are responsive and loving, relationships that survive one's loving and hating, one's aggression and destruction. These relationships include parenting (surviving the aggression of a child), friendships, mentoring and coaching relationships, marriage and other committed partnerships, and counseling relationships. Without a significant level of trust in a relationship, the necessary holding environment that allows for concern to set in cannot be established, and the risk of continuing a cycle of hate and hurt increases significantly. Many relationships fall apart before reparation can occur, as the false self seeks new relationships that protect against hurt but also inhibit transformation. Online, one can move from one comment section to another to troll and bully victims. It is grace that some counselors, life coaches, and other professionals are trained to survive one's ruthlessness and to facilitate the integration of loving and hating. The effect of living with hate and ruthlessness is often underestimated as cycles of hurt and exploitation continue. When an infant or child receives the gift of reparation, facilitating the reparation of others comes naturally.

Frozen Moments

When wounded, especially without reparation, the self does something with the hurt. "No one knows how deflated and devalued the child feels inside, and how its heart sinks, and in time it probably learns to cover over its hurt by a hard, naughty, or defiant exterior, or else shrinks into itself like a snail into its shell from the outside world that seems to have little use for it and apparently regards it as a nuisance," Guntrip writes.[26] The false self as caretaker of the self often chooses one of two paths: it channels the energy outward into defiant and even antisocial behavior, or it hides the hurt deep in one's inner world where the pain is kept frozen, for it hurts less in a solid state. The false self's primary goal is to diminish one's hurt, whether focusing the hurt outward or keeping it frozen inside. In discussing the need of some persons to regress to a state of dependency in a counseling journey, Winnicott writes, "One has to include in one's theory of the development of a human being the idea that it is normal and healthy for the individual to be able to defend the self against specific environmental failure by a *freezing of the failure situation*." Defense mechanisms are not pathological, but they can become so when they become a way of being and not a time-limited defense against a specific event. Frozen moments carry "the unconscious assumption . . . that opportunity will occur at a later date for a renewed experience in which the failure situation will be able to be unfrozen and re-experienced . . . in an environment that is making adequate adaptation."[27] We freeze to thaw later. When frozen moments are left frozen, they affect lives negatively because they ensure that one cannot show up as a person able to love, hate, and repair, especially in intimate relationships.

It is common to regress in moments of illness, when the need for being loved and cared for increases and curling up in the fetal position comes naturally. Likewise, it often takes going back to relationships of dependency, such as the ones found in a counseling journey, to thaw a frozen moment. Approaching a frozen moment increases a sense of vulnerability, often followed by anger at the environmental and relational failure that caused the wound. Thawing and remembering awaken pain as if someone's hate is experienced for the first time. The regression during illness, if situated in a caring environment, can thaw earlier deprivation. In addition, failure situations can be "reached and unfrozen by various healing phenomena of ordinary life, namely friendships, nursing during illness, poetry, etc."[28] The false self, in an attempt to enliven us in the face of emotional energies flowing toward the frozen moment, may seek sensual pleasure with short-lived effect. These experiences are bound to feel unreal and even futile. As powerful emotions are held in a holding environment where thawing takes place, a new sense of independence originating from the true self can set in. Vitality returns and the false self can resign its caretaking function.

The image of harboring and thawing frozen moments is provocative. It provides a glimpse of what the work of reparation entails. Alice Miller tells of Johanna, a twenty-five-year-old first-time mother to Michael.[29] While parenting him, she developed mastitis, a hardening of the nipples that made nursing very painful, with an accompanying fever. This happened suddenly and without apparent reason. Working with Miller, Johanna revisited sexual trauma she experienced in childhood, trauma that Johanna felt robbed her of her maternal instincts. When Johanna addressed her past—thawing her frozen moments—it lowered her fever and the mastitis improved. Johanna's psyche-soma used her breasts as a psychic shelter. After some personal work, during which her infant received a bottle, she returned to breastfeeding. In therapy, Miller writes, Johanna "found repeatedly how important it was to her just being able to love, to express her love without being afraid that she could be betrayed, exploited, violated. This love gave her the feeling of being whole, as she had been before her integrity has been injured."[30] Harboring frozen moments makes us vulnerable to the feelings Johanna experienced: neglect, betrayal, and exploitation, as well as violation, fear of being smothered by love, or feeling one has no love to offer. One gift of parenting is the invitation to thaw frozen moments, a process that is less painful if one is held in caring relationships. "I think," Miller concludes, "that Johanna's struggle for her true feelings saved not only her child's future, but also her own."[31]

Imagining a person without frozen moments would be denial. These moments, in the paradox of life, create the possibility to experience God or the numinous. Donald Kalsched, a theologically trained therapist, helps us to understand how the self, in its wisdom, protects a person in moments of trauma where an experience—most often abuse, violation, or serious neglect—is more than what can be consciously managed. In *Trauma and the Soul: A Psycho-Spiritual Approach to Human Development and Its Interruption*, Kalsched explores the self-care system used by the false self "to keep an innocent core of the self out of further suffering in reality, by keeping it 'safe' in another world."[32] Trauma threatens a person's psychosomatic unity because in dissociation a split sets in-between the different parts of the psyche and between the psyche and soma. The dissociation, which allows some parts to experience the pain and other parts not to, covers and protects against non-being. The split leaves gaps in one's psyche and keeps the self from suffering as a whole even as some parts remain traumatized. The false self assumes its caretaking role and the true self goes into hiding, making the telling of coherent narrative impossible. "Ironically," Kalsched writes, "dissociative defenses save a vital core of the self while simultaneously losing it (or partially losing it)."[33] In the split, one part goes into hiding, where it often communicates with spiritual or numinous entities: God, angels, or the daimonic (the archetypal function of human experience and the drive to be a self).[34] "Survivors of early trauma often report that an essential part of themselves has retreated into a spiritual world and found refuge and support in the absence of such report by any human person."[35] Therapy facilitates the work of restoration, which is the thawing of frozen moments and the reintegration of a self split apart by trauma.

Kalsched introduces Jennifer, a woman who told her story for the first time in her fifties. She was sexually violated by her stepbrother for two years starting when she was eight. He threatened her with injury should she tell. Jennifer remembers sitting at a school playground and realizing that she was "damaged, no longer able to play, robbed of her innocence, broken." She felt alien in a world other children occupied. At odds with herself and with others, the self she knew went into hiding, to reappear briefly when she was painting alone or spending time in nature. Her emboldened hated denier (see chap. 2, "Relational Intelligence") fueled her inner voice of self-criticism and shame, leaving her filled with despair and loneliness. This voice told her "don't let [Kalsched] see how sick you are; don't speak, it'll be wrong, change your clothes to look ridiculous, you can't have that—it will be taken away from you, you're too fat to attract a man."[36] She was an engaging survivor, but she rarely felt alive.

In relationship with Kalsched, where together they held the tragedy and triumph of her life, she began reconstructing a personal story and revisited another key moment in her life. As her compassion for herself as a young, confused, and helpless girl grew, she remembered a light visiting her at the time her abuse started; she thinks it was an angel. Shortly after the light visited her, as if to prepare her for what she was about to face, she was in the hospital with internal injuries after her stepbrother raped her. Life was leaving her, and her parents and nurses went silent. She remembered the light that visited her earlier, saw brightly colored crayons in her mind's eye, and decided she wanted to color and paint. Against expectations she made a miraculous physical recovery, but her frozen hurt remained. A few months later, in the midst of winter, an angel appeared to her, saying: "You do not have to continue; it's all right to let go. . . . If you decide to stay, it won't be easy." Her eyes fell on a box of watercolors, especially the color Rose Madder. She told the angel, "How can I leave without using this color? I must stay to paint—to use my colors."[37] Feeling held by a serene intelligence beyond her comprehension, she chose life. The trauma Jennifer experienced caused a gap in her sense of being, and in this gap the numinous appeared. Surely this is grace. The light and angel that visited Jennifer provided a soothing presence in the absence of a holding environment and prepared the way for the work she did with Kalsched.

In a tripartite view of reality, where one lives with the Me, the Not-me, and the transitional space between what is subjectively experienced and objectivity perceived, the wounds behind frozen moments impinge on one's capacity to experience the aliveness found in the in-between world. "When trauma occurs in a child's life," Kalsched writes, "one of the most tragic results is the foreclosure of the transitional space."[38] The true self goes into hiding with a bolstered false self. Wounded, one oscillates between the deeply private world one cannot share and the world where power, money, consumption, and prestige indicate success. In the private world one wrestles with the hated denier and inner demons, and dreams communicate dependency needs and a hope for reparation. In the outer world one can find relief in consumption, manic activity, procrastination, and independence or in fleeting relationships.

The work of reparation begins with counseling, therapy, or another relationship where the transitional space can be reconstituted. The work includes regaining the capacity to enter into the transitional space where the self and the Other can be discovered anew. Because every relationship, including one with a counselor, ruptures, breaks in the relationship can be explored and restored. It is this back-and-forth dynamic that is difficult to replicate in other settings, especially in online settings. It is in a resilient, caring holding environment where innocence and a sense of the sacred—which Kalsched identifies as the soul—is reclaimed and awakened. Kalsched identifies how liminal experiences and numinous entities bring comfort and transformation, awaken hope, and open endless possibility.

Thawing her frozen moments by walking toward her pain, Jennifer not only reintegrated her self and revisited the deeply spiritual component often inherent to trauma, she also restored her sense of aliveness. Jennifer and Johanna are courageous women who portray Reparative Intelligence and recognize the wisdom of thawing frozen moments. While drawing on other intelligences—of the self, relationships, and transitional experiences—they transformed frozen moments into moments of relationship, of meeting, and of feeling alive.

Forgiveness and Acts of Reparation

Living between loving and hating causes ambivalence, a sense of guilt, and the need for reparation. As the opening quote from Turkle suggests, the ability to say "I'm sorry" is an opportunity to reclaim one's humanity and deepen relationships through conversation.[39] She is concerned that our tendency to communicate through texting and other digital means is removing our ability to express regret, which requires empathy. Just as the transitional object as first possession can withstand loving and hating, the primary caregivers must be able to withstand the aggressive impulses of the infant, returning as the loving, quiet parent. Infants partake in this process by offering spontaneous gestures as the beginnings of empathy. "The attainment of a capacity for making reparation in respect to personal guilt is one of the most important steps in the development of the healthy human being."[40] Whereas reparation as a sign of health has internal origins, reparation made by the false self in compliance to the needs of others leads to despair. Reacting to the wounds of others can be an escape from one's own pain, as the illusion that one can repair oneself by engaging with the wounds of others seduces easily. Sometimes the false self tries to keep up appearances by projecting a solid self in some settings, such as school or work, but the self becomes undone, angry, frustrated, and depressed at home and in intimate relationships.

Reparation in a technological world is a challenge because exploring ruptures in the holding environment is difficult, and one cannot take back or delete what has been posted or sent. Still, one finds restoration, care, and empathy in question-and-answer sites, a care page, a crowdfunding cause, or in respecting the views of others. Diminishing care to respect can be questioned, but it may be the most common way care can take shape in online relationships and communities. Whereas care and empathy require the ability to feel with someone or to imagine oneself into the shoes of another, respecting may not need Transitional Intelligence or Relational Intelligence so deeply. The question of where virtual people and digital citizens will learn empathy remains. Empathy flourishes in intimate relationships where one face calls the face of another toward ethical behavior. Being at home in virtual spaces does not remove the urgency of achieving the task of integrating one's loving and hating. This task, especially for adults, often leads to expressing or seeking forgiveness, a reparative act.

The work of forgiveness is allowing love and hate to meet in the transitional space where hate cannot destroy love, a space where the self and the Other are discovered anew (see chap. 3, "Transitional Intelligence"). When love and hate meet in the transitional space, that area of experiencing where subjective and objective elements are woven together, forgiveness surprises as a spontaneous gesture. Life-giving forgiveness happens when it is not sought, forced, or seen as a step-by-step process, but discovered or found. The work of forgiveness, as with thawing frozen moments, relies on being surrounded by loving, caring, and reliable faces forming a holding environment. This work restores belief in stable, reliable relationships and communities where one can have a meaningful existence, a world that can survive hate and where trauma cannot annihilate even if it persists. Reflecting on forgiveness, however, whether through a theological, psychological, social, political, or other lens, shows it is a complex dynamic and possibly even a "problem."[41] Forgiveness easily serves power, privilege, and patriarchy and has no set process or normativity. Yet perceptions of "ideal" forgiveness, where a perpetrator comes to deeper awareness and asks the victim for forgiveness, possibly with a restored relationship, remain.

In *Trauma and Forgiveness*, trauma theorist Fred Alford explores the origins of trauma and forgiveness through a psychodynamic lens.[42] Alford locates forgiveness in the transitional space because it is a space where the psychological and the social are interdependent. Forgiveness anticipates the letting go of bitterness, anger, and hatred so that life can go on. In letting go of the illusion of omnipotence that one can ensure one's own happiness or force others to act according to one's wishes. Forgiveness, like thawing, requires being in a community where the wounded true self can risk vulnerability and trust. "When one is in a transitional relationship, then one need not hold on so tightly," Ford writes. "Forgiveness is easier as letting go becomes easier: we can let go of our hatred and fear of disintegrating or endlessly falling."[43] In the transitional space the false self no longer needs to be compliant to the trauma or external world. Here, internal objects can be repaired, even if external relationships or persons remain unrepentant or absent. In transitional relationships the distinction between the self and the Other can dissolve, and the perpetrator moves out of sharp focus. Furthermore, the transitional space is protected from impingements of normative ideals by reality ("You must forgive . . .") or a collapse into the silence of a traumatized self ("I probably deserved what I got . . .").

Because the experience of forgiveness anticipates revisiting experiences of vulnerability in thought, speech, and affect, doing so without a holding environment is rare. One can be surprised by forgiveness when held in caring relationships. "*Forgiveness,*" Alford writes, "*is something that happens to us at a certain point almost as a by-product of living in the world in a certain way.*"[44] The space itself and the relationships might be sufficient to bring restoration. By being held, one can grieve, for there is no work of forgiveness without mourning the loss of the self, the loss of relationships, the loss of the other, and the loss of the world as a benevolent place. The work of mourning, French philosopher Jacques Derrida reminds us, is "to reckon, to recount, relate, or narrate, to consider, judge, or evaluate, even to estimate, enumerate, and calculate [the loss or trauma that occurred]."[45] This work takes time.

The act of forgiveness, one can argue, is the spontaneous gesture that follows successful mourning. It almost never follows a step-by-step process, and sometimes forgiveness just happens, or it does not. "In mourning," Alford writes, "we mourn the loss of those parts that are lost forever (or so it seems, and it is often true) with the loss of the other."[46] One mourns the loss of anger and hatred, feelings that empower, but also the giving up of self- and other-loathing, dehumanization, intolerance, violence, apathy, and even judgment. In the transitional space, one might even relinquish the wish that the offender will come to a full realization of the hurt caused and then apologize and ask for forgiveness. Cheap forgiveness asks no mourning, which can be a slow, meandering process. The work of mourning, when circumvented, awakens nostalgia for an innocent self and past. Premature or pressured forgiveness offers cheap grace. Forgiveness guided by Reparative Intelligence, on the other hand, recognizes that life with its loving and hating is fragile and worth protecting. It accepts an uncomfortable truth: "There is no safe place, no secure harbor, only the appreciation of life and its goodness in all its forms, from a beautiful sunrise to a welcoming smile, all mixed up with a darkness that never goes away, but may recede into the background or even disappear for longer or shorter periods of time."[47] Forgiveness reminds us that there is no perfect world, only a good enough one worth taking a chance on.

When one engages in acts of reparation, one is instilled with the virtue of "forgivingness," which is the giving up of anger without giving up judgment.[48] It is to forgive but not to forget. Forgiveness almost always meets unattainable visions of wholeness. Alford suggests that practicing forgivingness is important because living with anger or resentment catches up with a person, especially in old age, where psychological barriers tend to break down.

Trauma and Forgiveness identifies individuals who found reparation and forgiveness in the transitional space and those who found forgiveness elsewhere. Eva Kor, a Holocaust survivor, forgave her perpetrator Josef Mengele and the Nazis, yet she seems not to have developed concern. Eva and her twin sister, Miriam, were taken to Auschwitz, where they were experimented on with significant trauma. During the fiftieth anniversary of the liberation of Auschwitz (January 27, 1995), Eva stated, "I, Eva Mozes Kor, a twin who survived as a child of Josef Mengele's experiments at Auschwitz 50 years ago, hereby give amnesty to all the Nazis who participated directly and indirectly in the murder of my family and millions of others." One needs to forgive but not forget, she stated to the shock of many, naming forgiveness as "nothing more and nothing less but an act of self-healing, an act of self-empowerment."[49] A few years later, Israeli peace activists took Eva to Gaza, where she was unable to listen to the stories of six Palestinian educators. The educators felt that the Holocaust experience should have awakened empathy in Israelis, empathy that would speak to settlements, blockades, raids, and more. Eva said that she felt threatened by the educators as she listened to their stories, afraid she would be kidnapped. Giving amnesty to the Nazis, Eva's act of forgiveness, gave her a sense of control over the Nazis, but not compassion and care toward others. It was not an act of reparation.

Alford also introduces Terri Jentz, someone who knows trauma intimately. While a nineteen-year-old student at Yale, she was on a cross-country bicycle trip with a friend when a man ran over their tent with his truck while they were sleeping and then attacked them with an axe. Holding on to life, Terri was first locally hospitalized and was moved closer to her family when her condition stabilized. Fifteen years later, she returned to Redmond, Oregon, and did so annually for eight years, saying that the event traumatized the community, too, even though the community had a strong suspicion of who the perpetrator was. He killed his girlfriend a day after he attacked Terri and her friend. She returned not to find the perpetrator, but to revisit the community that took care of her. In Redmond she created a community that held her, finding deep connection with the nurses and other members of the community willing to hold her pain. Held in the relationships around her, Terri forgave the community even though it had knowledge that could have prevented her attack after her relationship with the community deepened. The community also did not inform the police about its suspicions as to who the perpetrator might be. Members in the community in turn used their relationship with Terri to let go of the guilty feelings that plagued them. They could apologize for their sins of omission. In the community that Terri and the people of Redmond built, evil was stripped of its destructive powers. Terri forgave the community but not the offender, identifying him as "evil incarnate."[50] Still, Terri confessed she too was vulnerable to the allure of the power her perpetrator yielded. Indeed, vulnerable to many forces, forgiveness is found and cannot be forced.

The ways Reparative Intelligence manifests are diverse. To care or mind and to accept responsibility toward persons and nature are key human traits.

Circles of Empathy

"Online culture increasingly resembles slums in disturbing ways. Slums have more advertising than wealthy neighborhoods, for instance. People are meaner in slums; mob rule and vigilantism are commonplace," writes Jaron Lanier, a computer scientist often described as "the father of virtual reality."[51] Lanier's *You Are Not a Gadget* argues, as *Growing Down* does, that our technological world should fuel questions about human nature. Lanier identifies the "circle of empathy" as a heuristic device that speaks to Reparative Intelligence. This imaginary circle describes people and things deemed worthy of empathy. Whatever falls outside the circle carries little value, whether it is a person, a fetus, an animal, or an object. Slaves were placed outside the circle for hundreds of years. Women, children, the poor, immigrants, victims of interpersonal violence, and even the elderly are often placed outside this circle.

When one places oneself outside the circle of empathy, one cannot love one's neighbor as oneself. We are best reminded that the prophet Joel writes, "For God is gracious and compassionate, slow to anger and abounding in love, and God relents from sending calamity" (Joel 2:13). Jewish scholar Abraham Joshua Heschel argues that the prophets reminded people of God's pathos—God's love—for being a prophet is feeling what God feels. "[God] is moved and affected by what happens in the world, and reacts accordingly," Heschel writes.[52] The apostle Paul also knows this God when he writes about God as "the Father of compassion and the God of all comfort, who comforts us in all our troubles, so that we can comfort those in any trouble with the comfort we ourselves have received from God. For just as the sufferings of Christ flow over into our lives, so also through Christ our comfort overflows" (2 Cor 1:3-4). Lanier's circle of empathy is an age-old tradition.

The practice of Reparative Intelligence leaves one openhearted. One can risk being kind, gracious, generous, compassionate, empathic, and benevolent. Without Reparative Intelligence, loving a neighbor as oneself is nearly impossible. Being kind and openhearted "looks distinctly old fashioned, indeed nostalgic, a vestige from a time when we could recognize ourselves in each other and feel sympathetic because of our kind-ness, " write Adam Phillips and Barbara Taylor in

On Kindness.[53] One person needs another, "not just for companionship or support in hard times but to fulfill their humanity."[54] "Today, it is only between parents and children that kindness is expected, sanctioned, and indeed obligatory."[55] Of course, few would argue against all of society and the natural world being in need of kindness. The vulnerability inherent in being open-hearted is rarely seen; it is often viewed as a virtue of losers and is easily identified as an object of suspicion. Grown-downs know differently, for kindness comes naturally to children who need the care of their parents or caregivers and to adults when the work of reparation has been engaged.

Reparative Intelligence calls on one to assess one's circle of empathy and to expand it. When love and hate are not integrated, when love does not step in to thaw frozen moments and engage in acts of reparation, the events of the past are often repeated, and persons and communities continue to hurt. With Reparative Intelligence creative ways can be found to address personal, professional, and even political needs. Moreover, the sense of omnipotence that leads to violence, that mental state of undifferentiation where one cannot accept the autonomy of the other person, diminishes. "Violence," analyst Jessica Benjamin reminds us, "is the outer perimeter of the less dramatic tendency of the subject to force the other to either be or want what it wants, to assimilate the other to itself or make it a threat."[56] In violence the Other cannot be seen without dissolving the Other into one's own image.

"[A] sign of health in the mind," Winnicott writes, "is the ability of one individual to enter imaginatively into the thoughts and feelings and hopes and fears of another person; also to allow the other to do the same to us."[57] This is empathy, a crucial human trait many lack.

5

PLAYGROUND INTELLIGENCE
Toward a Theology of Play

What do ducks do before they grow up? They grow down.

— Debrah Aaron, *Jokes and the Linguistic Mind*[1]

"**N**ecessity is not 'the mother of invention'; Play is." With this powerful statement, made in 1935, Scottish psychoanalyst Ian Suttie distanced himself from Freudian theories of pleasure and aggression as sources of social construction. Play steps in as an infant separates from a mother or a primary caregiver, awakening physical and mental capacities and social skills needed for survival and human success. The playing of children, which is inextricably tied to their self-preservation, extends into adulthood as cultural expression and experience. Language and conversation, Suttie concludes, are forms of mental and verbal play every person engages in, though research suggests that the art of having a conversation is weakening in a texting culture.[2]

The well-known proverb that necessity invents, ascribed to Plato and his *Republic* (360 BCE), never reckoned with play.[3]

Play personifies a grown-down life. Johan Huizinga, a Dutch cultural historian and contemporary of Ian Suttie, wrote in 1938, "We moderns have lost the sense of ritual and sacred play. Our civilization is worn with age and too sophisticated." One can only imagine what Huizinga would say about contemporary society and culture . . . For Huizinga, play exceeds being serious because seriousness seems to exclude play, whereas play can include seriousness. "What is the right way of living," Huizinga asks. "Life must be lived as play; playing certain games, making sacrifices, singing and dancing . . ."[4] Huizinga argued for and introduced a foundational anthropology that challenges *Homo sapiens* (the wise person or the person as thinker): we are *Homo ludens* (a person at play).

We play, increasingly using our phones, tablets, and consoles, yet defining play is not easy. Resisting clear definitions, play, often seen as an absorbing, purposeless, unproductive, useless, yet restorative activity, is best defined by its attributes. One reason behind the challenge to define play is the many forms of play one finds: from solitary play to social play to symbolic play; from verbal play to object play to imaginary and motor play; from basic play to elaborate play to crude play; and from sophisticated to casual to even violent play.[5]

Play is best described in terms of its attributes: Play is voluntary, and it is pleasurable. It creates freedom from time and preoccupies and diminishes consciousness. Play awakens imagination, creativity, improvisation, and problem-solving. It is contextual and appropriates contexts. Play can be disruptive, and being autotelic, it follows its own goals. Furthermore, play helps one adapt to changed circumstances. It is crucial in the development of interpersonal skills and fostering community, and it instills the wisdom of holding on and letting go. In addition, play is a form of knowing. The ancient Greeks had only one word for play and for learning: *paideia*. Through play, young and old learn, discover, and are transformed, often without conscious awareness that such processes are taking place. And, a final trait that speaks to a grown-down life, play promotes neoteny, the ability to prolong juvenile characteristics into mature age.

As an embodied activity, play alters selves and relationships while meeting specific emotional, relational, and physical needs (see chap. 1, "Self Intelligence"). At the same time, play can undo past formations, including trauma, and open future possibilities. Play increases one's tolerance for closeness and community by making relationships less hierarchical or less controlling. By stimulating the cerebral cortex, where memory, attention, perceptual awareness, thought, language, and consciousness reside, play is important for optimal cognitive functioning. Play behavior activates the motor cortex, prompting one to move, unless the rules of the game or the social setting prohibit such physicality. In addition, play excites the hypothalamus, which controls our motivation, and the amygdala, which regulates our social behavior and assists in facial and bodily expression. And, as natural opioids are released through play behavior, the stress hormone cortisol is countered. It is impossible to imagine a person thriving or flourishing without play being an active part of life. The body not only anticipates, but fully participates in every act of play.

We often oppose play to work, which reflects a weak understanding of both play and work. Many—if not all—children still hear the command, "Finish your work first before you can play," or variations of the message that work is more important (and serious business) than play. Playing and being playful are best seen as ways "to be in the world . . . a form of understanding what surrounds us and who we are, and a way of engaging with others."[6] It is a mode of being human—an attitude—that informs every moment of life, irrespective of the circumstances. Without play a sense of feeling alive is impossible, as a mechanical or reactive life sets in. For most, play is rarely promoted, and children are often encouraged to place work above play. By adolescence, free play is left to special moments, weekends, and vacations when work is set aside. Many will spend considerable money to watch others at play, feeding off the vicarious nature of play.

Religion played a role in our misguided view on play. The Christian tradition, with its emphasis on original sin and a strong work ethic, generally disapproved of play and the freedom play instills. Whereas the Psalmist asks, "How can we sing the songs of God in a foreign land?"[7] theologians Hugo Rahner and Jürgen Moltmann ask, "May a Christian go on merrily playing when a stern and strict choice has to be made for eternity?" and, "Is it right to laugh, to play and to dance without at the same time crying out and working for those who perish in the shadowy side of life?"[8] Although Rahner and Moltmann answer their questions affirmatively, their questions betray a deeper distrust of play shared by Christians and culture alike. Contemporary theologians, drawing on especially Christian practices and the Hebrew Scriptures, see play (especially of children) as a blessing indicating that God's reign on earth—a period of shalom—has arrived.[9] Playing with toys, however, is rarely discussed by theologians, with the possible exception of Jerome Berryman and those teaching religion to young children.[10]

Playground Intelligence is the ability to rely on play behavior to build a sense of self, deepen relationships, move effortlessly between inner and outer worlds, and bring reparation to the self and others. This intelligence develops naturally in children until they have fully grown up. Grown-downs embody playground intelligence since the intelligences of the self, relationships, transitional spaces, and reparation discussed thus far inform a playful life. Conversely, achieving Playground Intelligence nurtures grown-down living.

Psychodynamically, playing is an important signifier that inevitably takes us to various playgrounds. On these playgrounds one plays but is also played.

We Are *Homo Ludens*

Before the first year of life is celebrated, an infant regularly engages in play behavior. The most common form of play is with a spoon, banging it on the table or on a bowl, dropping it over the edge of the table and waiting for it to reappear as mother, father, or a caregiver patiently picks it up from the floor. When a spoon is placed in the hand of an infant, it is promptly dropped again for the game to continue. By mouthing a spoon, the infant incorporates what is in his or her environment, just as mother's breast or a bottle was previously incorporated. As the physical act of playing with a spoon unfolds, significant internal processes are taking place as the inner world relates to the outer. Playing indicates a personal way of living, rather than a specific activity. Winnicott relied on "the spatula game," the dropping of a spoon or spatula, the first game most people play, to deepen his knowledge of human nature. He would place a spatula in front of an infant and observe how the infant engages with the spatula. Did the infant show interest in the spatula? Was the child hesitant to take it, or was the infant shy or coy? Was the spatula taken aggressively? Was it mouthed? Did the infant use the spatula to make noise or mimic feeding others? Did the infant show a sense of trust? Was there humor involved? Was the spatula held or dropped over the edge of the table?[11] If dreaming is the road to the unconscious, play is the road to one's inner world.

In an essay in which Winnicott explores the relationship between appetite and emotional disorder, he revisits the spatula game as play: "At the normal end of the scale there is play, which is a simple and enjoyable dramatization of inner world life; at the abnormal end of the scale there is play which contains a denial of the inner world, the play being in that case almost always compulsive, excited, anxiety-driven, and more sense-exploiting than happy."[12] From a psychodynamic perspective, one plays for the enjoyment thereof *and* to cope with anxiety, but play can be corrupted: "Threat of excess of anxiety leads to compulsive play, or to repetitive play, or to an exaggerated seeking for the pleasures that belong to play; and if anxiety is too great, play breaks down into pure exploitation of sensual gratification."[13] Play, especially in mouthing a thumb or fist, in bowel movements, and in masturbation, as well as in behaviors guided by fantasies, helps the child discover her body's sensuality as well as the power of holding on and of eliminating or letting go (see chap. 1, "Self Intelligence"). As such, "play is the alternative to sensuality in the child's effort to keep whole."[14]

When play becomes a purely sensual experience, as it can become with masturbation or when playing immersive video games, it loses its core traits and becomes compulsive. Play in the service of sensual gratification—as is often the case in experiences with virtual reality—does not draw on the transformative power of play, but in fact may show deeper anxieties in a person. Putting on a headset to play an immersive game promises sensual gratification and may even bring relief from anxiety, but it may not help facilitate creative living.

Through play one learns how to play alone in the presence of others and also how to play with others, which makes culture possible. Playing invites the destruction of preconceived notions of others in fantasy in support of "the initiation of emotional relationships, and so enables social contacts to develop" (see chap. 2, "Relational Intelligence" and chap. 6, "Technological Intelligence").[15] One learns ways to moderate aggression and to get along with others. Play is an important way to address the violence that is in the world, for play helps us to regulate aggression and hate in a trusting environment (see chap. 4, "Reparative Intelligence"). The wounding and even destruction of others, an inevitable part of life, has fewer personal and relational implications if done in fantasy. With maturation, play folds into art, religion, and the practices that assist an individual in moving between the inner and outer worlds. Winnicott concludes his brief essay on why children play by saying that play is essentially creative, always exciting, and occurs between the subjective and the objective (see chap. 3, "Transitional Intelligence"). It allows for closeness and separation to be experienced and communicates the psychodynamics of the self.

Both the onset and the end of play are often related to inner dynamics or the outer forces impinging on the self. When healthy play becomes compulsive, anxiety driven, or aggressive, a holding environment has failed, and faces and relationships no longer recognize the authenticity of all involved. At all times, we find ourselves somewhere on this spectrum from healthy to anxious play. Psychodynamically, the way of playing—can one lose oneself and escape in preoccupation?—and the content of playing—is it comforting, challenging, or violent?—are determined by one's developmental stage and a specific context. "Put a lot of store on a child's ability to play," Winnicott writes. "If a child is playing, there is room for a symptom or two, and if the child is able to enjoy play, both alone and with other children, there is no serious trouble afoot."[16] Play driven by a rich imagination is different from play soothing anxiety or frustration. Whereas the former allows for freedom and a personal way of living to unfold, the latter leads to compulsive and repetitive behavior.

Play is often transgressive and pushes against boundaries; it seems to invite rule breaking and exploring just how firm boundaries are. "Boundaries are to be deprecated; they resonate with everything that is petrified, stale, encrusted, immobile.

Boundary-breaking is to be admired; it resonates with everything that is fluid, fresh, unencumbered, mobile."[17] Play is inherently risky as its natural urge to transgress may not be responsible or ethical. With society's zero tolerance of rule-breaking, an innocent prank gets one in trouble, unlike in previous societies where the tension that boundary-breaking brings could be held. Foundational to breaking boundaries is play as make-believe. Musicologist William Cheng writes, "it's about re-making belief, redrawing frontiers of the imagination through performances of actions, identities, and ideologies previously unfulfilled (or assumed to have been outright impossible)."[18]

A satisfying life takes place in the overlap of various areas of play. This space can be between a person and imagination or between one person and another. It can also be the spaces between a person and a family, a community, or the Divine, or the spaces that culture and virtuality create.[19] Play without Transitional Intelligence is rigid or compulsive and can lack spontaneity as it serves either compliance or sensuality. Play's specific place, which is neither inside a person's subjectivity nor outside as an element of reality, but the space in-between, is filled with potential, which informs and transforms the inside and the outside. The importance of play in human nature is that no culture has existed in the past hundred thousand years where play and its extension into ritual have not been found. Play is a universal human trait that not only belongs to health, but facilitates it.

Corrupted Play

Play's precariousness is found in one's inner life fusing to the outer, a dynamic that excites more deeply than sensual pleasure. Due to its precarious nature, play easily becomes corrupted and is vulnerable to cultural forces.[20] Playground Intelligence can distinguish between what is play and that which feels like play. The way children played changed notably in the late 1980s. By

1987 there were more shopping malls than schools in America and the "malling of America" and the "franchising of America" (or "chaining of America") set in.[21] Children, teens, and adults would go to the mall where they met (or played) with their peers as consumers. As the number of shopping malls declined after the 2008 financial crisis, the play space moved to one's hand holding a phone or playing with a gaming console or computer. Here play stimulates, creates belonging, and allows shopping to continue. The cultural forces that increased consumption and decreased free play, initiated in the late 1980s, not only remain intact but are growing. Today we have the "gaming of America" and the "screening of America" as video games are increasingly popular. One gets badges for participating, and devices become central to our lives.

Play can become corrupted in at least six ways. For many, *consuming*–meeting personal, relational, and other needs through shopping and by taking in excessively—has replaced playing. Shopping, especially as a reward after a stressful time or hard work, functions as play does; it releases stress. For a virtual people that know commodification intimately, confusing playing and shopping or consuming should come as no surprise. Our shopping continues as we play games. Logging in requires setting up a credit card, and in-app purchases are optional, but in essence required. To distinguish oneself from another player, one purchases virtual clothing, accessories, and equipment. What is acquired gives pleasure and status. Whereas playing indicates a creative self brimming with the powers of imagination and creativity, consumption identifies a depleted self that is insatiable.[22] Taking in excessively—a form of gluttony—never satisfies an insatiable self.

When playing together is difficult or impossible, *control* sets in. This control mimics the controlled lives of today's children as parents overprotect, overinvest, overschedule, and overprogram their children's lives. This, of course, is done out of concern not malice, but trying to control a child's future comes at the cost of free and unscripted play. As psychologist Peter Gray writes in *Free to Learn*, "If we value freedom and personal responsibility, we must respect our children's rights to chart their own lives. Our ambitions cannot be theirs, and vice versa. . . . To learn responsibility, children must learn how to make their own decisions in the course of each hour, day, and year, and they can learn that only by practicing it."[23] When play is tied to a script written in a Disney studio or by a game developer, control as a corrupted form of play receives new meaning. Time is a commodity under tight control. Sociologists state that the way North American culture speaks about time—not having enough time, wasting time, buying time, killing time—reflects the language of people who lack basic resources such as food and safety. Grown-downs know that play is the one dynamic that suspends time and promises freedom from the clock.

Conflict, especially between persons with close emotional ties, imitates the intimacy and connection best facilitated by play. When persons cannot connect or when they feel distant from each other, conflict's pseudo-intimacy replaces the life-giving connection all long for. The differences between conflict and play are obvious, even if play fighting and real fighting can be hard to distinguish: "When play-fighting ends, children keep playing together happily. The stronger ones will hold back their full strength in order to keep things roughly even. . . . In contrast, real fighting involves hitting with fists, shoving, pushing, and kicking. At least one child is usually frowning or scowling, and another may be crying. Real fighting generally ends with the children unhappily going their separate ways. The stronger child does not hold back, and injuries are much more common."[24] In online gaming, of course, the purpose is often to be as destructive as possible, and should one die in combat, one merely resurrects one's avatar. In virtual worlds aggression and power are rarely held back. Where will we learn how to moderate our aggression if we spend much time in settings where the face of the Other never communicates hurt to us, where we cannot apologize for inappropriate words or actions? The lack of this space should concern society. Whereas play fosters connection, conflict brings distance to wounded and traumatized selves.

Criticism is playing to unreachable expectations. Similar to conflict, being critical of someone establishes a tie to the Other. Before another is criticized, however, one has fallen victim to the hated denier, that internal voice that only criticizes and never affirms (see chap. 2, "Relational Intelligence"). Far from the voluntary participation and freedom inherent to play, the "persecutory presence can haunt all of us from time to time with some form of self-doubt triggered by the sting of devaluation from without," writes Dorothy Martyn.[25] Martyn, a child therapist and advocate, calls criticism "demonic." Marriage researcher John Gottman, moreover, identifies criticism as one of the horsemen of the Apocalypse, for its presence announces the possible end of an intimate relationship.[26] When two persons cannot play together, one person can use criticism to rope the other person in.

Compulsion, one can argue, is a form of hyper-play that grows into rituals fueled by anxiety. Compulsive play or rituals do not bring life, even if these actions keep anxiety under control. Therapist Brian Grant reflects on persons he worked with who had compulsive behaviors: "The repetition, this unsuccessful but loyally maintained pattern, is sustained by constrictions at every level. Thought content is delimited: the person thinks about the same small array of mental content. Thoughts follow the same routes in dealing with one problem after another. The same overfocussedness . . . crops up in response to every situation.

The body participates in this rigidity [and] relational systems become fossilized."[27] Compulsive behavior protects against anxiety by providing well-rehearsed rituals, which mimic the continuation desire of healthy play.

Competition is a sixth way play becomes corrupted as it piggybacks on the transformative power of play. In this context, winning is seen as *the* determining power that shapes personal identity. A self that is built on winning, however, easily falls into a depression-like state when not winning, as an active hated denier berates the person. When competition and winning at all costs enter sport, it is a far cry from the ancient Greek ideal for competition and sport. Plato, we might want to remind ourselves, saw the purpose of sport as completion, coordination, and cooperation. Winning ultimately cannot sustain a depleted self.[28] The game of life is one of learning how to lose, where the self can get out of the way so that the selves of others can flourish.[29] Jesus played a losing game that was foolish to many. But so did persons like Sojourner Truth, Mahatma Gandhi, Martin Luther King, Rosa Parks, Mother Teresa, the Dalai Lama, Nelson Mandela and Desmond Tutu. In a culture where every yard gained, run hit or fumble made becomes a permanent statistic, competition is a defining trait. Coach Vince Lombardi famously said, "Winning isn't everything; it's the only thing!" This attitude leaves a world of grown-ups with a small number of winners and a majority of losers. It is not a welcoming space.

Grown-downs recognize that other behaviors and attitudes mimic play. Despite their attraction, however, these corrupted forms of play do not cultivate and support personal well-being. The word "play" stems from the Anglo-Saxon *plegan*, which gave English the words "plight" and "pledge." Grown-downs commit to warding off corrupted forms of play, which, as stated, seem just as natural as play itself. They are obligated to invite themselves and others into a play space where new discoveries about life and each other await.

Playgrounds

Play requires place. More precisely, it has at least two places. The first is the potential or transitional space that resides between the subjective and the objective. It is the space where losing oneself in fixed attention is possible. The second is a physical playground, which can be a forest, a park, a beach, a table, a living room, or a cyber playground or other virtual space. In his *History of Children's Play and Play Environments*, historian Joe Frost describes playgrounds starting with archeological Peru and China and ancient Egypt, Greece, and Rome, where play scenes or objects inform anthropological studies. Making his way through the centuries, Frost stops by a garden for children (a kindergarten), which is a natural play area and the pedagogical conception of German educator Friedrich Stroebel (1782–1852), in the town of Blankenburg, Germany. Stroebel, the son of a Lutheran pastor, saw play as "self-active representation of the inner life from inner necessity and impulse" and changed the way Western society thinks about playgrounds.[30] In the kindergarten, children's physical bodies were developed through calisthenics, and social skills were instilled through association with peers and some work. The senses were cultivated through playthings, and the mind was exercised through imitation. Stroebel discovered the power of play to educate and transform as he allowed children to teach him about play and their needs.

As one might imagine, there are vast differences between play in eighteenth-century Europe, kindergartens welcoming children, and contemporary recreational play. The biggest difference Frost identifies is what he calls a "multiple play-deficiency crisis."[31] Compared to children five hundred years ago, when children had many playgrounds, today's children and youth are limited to living rooms and screens, where they do have many choices in games, but games with limited genres. Other differences over the centuries include the following: children's games once had religious roots and served physical purposes; children from wealthy families played differently than those from families without resources, with the latter often being abused and neglected; play was fused with working, especially for slave or tenant farmer children; and Sunday was seen as a day of rest. Still, children played often and with a range of toys. Inherent in the devolution of playgrounds over the centuries is a shift from playing outdoors to playing indoors. "Children in America have become less and less active, abandoning traditional outdoor play, work, and other physical activity for sedentary, indoor virtual play, technology play, or cyber playgrounds, coupled with diets of junk food, fast food, and gorging all-you-can-eat restaurants," Frost laments.[32] He does not temper his concern as he faults a culture of overprotection and excessive safety standards, where the liability of a traditional playground is just too much and society is too dangerous for many. Playgrounds have been dumbed down with signs such as "No running, pushing and shoving," "Do not use equipment when wet," and "Do not use play equipment improperly."[33] The message implies: adults are dangerous, but so too anything that can be climbed, slid on, or crawled under. The child-saving movement may have cost children the gift of free play.

Frost tells how playing on the streets of New York City—even singing and playing marbles—was illegal in the early 1900s. Few playgrounds existed. Still, a flashlight study by four hundred observers in New York's Hell's Kitchen area at 4:00 p.m. on Saturday afternoon, April 19, 1913, counted 110,000 children at play despite a curfew against public playing.[34] Children placed lookouts and continued to play regardless of what authorities said. Such is the power of play's continuation desire.

The effects of play deprivation may not be easily quantifiable, but they are real and require deliberate societal steps to stave off what Frost sees as a humanitarian crisis. Direct effects are declines in fitness and general health, increased obesity, cognitive impairment (e.g., a physically smaller brain, attention deficit disorder), difficulty with social and interpersonal relations, the body disconnecting from the mind, and inability to cope with trauma. The histories of violent adults show the lack of childhood play or play that was corrupted. They often grew up in holding environments that failed, ones that cultivated weak interpersonal attachments.[35]

Modern playgrounds are living rooms, where the toys are communications and media technologies; the playground has become virtual and no longer only for children, as adults play games, too. One can hold on to the vision of children running wild in the woods, exploring streams, climbing trees, and building forts, but that would be nostalgia. Nostalgia is like a light too far away to read by but too close not to notice. From the Greek roots *nostos* (return, homecoming) and *algos* (suffering, pain, or distress), nostalgia is a process of mourning after the experience of change that remains incomplete. Reflecting on the relationship between transitional phenomena and virtuality found in gaming technology, professor of art Victor Burgin reminds us that "there is a tendency among British psychoanalysts to personify the ideal of *unfettered* play . . . a childlike *fou savant* they indulge with a mixture of condescension and envy."[36] Burgin exposes the danger of nostalgia that frowns on virtual play. Combining traditional and modern playgrounds is required. "Pretend play, supported by traditional play materials such as blocks, dolls, and soft toys, or through combining toy play with incentives of television, computers, stories, and songs, can lead to increased imagination and the love of play."[37] Frost sees modern technology as needing "scaffolding"—parents and teachers who monitor and engage the play—before it can contribute to the well-being play promises.

The concern is thus not so much with technology but with, as Winnicott argues, the content and way of playing. Play is best supported by a loving and caring environment. For children, that is a family, and for adults it is the family they created for themselves, with their extended family, friendships, and participation in culture. When modern playgrounds lack the necessary holding environment—gaming is a way to escape loneliness, for example—lives are compromised and play is corrupted. Imagining a North American child who does not play games on a computer, a phone, a tablet, or a console is foolhardy. Not only children but teenagers and adults too may be in need of conversation partners. Research by London therapist John Woods shows that pornography—the voyeuristic, compulsive, and sensual play with images—has a significant adverse effect on teenage boys and men.[38] It leads to risk-taking behaviors, increased oral and anal sex (as images found online are mirrored), erectile dysfunction, and sexual violence, as well as sexual partner dissatisfaction, infidelity, a dissociation of monogamy and marriage, and an increased appetite for more graphic sexual imagery.[39]

Technology has forever changed how a playground is perceived. Playgrounds are now virtual, having mostly replaced the playgrounds found in open spaces, such as woods and forests, and structured places, such as community playgrounds. Play in a postindustrial world is *converged* play, educational specialist Susan Edwards writes. For children, converged play is different from traditional forms of play where children have experiences that "build skills and understandings in areas such as fine and gross motor development, present and role play, and through craft- and/or construction-based activities such as painting, pasting, and block building."[40] The two forms of play can overlap, but they are increasingly differentiating from each other as gaming is commodified.

Converged play can be limited play that instills consumption and prescribed or scripted creativity. It is limited because the play narrative is provided and rarely rewritten. Children who play with Harry Potter Lego blocks do not create their own Hogwarts Castle; they reproduce the castle they saw in the movies or point to the glossy image of the castle on the Lego box. Inside the box they find a handy construction insert to help out should they get stuck. With prescribed scripts personal meaning is difficult to separate from the object, and the gifts of play, such as instilling problem solving skills, are minimized. Adult role-modeling and role-playing also diminish, as children follow the actors, who are often children like themselves, or reality television stars.

Children and adults have to be intentional to create their own toys to play with or to choose games where an open-ended script awaits them. Traditional forms of play *and* converged forms of play coexist in the blurring of boundaries. Both forms of play promote craft and fine motor skills (drawing, playing with stickers, creating a digital image), construction (playing with blocks, *Bob the Builder*, *SimCity*), music (playing an instrument, listening to music), pretending (dolls and toys, creating an avatar and associating with digital characters), and role-playing (unscripted and scripted narratives).[41] Traditional and converged forms of play each bring a unique literacy, with converged play often informing traditional play. The formational elements of each form of play are needed for all who desire flourishing while they engage with today's communication technologies. Focusing on the limitations of modern forms of technological play, Edwards warns, does not take into consideration that children play on more than one playground.

On the playgrounds of life, whether traditional or converged, learning and formation occur and friendships develop. A traditional playground teaches children to hold back aggression and force as shared converged play teaches a child to get along with a large number of other children, all of whom share the same interest. Both worlds need a holding environment with trusting relationships. Because one works off aggression in play, play fighting and even violent video games have a place. In both settings, however, things can go awry if a child is not held in loving relationships where the quality of face-to-face contact outperforms facing a screen.

Being Played and a Game with No Rules

Playground Intelligence knows about play and being played. It anticipates wisdom much deeper than whatever is learned about being a boy or a girl and sex. As a concept, being played is complex and can turn on a small nuance. It ranges from life-giving and playful interactions, such as flirtation, to being exploited and violated. Knowing the difference is crucial in providing personal safety and in maintaining relationships, whether personal or professional. Children constantly play their parents. Parents allow this unless the emotional manipulation undermines healthy personal and family relationships and the development of their children. Lovers play each other, seducing and coaxing, but also attempting to control each other. When control does set in to a relationship, so too do power and the potential for interpersonal violence. Venture online and one will quickly encounter trolls, individuals who find gratification in antagonizing others, often with mean-spirited comments posted to comment sections or on forums, as researcher Joseph Reagle indicates (see chap. 4, "Reparative Intelligence").[42] Scammers like to play naïve web users with invitations to rescue a friend suddenly in financial danger while traveling or the surprise news that one has won a lottery. Phishing catches innocent victims in nets of deception.

From a psychodynamic perspective, playing and getting played are inherent in all relationships. Grown-downs can allow others to play them. That is, they can allow others to project onto them any unwanted aspects within the other person without being reactive to it. They also play others by inviting them into a play space where personal transformation can take place. There is an easy back-and-forth movement between a grown-down and others that does not get bogged down with tension or conflict, or by enmeshment or emotional cutoff. This easygoing but playful interaction is seen in "the squiggle game," a therapeutic game Winnicott played with children and teens, often during the first meeting. The game can also inform relationships and is a metaphor for life. Its basis is playing together and being played and, as such, is not really something novel or artificial, but part of everyday living. As we live with our communications technologies, the squiggle game provides new meaning to our increasingly brief conversations via texts or tweets.

By saying, "Let's play something . . . a game with no rules," Winnicott invited a child into a safe, trustworthy holding environment. He took a piece of paper and tore it in half, showing that what they do was not all that important. With his eyes closed, he would draw a squiggle on the paper, saying: "You show me if that looks like anything to you or if you can make it into anything, and afterwards you do the same for me and I will see if I can make something of yours."[43] Going back and forth in a free exchange of doodling, Winnicott and the child or teen created a drawing. Some drawings had emotional and relational significance for the child or teen and other drawings were just a drawing. All along, Winnicott remained acutely aware of emotional development—the Intelligences described in *Growing Down*–believing that persons naturally seek health, and trust they will find it. Together Winnicott and a child drew up to thirty pictures during a consultation. Creating a relationship where partners can move freely is more important than being clever about what is being drawn. The squiggle game creates a space where integration can occur in the absence of interpretation by the clinician as the child discovers the emotional content of his of her life, content that was there all along. With no authority interpreting a drawing, the relationship Winnicott has with a child determines the mutuality needed to gain meaning from a drawing.

Winnicott played the squiggle game with children five to sixteen years of age. One boy, Alfred, demonstrates the power of relationship building through the game.[44] A precocious ten-year-old, Alfred came to see Winnicott because he had struggled with stammering for the previous four years. When Winnicott asked him about his father, Alfred's stammering increased to the extent that the conversation could not take place. So Winnicott switched to playing a squiggle game with Alfred. The stammering stopped. Together they drew faces and a witch, based on a dream Alfred had at the age of six and a half. They also drew a father with a violin he wanted to play, but could not. Alfred pushed his breath while doing so, as if letting out a sigh. The witch dream coincided with a move in which Alfred's father took a new job and was hospitalized for depression due to the stress he encountered in his new position. Alfred could not remember his father's hospitalization. Trying hard to help his father succeed (the dream of not being able to play the violin), Alfred started stammering when he tried to help his father succeed in his new position, a theme found in his drawing of his father unable to play the violin. Although Alfred was not cured of his stammering in his only meeting with Winnicott, Alfred showed that, given the right holding environment, he did not need to stammer. Alfred also showed that the holding environment that parents and caregivers create has a direct effect on their children. Two months after the squiggle game, the mother reported to Winnicott that Alfred's stammering had improved. The overlapping play of Winnicott and Alfred created possibility. Alfred's parents actually noted that improvement already set in shortly after they said they would visit with a doctor. Winnicott understood this response as a sign of hope that things would improve. The paradox in a squiggle is that neither Winnicott nor Alfred could claim ownership of the drawings. It belongs to that intermediate area of experiencing where ownership is ultimately shared and given away.

Families can draw squiggles too as they play each other and are being played. Therapist Matthew Selekman tells of Luis, a six-year-old Puerto Rican who was brought to counseling by his parents and fourteen-year-old sister. Luis did not socialize with other children and daydreamed in class.[45] The family lived in a crime-infested area, and Luis witnessed his father in a fistfight with his father's brother. Luis drew a picture of himself about to be run over by a truck. This alarmed his sister and parents, who joined in the drawing. Luis' father asked if he could draw a stop sign or a police crossing guard on the street. His mother drew an underground walkway so that he could cross safely. His sister placed a siren-blaring police car between Luis and the truck. The family was not aware that Luis had despair so deep that he contemplated taking his own life. When the family returned two weeks later, they reported that Luis had "happy spirits" and was "much more talkative."[46] Luis' drawing and the events around it prompted his father to make amends with his brother. The family had one more session before the counseling journey ended. Luis' false self—his caretaker self—successfully played his family, but he needed the help of a counselor who created a holding environment where play could occur.

Winnicott saw parallels between the Squiggle game, dream association in therapy, and adults having a conversation. In each activity a reality is coconstructed. Verbal squiggling is a powerful way to play and be played. Partners engage in this dynamic form of play, and as stated, parents do too. Family members coconstruct their world as they practice relationship building and meaning making. As discussed in the chapter on Transitional Intelligence, speaking to a group also calls on this back-and-forth movement between presenter and audience. Authors and poets rely on this same hermeneutic when they write a book or a poem, as do their readers, who find the written word meaningful. Scholars and writers not only play with other voices they encounter in their research, but also with the audience who will read their book. Teachers rely on this dynamic too as they create overlapping areas of play between themselves and their students. Stand-up comedians and improvisers are masters at playing the game; their humor and contributions feed off the response they receive from their audience. The squiggle game describes a hermeneutical model, a way of discovering the self, spontaneity, mutuality, and intersubjectivity. On the surface little is going on, but much is happening in the back-and-forth movement as it speaks to the self's desire to be transformed and the power of playing and being played. Life is best seen as various overlapping areas of play where a free-flowing attitude brings spontaneity, creativity, and integration. Such a life is not relative and without boundaries, for persons are not objects and relationships without boundaries inevitably fail.

Technology definitely promotes playing and being played. Texting can be seen as a form of squiggling as a narrative is created together. Teenagers, no longer visiting with friends after school due to over-controlled lives and dangers that lurk when one leaves the house, text (or squiggle) back and forth with their friends, building a conversation that does not always translate into skills for face-to-face conversations. On Wikipedia and Pinterest people play together, establishing databases of knowledge and images frequented by many. In immersive video games, such as *StoryMaker* or *Whyville*, and in strategy and survival games, creating a personal narrative is a form of playing and being played. The player remains an individual within the rules and relationships of a virtual community. What is created in these overlapping areas of play is something recognizable, shareable, and meaningful. A significant danger, however, is the lack of safety and trust in virtual worlds, for a virtual world creates an ever-present, but unreliable and possibly hostile holding environment (see chap. 6, "Technological Intelligence").

Being played indicates the work of integration or the lack thereof. It speaks of children's natural wisdom as they seek to survive and thrive.

Masters in the Art of Living

"Deep play," author Diane Ackerman writes, "is spontaneity, discovery, and being open to new challenges."[47] It is the kind of play that leads to transcendence, creativity, and a need for the sacred. Deep play is about challenge, exploration, and the search for one's limits. Inevitably it includes losing oneself in an activity and reaching one's boundaries, which opens the possibility of discovering something or someone sacred. This can happen when standing next to something majestically large such as the Grand Canyon, zip-lining through a tree canopy, or engaging in moments of intense concentration and creativity. Such play awakens the senses, and one is left more aware of one's place in the world and even the cosmos. Play, at its core, is theological: it tells of God, humanity, and our relationship with creation. Any activity can become deep play, for it is a state of mind more than a specific action. The toys of deep play vary, ranging from persons to things, such as cameras, hiking boots, board games, food items, books, handheld technologies, and computer consoles, and even to modes of transportation.

Life is definitely better lived if one has toys to play with. Toys, psychologist Erik Erikson reminds us, are used to "relive, correct, and re-create past experiences, and anticipate future roles and events with the spontaneity and repetitiveness which characterizes all creative ritualization."[48] Today's toys are traditional and technological, and played with on converged playgrounds. They come as blocks but more often so as screens. Within each type of toy comes a myriad of possibilities and ways to ritualize life. Play excites not only because dopamine and oxytocin are released in our brains or because it gets us moving, but also because of "the precariousness of the interplay of personal psychic reality and the experience of control of actual objects. This is the precariousness of magic itself, magic that arises in intimacy, in a relationship that can be found to be reliable."[49] Play is the stuff of magic as it draws on the potential that is hidden in the transitional space or the intermediate area of experiencing. A grown-down life, best lived in the overlap of persons playing together, becomes an adventure that can be trusted, for even in adverse moments one can feel alive. As one creates space for others to play, the gift is discovering a similar space opening for oneself.

Play, magically precarious, indicates a resting place for the self, a space where the false self can let go of its caretaking function and the true self can initiate creativity. It builds community without effort, belonging without compliance to someone's emotional needs, unless power and control corrupt the life-giving nature of play. In play one finds rest from the inner world's perpetual engagement with the outer world. It harkens back to resting in the loving arms of mother, father, or a caregiver as an infant, or being held by a counselor, a friend, or a community. Preoccupied in play, one finds rest *and* creativity.

Protecting these moments of rest, which are a Sabbath of sorts, has become a challenge as the notifications pushed by various apps and a barrage of new apps impinge on our selves and play spaces. This rest, the gift of losing oneself in play, is foundational to every other experience and activity of creative living. It turns the self into a toy, a plaything that can be handled and enjoyed by others.

Culture's emphasis on productivity, excellence, and expectations robs us all of a playful spirit. When children arrive home from school, where most often recess has been removed from the schedule and the inevitable after-school activities have ended, they are to sit down and complete their homework. When adults get home from work, they lose themselves in screens. Playground Intelligence encourages young and old to play. Play is an effective way to manage transitions, whether from waking to sleeping or from school and work to home. All work benefits when play enlivens the brain. Play is arguably the only behavior that can suspend time. It is truly the stuff of magic, but it requires intelligence to unlock its potential. The possibility for play abounds, and there are arguably more games available today than at any time in history, even if the number of playgrounds where free play can occur may have diminished. We find ourselves in a ludic century.[50]

"The master in the art of living," Oxford philosopher L. P. Jacks wrote in 1932, "makes little distinction between work and play, labor and leisure, mind and body, information and recreation, love and religion. The person simply pursues a vision of excellence in every action, leaving others to decide what is work or play. Masters in the art of living are always doing both."[51]

6

TECHNOLOGICAL INTELLIGENCE
Toward a Theology of Discovery and Devices

For the master's tools will never dismantle the master's house.

—Audre Lorde, *Sister Outsider*[1]

"Technology is neither good nor bad; nor is it neutral."[2] This is the "first law" of six historian of technology Melvin Kranzberg identifies as he reflects on humanity and technology. The maxim acknowledges that technological advances affect human nature in ways unforeseen by the development and purposes of those advances or by the practices they induce. Furthermore, technology's impact is greatly determined by context or whether short-term or long-term impact is assessed. What may be a concern in one context can be life-giving in another. The capacity to discern whether technology is good, bad, or neutral is a skill every person needs to gain in a virtual age. Kranzberg's sixth law also informs us of our reflection on human nature: "Technology is a very human activity—and so is the history of technology."³ Making and using tools as *Homo faber* (the person as maker), Kranzberg reminds us, has been central to the formation of *Homo sapiens* (the wise person or the person as thinker).⁴ Using technology is a basic cultural trait and has assisted in the development of language and abstract thinking. "[The] function of the technology is its use by human beings—and sometimes, alas, its abuse and misuse," Kranzberg writes.⁵ It is a person who enlivens a piece of technology and gives it meaning. Technology does not necessarily determine our actions, yet we assign much power to it. This chapter explores why we do this.

Neither good nor bad nor neutral: A three-year-old engrossed in a tablet while the family eats at a restaurant is different from a teenager playing a simulation game with friends on a Friday night. Breaking up with someone via a text message is different from doing so face-to-face. A couple texting a conversation that needs to take place in person is different from families split by continents relying on texting or video calls to remain connected. How one defines the "impact" of technology is equally important, for the impact might be personal, neuroscientific/physical, behavioral, relational, spiritual, moral, economic, or a combination of these areas of human living. Discerning technology's impact on human nature inevitably frustrates our dichotomous mind. Questions such as, "Do violent video games make us violent?" or "Can technology save the world from poverty?" require wisdom that a quick yes or no answer rarely provides.

Since we made spear points from stone flakes, learned how to control fire, and created the wheel, a plow, the telescope, and other technologies, every new technology awakens condemnation, celebration, fear, and skepticism. With the perfect vision hindsight brings, some fears are now laughable and reflect flat-earth thinking. For example, reading and writing, developed as Sumerian cuneiform around 4000 BC, were discouraged in

Egypt by sacred decree for fear of eroding oral memory and thus wisdom. Likewise, the first pedal-wheel sewing machines were feared for awakening sexual desire in women, who used them most. In the oral culture of the ancient Egyptians where memory was prized, writing could be a threat. And in the age of Victorian puritanism, human sexuality loomed large. Writing, one can expect, will be relegated to an art form as the creation of text becomes predominantly digital. With human sexuality now reflecting the complexities of human nature more than ever before, sexuality's relationship with virtual technologies especially also creates new potential and new fears.

Discernment regarding technology demands wisdom and insight into human nature. Who is the person using technology? Whose face is staring at a screen or is affected by the use of technology? These questions are foundational to any other questions technology brings, whether they are questions about risk or potential. Marveling at the fact that technology typically doubles in speed and power every two years—Moore's law—awakens hopes and fears as to where technology is heading, but it also obscures exploring human nature in light of technology. "Perception—looking at things . . . must never be separated from, apperception—seeing oneself" analyst Adam Phillips reminds us.[6] Seeing oneself as the one affected by technology is difficult, however, for it asks one to take a step back from oneself with a level of self-awareness that the use of technology rarely encourages. Because we are extended selves, as William James argued, with the self and technology inextricably linked, distancing oneself from what *is* oneself requires mindfulness and maturity of thought.

The previous chapters argue that technology allows the reexperiencing of intimacy with self, others, and the environment—a holding environment—first experienced in infancy. Technology is an extension of the self; it cultivates a reactive false self that is compliant to external demands but also allows the true self to be creative and act without awareness of rules of conduct. Communications technologies empower personal identity and independence but also overstimulate the male/female element of one's being. It functions as a transformational object, one pursued by adults to provide moments that alter the experience of the self and the Other and to reshape one's emotional life. Using technology often removes a sense of presence in face-to-face relationships and commodifies persons and their experiences. Technology provides opportunities for creative living in the inner world, the outer world, and the world in-between, but it curbs creative living because it releases us from the tensions of boredom, the gateway to self-knowledge and solitude. Technology fosters regression to dependence. In addition, it often exposes the lack of concern persons carry while rarely cultivating empathy. Lastly, technology has created new playgrounds for us, eliminating traditional ones.

Technology affects our bodies, which "are programmed to consume fat and sugars because they're rare in nature. . . . In the same way, we're biologically trained to be attentive to things that stimulate: content that is gross, violent, or sexual and that gossip which is humiliating, embarrassing, or offensive."[7] People today are at risk of becoming obese on technology and unhealthy digital diets, sociologist danah boyd warns. Language about being addicted to one's phone sounds sensational— there was a time when a now-obsolete phone was referred to as a Crackberry—but it exposes elements of truth and concern. Glancing at a phone's screen every few minutes reminds us of times when we were on the lookout for threats that loomed around every bush and in every cave. It also reminds us of a spoon that was dropped and magically reappeared. Our bodies release the natural opioid dopamine and the hormone oxytocin as we engage screens. Checking technology and entering virtual spaces provide a sense of relief and give one the feeling of connection and belonging, even to hundreds of friends. Research has quantified the use of handheld communications technologies. A study commissioned by phone maker Nokia in 2012 showed that persons check their phones every six-and-a-half minutes even if no notification has come in. If awake for sixteen hours, one handles a phone 150 times![8] Other research verified a high frequency in use of phones, but not as frequent as the Nokia study found. Psychologist Larry Rosen researched the behaviors of the Millennial generation (also called the Net or I-generation), Gen Xers, and Baby Boomers vis-à-vis their phones.[9] For the Millennial generation (born 1980–2001), between 62 and 64 percent checked their devices every fifteen minutes or less during waking hours, and 51 percent stated they become anxious if they did not check text messages immediately upon notification. These findings compared to 42 percent of Gen Xers (born 1965–1979) and 18 percent for Baby Boomers (born 1943–1964), who checked their devices every fifteen minutes or less. Rosen found that 27 percent of Gen Xers and 15 percent of Boomers became anxious if they could not check in with their device. Rosen describes the Millennial generation as being "obsessed with keeping constant tabs on the two most important connection vehicles in their lives—text messages and Facebook—and they do so with vengeance."[10] Clearly, what is needed is Technological Intelligence.

Technological Intelligence is the ability to discern the impact of technology on oneself as well as one's relationships to the Other, culture, and nature while engaging and being able to evaluate digital and virtual content and objects. It speaks to a practical knowledge that is deeper than following rules or knowing the history of technology, but is able to assess evidence and come to a reasonable decision as to the value and impact of an activity or artifact. This knowledge is thus not about objects, per se—a phone, or a tablet—but rather it describes the meaning, roles, functions, and spaces these objects occupy within human nature. It informs a theology of discovery and devices, a specific way of thinking theologically about technology. Theologies of technology are well developed and typically discuss humanity reflecting on God's creativity. The theologies also focus on human freedom, resourcefulness, and sinfulness; the belonging found in faith communities; the importance of reflecting godly values; and the anticipation of an eschatological future.[11] Technology is not alien to the Judeo-Christian tradition, as scriptural references to bronze and iron tools, Jesus being identified as a *tekton*—a carpenter—and the Apostle Paul using a pen and parchment indicate.

Technological Intelligence does not nostalgically long for prior times but embraces technology with the good and ill the devices we love bring. This chapter identifies technology as a "third element," a construct describing a transformative presence formed in the special holding environment (or relationship) created between the therapist and a client. Today, technology functions as an "e-third."[12] Whereas the third element in therapy heals and restores, psychoanalyst Michael Stadter sees the e-third as fragmenting personal identities, facilitating connection and relationships, and magnifying the narcissistic tendencies all people carry. For many, it is a destructive third entity in their relationships with others or with themselves. The e-third creates a sense of co-presence when presence (or a whole person) is required and functions as a transitional object that can lower anxiety. Whereas the therapeutic third facilitates, technology as the e-third often intrudes. Indeed, discerning and managing the powers inherent in the media and other technology is an achievement.

Psychodynamically, Technological Intelligence begins with a young child playing with spoons, soft toys, and other objects.

It speaks to provision and privation, to dependency and preoccupation, to presence, to discovery, and to the belief that provision will come, which is hope. Just as a counseling journey and free association create a space for rest, aimlessly surfing the web or browsing walls or galleries to discover what one does not even know one is searching for is an attempt at rest. When the contents stimulate, shock, coax, fool, and commodify, the potential to find rest disappears.

Provision and Privation

One's relationship especially with communications technologies mirrors the experience of provision and deprivation. Provision speaks to a holding environment where all one's needs are met. It is first experienced when one is an infant in a state of absolute dependence, but it follows one into adulthood's relative dependence. When one is provided for, natural maturational processes continue on expected paths. However, when privation sets in, when basic needs are not met and care fails, one can expect psychosomatic symptoms, "bed-wetting, stealing, telling lies. . . , aggressive behaviour, destructive acts and compulsive cruelty and perversion" in children and in adults.[13] For many, a life of seeking provision but experiencing privation is the only life they know.

In *Deprivation and Delinquency*, Winnicott tells of the oldest son of two musicians, who was unexpectedly caught stealing, both inside and outside the house. With the father skeptical of any psychology, the mother sought Winnicott's advice. "I therefore explained the meaning of stealing and suggested that she should find a good moment in her relationship with the boy and make an interpretation to him. . . . I said: 'Why not tell [your son] that you know that when he steals he is not wanting the things he steals, but is looking for something that he has a right to: That he is making a claim on his mother and father because he feels deprived of their love.' "[14] Winnicott, knowing the family, knew that the parents were preoccupied outside the home. The woman wrote Winnicott that she did as Winnicott suggested, and her son did indicate that he felt neglected. Both mother and father increased the frequency of telling their son that he was loved, with behaviors of belonging that supported their words. "And up to now," she commented, "there has been absolutely no more stealing."

Through tracking thousands of displaced children during World War II, Winnicott and his colleagues deepened their understanding of the relationship between provision, deprivation, and what they referred to as the antisocial tendency. Perfectly healthy and happy children turned into unmanageable nuisances as they were evacuated to group homes away from big cities, as those were bombed by Nazi Germany. Provision speaks of hope—that good will always be readily available. It speaks of boundaries strong enough to receive pushback, without being rigid, punitive, dangerous, or too porous. Privation almost always leads to behavior that is edgy, dysfunctional, unethical, and even injurious to oneself or to others. The contribution of the antisocial tendency is that it identifies a dynamic present in every family and society, because perfect attunement in a holding environment is impossible.

It is important to remember that the impetus behind any antisocial behavior is not to transgress boundaries, to get into trouble, or just to be a nuisance. Rather, it is an attempt to get behind the privation, to restore a setting and relationships where needs can be met. Winnicott saw unsettling and transgressive behaviors as acts of hope, the hope being that provision will return. Of course, there are those individuals who are criminally minded, who move beyond the antisocial tendency to become delinquent, who carry a *clinical* diagnosis of having an antisocial personality disorder. These persons, typically above the age of eighteen, are egocentric, apathetic, manipulative, deceitful, unremorseful, hostile, and irresponsible, as well as unable to sustain intimacy.[15] Antisocial adults have lost touch with the original deprivation they experienced and live a life of despair.

The term antisocial tendency, used here in a psychodynamic context, refers to normal persons reacting to extraordinary deprivation. Despite all societal progress deprivation remains an interpersonal evil. In a world where children experience zero-tolerance authorities, where authorities do not survive the natural pushback of children and adolescents, where the majority of adult relationships are likely to fail, and where families are more complex than ever, the search behind privation is powerful. Likewise, because longed-for employment evades many, financial concerns lurk, and societal violence and extremism remind us of work yet to be done, communications technologies offer new ways to experience provision but also expose personal and relational privation.

The self longs for provision in the face of deprivation. In *It's Complicated: The Social Lives of Networked Teens*, danah boyd shows how privation creates new behavior. She calls the depiction that teenagers are addicted to technology unnecessary sensationalist. Teens still long for a holding environment that recognizes them, one where they can experience life and deep belonging, but also one where they can push against boundaries. boyd's interviews with teens found that for many, fear is a common mechanism used by parents and adult authorities to restrict the freedom of children and adolescents. Keeping children safe on playgrounds and online informs the holding environment of today's younger generation, despite research showing a child is most likely to be hurt by someone he or she already knows and trusts.[16] boyd admits that one can develop an unhealthy relationship with technology but states that especially social media offers teenagers a chance to experience what teens in other generations experienced in a different way. Parents restrict their children's mobility—walking or bicycling to meet friends is rare, as playdates and sleepovers are arranged. Add expectations of being the best and overprogramming of children's lives and they are confined to parental taxis and the home. Where children born before 1980 went over to a friend's house after school or played in the woods, today's children and teens stay in their homes, spending brief moments of freedom texting with friends or going online, often to meet friends there. In the absence of face-to-face meetings with friends, apps, social media sites, and online gaming are how and where teens meet. Technology provides a virtual context of freedom when the holding environment has become too restrictive. "Childhood has changed," boyd surmises. "Social media has become a place where teens can hold court. Their desire to connect, gossip, and hang out online makes sense in response to the highly organized and restricted lives that many teens lead."[17]

Communication technologies are technologies of provision and hope, promising new settings perceived as reliable. Danger does lurk, but it can be minimized. What are provided are experiences that respond to the drive to be in relationship and spaces where ruthlessness and violence can be tolerated. As these needs are being addressed, the lure of technology identifies two privations: First, it demonstrates the privation of face-to-face relationships, of life-giving holding environments, and of the freedom and grace to become someone in the presence of others. Second, it identifies privation that sets in when a person is held by a screen. Humans live a facial existence, and no other life is possible (see chap. 2, "Relational Intelligence"). It is self-evident that electronics cased in plastic, aluminum, and glass cannot replace the holding environment established by persons who survive one's attacks, who love and care as authentic relationships are built.

Toys, Games, and Apps

The first possession one has in infancy plays a central role in initiating Transitional Intelligence (see chap. 3, "Transitional Intelligence"). That object, often a pacifier or a soft toy, helps the infant to *remember* mother and keep her *in mind*. As one matures, these transitional *objects* are replaced by language and other cultural *experiences*, including religion. Toys, however, remain important possessions that adults pursue. For psychodynamic theorists, it is the *experiences* of participation and reception one has in culture that are central to healthy and creative living, to feeling alive. These experiences mimic the role as the first possession: they facilitate memory, keep a holding environment in mind, and allow for changes in self-experience. As stated, it is in these aspects of early experience that the power of especially communications technologies is found. Engaging with a phone or tablet, whether to text, call, or browse, awakens memory of a time when one lived with the fact of dependency. We remember a time when a holding environment assured survival and fulfilled needs, when one needed support to face transitions, whether from waking to sleeping, from sleeping to waking, or from being together to being alone.

The symbolic meanings of toys, one's phone, and one's use of handheld technologies are similar. The boy who played with string (see the introduction) teaches us that the use of a rope has emotional and relational meaning.[18] Struggling with separating from his mother and oscillating between desires for dependence and independence, the boy tied himself to objects. At other times he included his sister in his tying activity, behavior that diminished greatly when his holding environment paid attention to his emotional and relational needs. String reflected the inner world of the boy, who may have experienced the holding environment he longed for. A note about the boy as a teenager indicates he became addicted to drugs.

Being held and holding toys and objects are elements of a holding or facilitating environment. Receiving toys and other objects to discover describes the world of infants and small children. When we reach our teen years, we begin to pursue those objects, a skill we typically achieve as adults. However, even very young children are using technology to alter their self-experience. Caregivers, who are the ones placing technology into small hands, need to reckon with the cost of this change. In *Reclaiming Conversation: The Power of Talk in a Digital Age*, Sherry Turkle continues her decades-long exploration of human engagement with technology. After listening to the experiences of children, she faults adults: "So children, from an early age, complain about having to compete with smartphones for their parent's attention . . . this is the complexity of our moment."[19] Apps promise to facilitate effectively the emotional and cognitive lives of children. This promise is false. "Our mobile devices seem to grant three wishes, as though gifts from a benevolent genie: first, that we will always be heard; second, that we can put our attention wherever we want it to be; and third, that we will never be alone."[20] All three wishes remain just that—wishes. "Parents wonder if cell phone use leads to Asperger's syndrome. It is not necessary to settle this debate to state the obvious. If we don't look at our children and engage them in conversation, it is not surprising if they grow up awkward and withdrawn."[21] Adults may not show symptoms of Asperger's syndrome, but they check in with their phones every few minutes even if in the company of others. Many adults have fleeting minds and are inappropriate in social contexts. What has become everyday behavior calls for conversation and discernment.

As Transitional Intelligence indicated (see chap. 3), one of the first toys infants play with is a spoon. Possibly mouthing the spoon and dropping it, the infant patiently waits for mother or father or someone else to pick it up and then repeats the cycle.

Initially an infant with a sense of omnipotence believes that she created the spoon as it reappears after disappearing over the edge of the table. The mechanism of disappearing and reappearing is a central dynamic of human nature. It prepares the infant to sustain personal well-being if mother or a primary caregiver leaves the room and thus disappears, for there is a sense of trust that mother will reappear. If mother or father fails to reappear, trauma can set in, at which point a toy or an object can become a fetish object—an object that replaced the face of another—defending against anxiety and around which rigid behavior patterns often develop.[22] No longer is a spoon held and dropped on the floor to magically to reappear when mother or father picks it up, but a screen goes blank and is awakened by notifications or the press of a home button. As a phone or tablet is held, fingering or touching the screen becomes a new form of handling with the promise of experience and discovery. In the regression technology can bring, waking and putting a screen to sleep are compulsive rituals. With a phone-as-fetish, what should be kept in mind—the holding environment can be relied upon and thus one can live with a sense of belonging and with less anxiety—has become an object that weights *on* the mind: one remains anxious when not handling the fetish object. Forgetting one's phone at home or losing it causes significant emotional distress.

Saying that a phone, a tablet, or social media imitates the psychodynamic functions of an infant's first toy and holding environment does not diminish the imagination and entrepreneurial genius that creates today's objects of desire. Grown-downs recognize the engineering skill, artistic design, and economic models that drive tech giants and social media dynasties. They also know that whether a child or an adult, one longs to recreate the holding environment of deep belonging where one's identity is recognized and shaped. It takes Technological Intelligence to handle technology, for the code behind apps and games aims to exploit human need and induce dependency.

Entrepreneur and technology angel investor Nir Eyal consults with persons who seek to create apps that hook people—in his context, successful apps. Eyal states that the inventors especially of handheld technologies study human nature and are "conversant in psychology as much as technology."[23] As an industry insider, Eyal reminds us that apps are engineered primarily in four ways to make sure one remains engaged. First, the apps rely on internal and external *triggers*, such as boredom, loneliness, or large "Like" or "Log In" buttons to bring users to them, and then offer solutions for that trigger.[24] Second, triggers are followed by *actions*, "behavior done in anticipation of a reward." Clicking on a link or activating a game or app is a popular action choice.[25] Through actions one seeks pleasure and avoids pain, awakens hope in the face of fear, and seeks acceptance while avoiding social rejection. Third, the action is associated with a *variable reward*—intrigue, curiosity, or a craving that activates the brain's reward system (the nucleus accumbens), which releases dopamine and oxytocin.[26] The rewards one seeks can be relationship-based (tribal), aimed at finding and acquiring (the chase and the hunt), or the pleasure of gaining competency or completing a task.[27] In the process the self is "gamified"—one's skill level or numbers go up, gold color badges are received, or community points are awarded.[28] The fourth element in Eyal's model is *investment*.[29] As app users and gamers invest "time, data, effort, social capital, or money," the chances that they will repeat the cycle increase. One remains hooked through personal needs, investment of time and energy, and receiving rewards.

Many people today may not be addicted to their phones, but they are certainly hooked, tied compulsively to a technology that provides a holding environment they are unable to escape. They experience an imploding world should they be cut off from their phones or communications technologies. Toys are no longer an inanimate spoon or a wooden horse that receives animation through the power of one's imagination. Apps are dynamic and, like many websites and games, rely on some version of the Eyal's Hook Model. Between e-mailing, texting, tweeting, posting, blogging, uploading, reading, downloading, and watching, the need to remain reactive to the "toys" one handles deepens.

Fantasy, Illusion, and Virtuality

Grown-downs live fantastical lives. They also live with illusion. Through *fantasy* one's subjectivity assigns emotional and relational meaning and purpose to others and experiences in an attempt to control the outer world. In fantasy, perceptions of the Other are destroyed so that the Thou in the Other can surface. This dynamic requires time and maturation as the Me separates from the Not-me. Through *illusion* one can enter into the potential space where symbolic meaning is assigned to transitional objects (see chap. 2, "Relational Intelligence"). Because symbols invite one into a world where one thing represents much more, where this stands for that, life receives meaning and realness. Culture, art, and religion thrive on this ability. The place where one lives is a hybrid of fantasy and illusion as well as a combination of the inner world, the outer world, and the world in-between. The transitional space is also "a space of simulation: in which, for example, the child may safely test the object's ability to withstand attack."[30] Through simulation the relationship between transitional objects, phenomena, and computer-generated *virtuality* is established.

Fantastical and illusional, grown-downs are virtual people. Virtuality was not created by computer technology, for "immersive experiences delivered through the human imagination have their origins in deep prehistory. Whether these varieties of nonphysical, dreamlike realities were communicated by our ancestors through the imitation of animals, the incarnation of spirits, the painting of scenes on the stone canvasses of caves, the holding of ceremonial rites in temples, or the elaboration of the human story through the fount of theater, humans have craved and crafted virtual-world experiences from the dawn of artistic and linguistic expression."[31] Entering a three-dimensional world, whether the world was created by one's imaginative capacities or computer technology, comes naturally. Here, the self is reoriented through virtuality's power of indexicality, taking the self to a new location. Of course, not all that is digital is virtual. What is digital is built on zeroes and ones, and what is virtual is also built upon zeroes and ones, but the virtual includes something deeply personal and emotional, something existential, an investment of sorts as physical, relational, and spiritual energies flow across three worlds. Between virtual *reality*–referring to augmenting tools such as head-up displays, gloves, and sense stimulation—and virtual *worlds*–places that do not necessarily require sensory immersion—virtual people find new caves to inhabit and walls to paint.

There is a natural progression and relationship between the fantasy and illusion one uses to appropriate life and the technology one seeks to enter virtual worlds. There is a reason why the gaming industry remains vibrant despite financial downturns. The highest-grossing video game, *Grand Theft Auto V*, was released in 2013 and earned $800 million on its first day and reached $1 billion in sales by day three despite the game's questionable depiction of women and its inclusion of a hostage torture scene! Sales by June 2015 exceeded $2 billion as more than 52 million copies of the game have been sold. Grown-downs know, however, that vital living demands the traversing of the inner and outer worlds and the world in-between. None of the worlds can become a permanent home that facilitates flourishing. Because of gaming's popularity and its orientation toward violence, it is no surprise that there are strong opinions about the impact of virtual reality on human behavior.

In *How Fantasy Becomes Reality*, social and media psychologist Karen Dill explores how exposure to media violence and gender and racial stereotyping, especially in video games, shapes lives. Most people today do not believe advertising or mass media has a significant influence on them, contrary to what research shows. Media affects users through a mechanism called "transportation," being swept into a game or a story so as to feel part of it, suspending any disbelief. Through transportation what "could" happen "should" happen, as media shapes behavior and attitudes. A study done by researchers at the University of Maryland showed that those who are most vehement in their belief that violent video games are consequence-free also played such games the most.[32] Those persons modeled the "third person effect," the belief that people other than oneself are affected by media. "Playing at harming someone increases the chances that you would *really* hurt someone. Fantasy creates reality."[33] Dill references research that shows when people are exposed to violence in the media, they are more aggressive than others who were not exposed to that content. In a game such as *Grand Theft Auto V*, a player physically assaults characters, shoots civilians and police officers, and kills and dismembers a prostitute while continuously using foul and derogatory language and engaging in antisocial behavior. When a female character dressed like a prostitute is hit, she responds, "I like it rough." Players and characters engage in a variety of sexual activities.

The same mirror neurons, important for all face-to-face interactions, are active here too, making imitation an unconscious activity. Playing violent video games causes physical arousal (e.g., increased heart rate, blood pressure, hyperalertness) and increases aggressive *thoughts* of hurting others, aggressive *feelings* (e.g., anger, hostility), and aggressive *behavior*. In addition, violent games decrease empathy, care, and helping attitudes and behaviors.[34] Although human nature is too complex for linear causes and arguments, Dill's argument does receive some support from authors who show that in numerous violent shootings, including Columbine (1999) and Newtown (2012), the shooters were avid players of violent video games.[35] In seeking a link between societal violence and violent video games, however, society neglects to see that sport, whether football, ice hockey, or cage fighting, is also violent and fully sanctioned.[36]

The relationship between violent video games and our behavior is complex, yet it reflects infantile omnipotence to argue that one is beyond being affected by playing violent games. Psychodynamically, one cannot engage with transformational objects—virtual games—without change coming to one's feelings, attitudes, or behaviors. The lobby convincing people that video games, even violent ones, are innocent fun and an expression of free speech are well funded and connected to power brokers.

Dill uses the analogy of eating nutritious food and being heart-healthy and aware of the risks of consuming trans fats to describe the effects of a media diet. It is unlikely that death will set in after eating a large portion of French fries, but one's health is compromised. Referencing research that shows that violent video games lowered empathy in fourth- and fifth-grade boys and girls, she concludes, "You consume media. You take it in and it becomes part of you."[37] It should be no surprise that a generation that grew up with technology shows less capacity for empathy compared to previous generations (see chap. 4, "Reparative Intelligence").[38]

The relationship between fantasy, illusion, and virtuality is not necessarily a negative one. A person needs illusion for creative living. Jane McGonigal, in *Reality Is Broken: How Games Can Make Us Better and How They Can Change the World*, argues for increased virtuality and simulation. "The fact that so many people of all ages, all over the world, are choosing to spend so much time in game worlds is a sign of something important, a truth that we urgently need to recognize," McGonigal writes.[39] As illusion is needed for creative living, so virtuality may also be needed to address today's problems, whether poverty, hunger, or war. Gamers, music lovers, and virtuality buffs can teach us about being fully alive, focused, and engaged in every moment, states of being not easily found in the outer world. Furthermore, virtual games can teach society something about being true to oneself and having passion, about being motivated, and about problem solving. The benefits of having the collective wisdom of millions of people engaged in a single activity—playing a game—with millions of years of cumulative hours spent online can be immense. Virtuality is not always escapist; it can be purposive and enable a future because games teach problem solving, engaging obstacles, and collaboration. The cultural bias against virtual gaming is strong, McGonigal warns, as if people are gaming the system.

Games typically have four defining features, which function similarly to Eyal's hook model: (1) *Goals* provide a *sense of purpose*; (2) *Rules* and *obstacles* inhibit but also unleash *creativity and strategic thinking*; (3) A *feedback system promises* the goal can be reached, as it *motivates, instills optimism, and satisfies*; and (4) *Voluntary participation* provides *a sense of safety, pleasure, common ground, and community*.[40] Engaging with the features of virtual (and other) games leaves one with pride or *fiero*—an Italian word describing a sense of satisfaction and happiness after completing a task. *Fiero* activates one's emotional system, which is foundational to McGonigal's argument that playing virtual games can enrich the material world. Among the games she identifies is *Chore Wars*, an alternate reality game (not virtual) and gamified app, where doing common household chores can earn one points, badges, and in-game prizes. Dusting is worth ten points, but cleaning the bathroom is worth one hundred. Couples, families, and roommates play the game while achieving real world consequences—a clean home, apartment, or office.[41] The game convinces people to do tasks typically found to be unpleasant and can make difficult tasks more rewarding. "We can no longer afford to view games as separate from our real lives and our real work. It is not only a waste of the potential of games to do real good—it is simply untrue," McGonigal concludes.[42]

Games can build, uplift, and facilitate the good. They need not be violent or racist. Technological Intelligence reckons with the fact that media, in whatever form it arrives, shapes one's reality and has unintended consequences, for it is never neutral.

Preoccupation and Attention

To be preoccupied—a sign of maturity—is to have one's thoughts and attention dominated in such a way that other thoughts and sensory data are excluded. For grown-downs, preoccupation takes at least four forms. First, there is the preoccupation a new mother has vis-à-vis her newborn, aptly referred to as primary maternal preoccupation.[43] Fathers and caregivers can be preoccupied in a similar way. A mother and her infant enter into a dual union of baby-is-mother and mother-is-baby that allows the infant to thrive and slowly separate from mother. It is a mother hearing her baby cry in a nursery, where many babies might be crying, or mother checking in on baby to find her baby in distress. This kind of preoccupation reflects unconditional love and a deep devotion to an infant totally dependent upon adult care. There is an ordinariness about it, for this state of heightened sensitivity comes naturally to almost all caregivers. Typically, the intensity of the preoccupation diminishes after a number of weeks as the holding environment that was formed holds both the mother and the infant. It is primary maternal preoccupation that initiates an infant's sense of self or "going on being."[44]

Second, there is also the preoccupation one finds in play behavior (see chap. 5, "Playground Intelligence"). In playing, Winnicott writes, there is "the near-withdrawal state, akin to the *concentration* of older children or adults. The playing child inhabits an area that cannot be easily left, nor can it easily admit intrusions."[45] While preoccupied, a child can discover and strengthen his or her sense of self while many other faculties are built and strengthened. Parents, caregivers, and partners know this kind of preoccupation well, for trying to get someone's attention while in this state inevitably falls on deaf ears and most often frustrates. Time is suspended and other worlds do not matter for one is engrossed in play. Entering the transitional space supersedes everything else.

Third, the preoccupation found in play behavior extends into creative living, the act of creating and the experience of feeling alive. It reflects a natural drive toward health and draws on the creative imagination of infancy where infants, with their sense of omnipotence, create the world. The preoccupation of the creative act takes one to the transitional space (see chap. 3, "Transitional Intelligence"). Here the dichotomy of the self and the Other, or being gifted or not, collapses in the face of paradox. Every person can live creatively. Getting lost in the creative act supports apperception and purpose: new experiences are integrated into the self, so that the act of creating itself transforms the experience of the self and the Other. Artists, captivated by the act of creation, attest to feeling alive and having other needs lose their power. Psychologist Mihály Csíkszentmihályi writes about preoccupation as flow, a state of complete absorption when engaging in an activity or experiencing a situation.[46] Artists, solo seafarers, marathon runners, long-distance drivers and riders, and even persons doing repetitive manual labor can experience flow.

A fourth preoccupation *inhibits* personal vitality and may be described best as a compulsion driven by anxiety. The boy who played with string was preoccupied with rope. Whereas normal play develops a sense of being, the boy's sense of self and self-in-relation were stunted. His preoccupation became a dramatization of his inner life. Communications and media technologies, through their power as transformational objects, can induce this kind of inhibiting preoccupation. Constantly holding a phone or handling a screen does not facilitate vital relationships or living. Unlike the preoccupation parents have with their infants, which diminishes over time, the preoccupation that develops around technology is intensifying.

A central dynamic within the preoccupation of parents with newborns, those captivated by play, an artist transfixed by creation, and a person preoccupied with his or her phone is *attention*. Attention—the ability to focus on a single task, or the lack of fleeting thoughts—is a distinguishing feature amongst the varieties of preoccupation. As communications technologies have eradicated boredom, so too did they diminish attention. Social media writer Howard Rheingold calls this "attentional shift." In the face of ever-present technology, access to media, and unfettered ability to contact others—the forces behind attentional shift—"relatively few people appear to use ubiquitous informational access and social connectivity politely and productively."[47] Attentional shift, which includes responding to the notifications on communications technologies as they arrive or checking in frequently to see if a new tweet or e-mail or text is waiting, comes at a cost deeper than developing a false self (see chap. 1, "Self Intelligence").

In *Net Smart: How to Thrive Online*, Rheingold discusses attentional shift in the context of multitasking. Multitasking is notoriously difficult, if not impossible, for most because it requires parallel processing. Research suggests that fewer than 2.5 percent of the population is able to engage in multiple tasks without a decrease in skill and competence. Fighter pilots and airport control officers are among the few who can truly multi-task as they tabulate, consolidate, aviate, navigate, and communicate. It is now common knowledge that texting and driving is a failed attempt at multitasking. "Attention, memory and executive control are the fundamental components of thinking," Rheingold reminds us.[48] Executive control is the part of the brain that retrieves memories and keeps five to nine chunks of information in one's working memory. Rheingold uses the metaphor of an orchestra conductor to describe executive control, removing attention on a specific task and placing it somewhere else. It is a capacity that matures over the first twenty-five years of one's life.

Multitasking breaks the flow between attention, memory, and executive control. As such, what we perceive as multi-tasking is really task-switching. "It is not that multitasking is always bad (except when it is—like when one is driving a car), or continuous partial attention (such as surfing the Web while talking on the phone) is always rude and inefficient. It's that too few have learned and taught to others the skills we need to know if we are to master the use of our attention amid a myriad of choices designed to attract us."[49] With an infinite number of choices present when one ventures online, the self can get lost.

After each switch or shift, one needs "to reorient, refocus, and filter out competing information in order to move from one stable theme to another."[50] It can take up to thirty minutes to regain concentration on a central task after an "attentional blink." While the human brain receives an estimated eleven million bits of information per second, it can be aware of no more than forty bits of information per second. Attention is being mindful not to deplete the forty bits of information awareness can manage.

This is difficult because one's mirror neurons fire up when using e-mail, reading tweets, or posting to walls. Unless mindfulness intervenes, attention diverts almost automatically from the task at hand to what arrived in digital form. Online activity, Rheingold warns, erodes awareness of one's attention to the extent that even one's breathing is affected. "E-mail apnea" is the tendency to breathe less when reading e-mails.[51] "Continuous partial attention, an always on, anywhere, anytime, any place behavior that involves an artificial sense of constant crisis . . . hampers opportunities for reflection and authentic social connection."[52] Breathing deeply and being mindful about one's attentional blinks are central to growing down in an age of technology.

Reclaiming the focused preoccupation shown by parents of newborns, children playing, and artists creating is a skill worth gaining. Attention training can get one a long way toward this goal. When teaching, Rheingold helps his students gain mindfulness by beginning with a meditative moment where they notice how easily their attention can drift. He records students from the front of the class to show them how their attention lapses when engaging with social media in class. In a class of fifty, he allows five students to have their laptops open at any given time. If someone appropriates a laptop, the other students are affected. "Thinking about what you are doing and why you are doing it instead of going through the motions is fundamental to the definition of being mindful, whether you are deciding to follow someone on Twitter, shutting the lid of your laptop in class, looking up from your [phone] in a meeting, or consciously deciding which links *not* to click."[53] Healthy preoccupation is a skill that does not easily admit intrusions.

Presence and Copresence

Presence speaks to place and being present, exuding or feeling an aura, or having a state of mind. The experience of presence does not rely on a person being physically present, as communications and virtual technologies create mediated experiences best described as being there or experiencing a sense of presence. Though mediated, these experiences feel unmediated like face-to-face experiences. Psychodynamically, presence is a paradox, for one is always alone in the presence of others (see chap. 2, "Relational Intelligence"). Within a good enough holding environment, infants and young children can risk to feel and emote, for they intuitively know that those who love them are stronger than any feelings experienced.[54] For adults, being alone in the presence of others implies holding one's feelings or emoting appropriately and reaching out to others when that is asked for. Neither spilling over nor taking one's feelings into one's body brings life. Loneliness is a sign that being alone in the presence of others has not been achieved. In play behavior, where powerful feelings are experienced, children practice how to hold emotions internally and provide a sense of being an "I am" that can be secure and vulnerable, protected yet exposed, alone but together. With the onset of the computer age, the paradox of being alone while in the presence of others received new meaning. While one certainly can experience a deep sense of presence online, the use of technology in the presence of others communicates withdrawal and a sense of co-presence, which is non-presence.

The question of presence comes into sharp focus in any discussion of online therapy. "Does presence necessitate a body?" asks therapist Haim Weinberg in *The Paradox of Internet Groups: Alone in the Presence of Virtual Others.*[55] His research found—and experience confirmed—that whether persons meet face-to-face in a group setting or in a virtual group, having a voice and hearing voices as well as seeing and being seen are central to having a sense of presence. Questioning the "perceptual illusion of non-mediation," Weinberg sees all communication as mediated.[56] The gap between the self and the Other has to be bridged, whether it is air and space that spans the gap or the Ethernet. A sense of presence emanates from settings with social richness, warmth, sensitivity, intimacy, immediacy, and a perceived accurate representation of persons, objects, and events. Such settings can be real or virtual. Whether offline or in a virtual space, presence is increased by the feeling that one is taken to another place (the idea of transportation) with a sense of emotional and relational immersion (which suggests a trusted place). When presence has set in, the fact that the other person (or a social actor) comes in a mediated form diminishes, leaving one with a sense of the person only through the perceptual illusion of non-mediation. It is important to remember that Weinberg does not refer to the fleeting engagements one finds online. He is talking about a set group of people (e.g., a therapy group) meeting regularly in a sustained conversation.

The fact that the medium is computer-based can become irrelevant, as seen in the definition of presence by the International Society of Presence Research: "Presence (a shorter version of the term 'telepresence') is a psychological state or subjective perception in which even though part or all of an individual's current experience is generated by and/or filtered through human-made technology, part or all of the individual's perception fails to accurately acknowledge the role of the technology in the experience."[57] It is the power of presence that allows Weinberg to run therapy groups online. Still, the practice remains anathema for many traditional clinicians where the physical presence of the counselor and counselee are foundational to therapy.

When one sees presence as "the perception of successfully transforming an intention into an action," as Gillian Russell does in *Screen Relations: The Limits of Computer-Mediated Psychoanalysis and Psychotherapy*, the capacity for presence in virtual spaces diminishes.[58] For Russell it takes a shared space to read intention—verbal and bodily communication, for example—and to act on the communication. As a mother has to survive the attacks of her infant, so too do members of an online group have to survive each other. In virtual counseling—and, by extension, online relationships—survival is greatly diminished, but possible. For Russell, presence also depends on internal and external experiences. Although the internal experience of virtuality is powerful, the ability to understand the intentional mental states of the other person—needs, desires, beliefs, purposes, and reasons—is most often circumvented.

The two-dimensionality and pixilated nature of screens cannot hold or represent the three-dimensionality of human nature. Russell quotes a clinician on using technology to facilitate a person's journey to restoration: "It is like you're trying to get closer to someone using the wrong tools. . . . It's like trying to see someone better by shouting."[59] Russell's research showed that clinicians tended to remember less of a technologically mediated session than a traditional session and that therapists were distracted more frequently. Therapists also felt less intimacy with their clients, often hitting a wall in the therapeutic journey that could not be broken through. Being present to someone—or copresent in Russell's vision—takes courage. Able to take (or meet) their clients everywhere, therapists using technology began to see their clients as portable. Russell draws on British psychoanalyst Wilfred Bion's concept of *reverie* to enhance the holding environment needed: "[Reverie] is a shared process between analyst and patient in which the unconscious interplay of both their states of mind creates an overlapping intersubjective experience."[60] We need a sense of reverie to thrive.

Whereas Weinberg is optimistic about online group therapy, Russell highlights the limits of computer-based experiences. Weinberg's optimism echoes what was stated in the first chapter, that the self is extended into cyberspace. He concludes that "maybe we can adopt a new definition of therapy that involves two *selves* (or a group of selves) in interaction instead of two embodied persons. The self is not equivalent to the body, is not contained by the body and even does not necessarily reside in a body. . . . The new approach to therapy, enhanced by a new understanding of human connection appearing on-line, portrays two decentered selves, partial, subjective, and polymorphous as they are trying to connect over a mediated space, having rare moments of close-touching connection."[61] Russell, on the other hand, emphasizes the importance of the face and the dynamics found in the holding environment. The self needs the physical presence of other selves to thrive. For her, me-ness has to engage we-ness.

Technology can facilitate a qualified sense of presence. However, it cannot easily induce the full experience of presence where a self's past and future are incorporated in the here and now, where consequences and the significance of events are placed in wider frameworks.[62] However, when communications technology physically comes between relationships, say between parents and children, presence diminishes, especially for the children. British theater director and neuroscientist Jonathan Miller reminds us, "Until we see ourselves reflected we haven't the faintest idea of what the most recognisable part of us looks like."[63] The need to be seen and recognized, to be mirrored in face-to-face relationships, is essential for human flourishing (see chap. 2, "Relational Intelligence").

British psychotherapist Anita Colloms writes about a mother who brought her infant with her to therapy. The mother tells her therapist that she is frustrated with her baby, who grabs for her phone while she is breastfeeding. "All he wants is the phone," the mother states. Her solution is to put a cloth over her breast and her baby's face, like a curtain, so as not to be disrupted.[64] The infant boy, struggling to gain his mother's attention while she is on the phone, cannot see her face and is not mirrored. Protecting her relationship with her phone, the mother fails to be reliable as her infant's false self gains strength (see chap. 1, "Self Intelligence"). In an observational study of mothers with infants at outdoor cafés, Colloms saw a mother, one who had been talking on her cell phone for an extended period, interrupted by her fussing baby. The mother, still talking on the phone, picked up her infant, who turned her head back and forth as if to gain her mother's attention. The mother kept talking on the phone. The baby heard her mother's voice and saw an animated face, but had no access to either. "Eventually the baby gave up and went limp."[65]

In *The Big Disconnect: Protecting Childhood and Family Relationships in the Digital Age,* psychologist Catherine Steiner-Adair refers to research that echoes Colloms' and Turkle's observations. Technology is shattering a sense of presence among, especially, parents and their children. This break can begin early, as Colloms indicated. Steiner-Adair refers to a study showing higher incidences of behavioral problems in children where mothers regularly used cell phones during their pregnancy and then continued to introduce technology to their children at an early age. It seems that the problem is not only children engaging with technology at a young age, but also parents and adults being poor role models for the younger generation and setting no boundaries around the use of technology.

A seven-year-old told Steiner-Adair, "My mom is almost always on the iPad at dinner. She's always 'just checking.'" Another said, "A lot of time when my parents are at home and on their computers, I feel like I'm not there, because they pretend like I'm not there . . . they're like not even talking to me, they just are ignoring me. I feel like ughhh, sad [sigh]."[66] Other children told Steiner-Adair they felt lonely and unrecognized by their parents, or at least less important than the "stupid" notifications that grabbed their parent's attention. When children draw pictures of their families, adults have cell phones in their hands. And as voices are streamed over Bluetooth connections in cars, children overhear conversations not meant for their ears. "Parents' chronic distraction can have deep and lasting effects on their children," Steiner-Adair reiterates. The message being sent is: *"Everybody else matters more than you. Everybody matters more than you. Whatever the caller might say is more important than what you are telling me now."*[67] Sherry Turkle supports Steiner-Adair's research. In her discussion of the impact of phones on friendships, she states that "By having our phones out, we keep conversations light and we are less connected to each other in the conversations we do have. And we rarely talk to friends about how we feel when they turn away from us to their phones."[68] Technology has created a sense of co-presence that tries hard to imitate the preoccupation inherent in an infant's holding environment. What is lacking, though, is life-giving and life-sustaining connections between persons—faces that signify conversation and care.

Research by the Annenberg Center for the Digital Future at the University of Southern California showed that 56 percent of users stated the Internet and mobile communication strengthen their immediate relationships, and 25 percent felt that going online had no effect on those relationships. However, 92 percent of respondents felt ignored by family members as those members engaged their cell phones.[69] As the Annenberg longitudinal study shows, the high percentage of persons who have felt ignored is no surprise, for the average amount of hours spent online each week while at home increased from 3.3 hours in 2000 to 14.1 hours in 2012. Many family members are caught in a screen and only co-present to others. Steiner-Adair is correct; we are lost in connection. In families and relationships, one needs to create "a fabric of connectivity that is strong and many-layered. It can deal with a crisis with elasticity, without unraveling. It is flexible, not brittle, and has a high tensile strength forged by spending time together. It values family life above life online."[70]

Grown-downs know that belonging to a group is a need all people share. Deep connection, not the kind that can happen over the brim of a laptop screen, in a quick text that disrupts thought until another notification replaces it, or in conversations that last but a minute, remains a desire. Friendship, partnering, family, being a member of a group, and partaking in culture are places and relationships that portray deep connection. When one feels one is a burden and has to interrupt to be recognized, persons and relationships flounder. Infants and children and the adults who provide their care do know naturally how to establish and enter into relationships. Technology, however, is changing our priorities. Outside the preoccupation inherent in caring for an infant, grown-downs have to work at preoccupation and presence, and that work has become all the more difficult due to technology's power to demand attention and set new expectations for one's relational life.

Discovery

From the moment a newborn discovers her new world, she embarks on a never-ending journey of discovery. The acts of discovering and interpreting are central activities of grown-down living and make life feel real. Initially, discovery is found when the infant Me discovers the Not-me, lets go of omnipotence, and, in fantasy, destroys any preconceived notions she had of mother. Later, discovery is found in play behavior, where one discovers that "an object can be destroyed and restored, hurt and mended, dirtied and cleaned, killed and brought to life, with the added achievement of ambivalence in place of splitting the object (self) into good and bad."[71] Playing with others diminishes when one approaches partners as objects to be controlled and manipulated or if situations cannot be interpreted. In a lecture given in New York in 1968, Winnicott described the importance of a person learning how to "use" the self and the Other. *Use* in psychodynamic theory, remember, is not exploitation, but it carries connotations of discovering, uncovering, finding, and recognizing the Other (see chap. 2, "Relational Intelligence").[72]

Discovery is an achievement, for naturally what one discovers comes fused with preconceived notions and ideas, warping one's interpretations. In his lecture Winnicott stated that a therapeutic journey does not begin before all preconceived notions of the analytic journey, the therapist, and even the counselee are stripped of any subjective phenomena. The subjective phenomena in question are dynamics such as projection, where fears and other unwanted elements of oneself are identified in others but denied in oneself. Projection is the most commonly used defense mechanism in online and virtual worlds. In projective identification, a person receiving the projections of another begins to identify with those projections, altering his or her sense of self. People also split their experiences and reality, seeing others or an event as either all good or all bad, when in reality, people and experiences are neither good nor bad nor neutral. When these defenses are present, Winnicott argues, one *relates*, unless one engages in the hard work of discovering and finding the Other in *usage*, which implies destroying the preconceived notions in fantasy. Whereas relating seeks to manipulate and exploit, usage finds, discovers, and recognizes. Discovering and finding is how one's inner world relates to the outer world. One can either find the Other and discover mutual recognition or one can see a person and be affirmed in what one already knows. The latter isolates and alienates persons and relationships. For many, Winnicott concluded, achieving the ability to relate authentically subject-to-subject and to feel real are the reasons persons seek counseling to begin with.

Virtual worlds are vulnerable to *relating* as seen in a game such as *Grand Theft Auto* and in the comments sections of websites. Discovering authenticity and recognizing the independent existence of another online is difficult. This is the argument of Kishonna Gray, an African-American gamer-academic who explores media, gender, and justice in her book *Race, Gender, and Deviance in Xbox Live*. As the title suggests, Gray explores how racism, sexism, and other antisocial behaviors are portrayed in video games played on Microsoft's gaming platform. She approaches games from the view of the marginalized. "Video games, as an interactive enterprise, represent a sophistical, virtual form of fantastic play. . . . [They play] on peoples' desire to experience the Other, breaking down real boundaries between communities, between the real and the unreal, all while normalizing racial and gender stereotypes."[73] Games provide freedom—to be someone else, to explore, and to be exposed to other worlds. Games also reinforce stereotypes around race, gender, and sexuality while sanctioning microaggressions, crime, entrenched inequality, bigotry, violence, and other injustices.

Gray, engaged in a multiplayer online game, was called out by her team leader after she was unable to ward off enemy combatants, and as a result, her team died (only to be brought back to life in an attempt to avenge her and her team's deaths). Her leader, speaking harshly into her headset, prompted Gray to reply apologetically into her microphone, exposing her as a woman, something her avatar hid:

> Oh you guys hear this? That's why you suck. You are a fucking girl. What the fuck are you doing in my room? . . . Wait wait wait. You're not just any girl. You're black. Get this black bitch off my team. Did you spend all your welfare check buying this game? Why aren't you doing what you love? Get back to your crack pipe and your crack babies.[74]

The game, which Gray played for fun, often became a place of hatred and bigotry. Women of color were not welcome in this space that was created for white, middle-class men. Game developers give players freedom of choice and have feedback systems where inappropriate interactions can be flagged. Still experiences like Gray's abound online. The power structure within the gaming world is predominantly white and male. The result is that women and persons of color are often exploited, and their contributions as players and purchasers are rarely recognized. Research indicates that 47 percent of all gamers are women.[75] Add persons of color and they outnumber white males, yet the racism and homophobia continues. In this context of hegemonic power, discovering and recognizing the Other is nearly impossible. Minority gamers are not seen as true gamers, and games are marketed to boys first, with girls a mere afterthought.

"Race and racist practices are embedded into the social fabric of the American social order, validating racialized practices in many institutional settings, and video games are not exempt from this trend."[76] In the majority of first person shooter, action, and sports games, where a player can control his or her actions and also the progression of the story, the dominant narrative within culture is maintained and even built upon. This allows for a strong emotional attachment between a player and a narrative that serves white male privilege with the concomitant stereotypes that surround women, persons of color, or other minority groups. The danger of this narrative is that it "hides and makes invisible the operation of power relations masking the relationship between subjection and coercion."[77] This power seeks social control, colonizes consciousness, and maintains hegemony. It is this power W. E. B. Du Bois warned against as universities seek to produce grown-up alumni who are part of the elite and powerful, instead of growing down and exposing the narrative for its ideological, taken-for-granted domination, the domination by white masculinity (see the introduction).

Gray's project, in which she discusses a number of the most popular video games, shows how subjective phenomena and preconceived and entrenched notions of race, gender, male power, and perverse sexuality permeate video games. The dominant cultural narrative rewards persons whose subjective phenomena continue to determine behavior and relationships as they abuse and malign people. At best, growing down to discover the Other as a subject will cause significant ambivalence in someone frequenting settings where race and gender stereotypes fused with violence, sexual exploitation, and other antisocial frameworks are the status quo. The gaming industry is unlikely to bring change and protect human nature. As womanist scholar Audre Lorde warns, "For the master's tools will never dismantle the master's house."[78] The power relations within technology are such that masculinity and masculine worlds are not only protected, but built.

Gray exposes the challenge of discovering the Other when immersed in popular video games with their hegemonic nature. Discovering the Other, however, is not the only form of discovering one engages in: Google provides answers when knowledge is sought. This form of discovering adds a layer to the relating that comes naturally to all and is the focus of Eli Pariser's The Filter Bubble. Pariser is curious and concerned about how and what one finds and reads online.[79] Filtering is not new, as humans have done so for thousands of years. Relating to others through subjective phenomena, as the previous paragraphs stated, is a form of filtering. What has changed, however, is the nature of filtering. No longer is filtering—a form of interpretation—the work of unconscious processes that can be made conscious; instead, it is done through personalized algorithms controlled by companies such as Google, Microsoft, Yahoo, and Amazon.

Most persons accept personalized searches and the vision of a custom-tailored world that saves all from boredom. However, Pariser warns that searches determined by algorithms based on prior searches and purchasing histories come at significant personal, cultural, and societal costs. He describes the personal cost as "a kind of invisible autopropaganda, indoctrinating us with our own ideas, amplifying our desire for things that are familiar," while leaving little room for discovering insights and learning.[80] Rather than discovering the self and the Other anew, the self becomes a commodity to be exploited by "persistent, personalized advertising."[81] The self becomes a copy of what was found online.

"Ultimately, the filter bubble can affect your ability to choose how you want to live," Pariser concludes.[82] In the filter bubble (also called "chamber echo"), every person becomes a victim as personal data is aggregated and repackaged to follow one from computer to phone to tablet and from website to website. Personalized products, news, notices, and things bound to be "liked" ties one to the familiar. Personalization gets in the way of creativity and innovation by limiting one's "solution horizon" — the mental space within which one searches for solutions to problems.[83] Algorithms tend to offer unverified information and encourage a passive approach to acquiring knowledge. Furthermore, the ease of searching removes the importance of memory and upsets the cognitive balance between strengthening existing ideas and acquiring new ones. It raises the question, just what is worth remembering? Filter bubbles surround us with familiar, agreeable ideas and often ignore "real" inconveniences such as violence, war, hunger, and poverty. It is difficult to "like" interpersonal violence, murder, or genocide. Facebook's effort to expand its respond buttons and fight fake news are acknowledgments that its platform does not function as envisioned.

Discovering persons or knowledge is the achievement of discovery and interpretation. It requires a new kind of practical wisdom or *phronesis*: Technological Intelligence. Technological Intelligence is the ability to discern the impact of technology on oneself as well as one's relationships to the Other, culture, and nature while engaging and being able to evaluate digital and virtual contents and objects. For the Greeks, *phronesis* was a virtue recognized in reasonable people who could *reinterpret* what they received or experienced. For all engaging communications and media technologies, the practical wisdom of Technological Intelligence as a grown-down trait determines the difference between living a creative life of justice and equality and merely receiving the data online worlds provide, data that inevitably maintains the status quo.

Seeking Ego Orgasms

Communications technologies support and strengthen the false self, even as they beckon the true self, unencumbered by rules, expectations, or concerns, out of hiding. The virtual spaces and immersive communities one enters blur boundaries and confuse roles by inviting us to tell about the self in widely different settings with different rules and expectations. It is such blurring and confusion that births the false self, a malleable self because of its compliant nature. One reason for role-playing games' popularity is the fact that players are given clear roles, follow set community rules, partake in circumscribed rituals, and have the ability to create their own narrative within a larger one. In technology the false self finds an ubercaretaker, always present and ready to fuel reactivity. One thus naturally enters into a relationship with technology. Like a mother deeply attuned to her infant, ready to provide when a need arrives, technology provides a holding environment with images and information sought previously. Without Technological Intelligence, one is fed not by a caregiver and in a state of rest, but by multinational corporations that both create and address need while profiting from doing so. The power of these corporations reminds us of the Old Testament prophets who exposed the attraction, but also the powerlessness, of idols.[84] As stated, Technological Intelligence carries much potential to inform theologies of technology. The technological holding environment serves select interests and keeps one from growing down toward mature adulthood. Gaining the know-how or mental discipline to consistently engage virtual worlds in life-giving ways takes intentionality. Between checking in with phones and status updates and surfing the web, the false self thrives.

Technology relies on the compliance of the false self birthed in infancy and early childhood. It also relies on the true self that seeks pleasure with spontaneity without a sense of boundaries or ethics. A person who cannot risk boredom or uncertainty often finds relief in reading one notification after another, fingering a screen or keyboard surfing the web or handling a gaming console. The outer world has become an always-on, digiphrenic place of digitally induced mental confusion, as we are in multiple places at the same time, and this world constantly demands attention.[85] Notifications create a sense of urgency, giving the impression that the world is moving at a rapid pace that leaves people behind. The false self finds meaning in such urgency; the true self goes deeper into hiding.

The cost of living with a false self is growing up too fast, feeling unreal, and chasing goals that never fulfill even when reached. One might fool others about one's identity, and corporations might love the false self, but the true self knows better. The desire to be authentic, vulnerable, and able to enter relationships with empathy and intimacy, which the false self cannot bear, becomes a fascination that remains out of reach. It is grace that the desire to experience life-giving intimacy and to claim creativity remains. The fantasy that one can find such vitality by touching and fingering a phone, staring at a screen, or purchasing the next object is powerful.

Technology does bring pleasure by providing moments of ego orgasms—experiences of joy, of happiness, and of feeling real. These moments are first experienced with mother and later in play behavior, in friendships, and in going to the theater or a music concert.[86] It is the *fiero* gamers' experience when they escape the outer world or are immersed in a battle or a race or when they come through a challenge after solving a problem. Ego orgasm is the pursuit of happiness, a search that has changed as we live with technology. Often physical orgasm is a way to seek an ego orgasm, which reflects the popularity of online pornography and virtual infidelity. Technological Intelligence guides and protects the self in the virtual world, which is the new last frontier.

CONCLUSION

Human nature is almost all we have.
— D. W. Winnicott, *Human Nature*[1]

The lure of modern technology and being constantly connected to online and virtual worlds is memory and hope: technology mimics the holding environment established between infants and children and their mothers, fathers and primary caregivers; we hope for the reestablishment of a life-giving environment, reparation of wounds received, and a creative life. One remembers: being held in such a way that the self was recognized and basic needs were addressed; receiving experiences that transformed the self; discovering the Other and oneself anew as subjects; feeling comforted when what disappeared reappeared; receiving wounds and reparation never came; discovering and exploring new worlds; and being invited into playful potential spaces where one felt alive and real. Growing down as a person, all the way to embracing the dependency of death, as Winnicott writes, is inherently mimetic. Psychoanalytic thought, starting with Freud, has shown our tendency to imitate or repeat past events, especially trauma. One's behavior is repeating a previously forgotten experience rather than recognizing that the experience belongs to the past, as Freud writes.² Or one mimics desire and notices the other person is holding back and refusing to provide, which leads to violence.³ Discussion of a third kind of mimetic desire fills these pages. Deeper than the longing for another person who will provide or who can be scapegoated and killed is the desire for a holding environment that will recognize, comfort, and contain—a place where one can become. It is the loss of this environment, first experienced in infancy and childhood, that is consciously forgotten but psychodynamically remembered.

On Mimesis

Mimesis is "the nature that culture uses to create second nature, the faculty to copy, imitate, make models, explore difference, yield into and become Other."⁴ With its wide range of understandings, mimesis is foundational not only to human nature, but nature itself. The German philosopher Walter Benjamin wrote in 1933 that one of humanity's "highest faculties" is the ability to mimic, a dynamic he linked to nature and play: "Nature creates similarities. One need only to think of mimicry. The highest capacity for producing similarities, however, is man's."⁵ Through the visual trickery found in nature—the original mimetic act—species survive. In play, one person, often a child, mimics another or an adult. Adults extend this mimicry to art and politics. For Benjamin, "language may be seen as the highest level of mimetic behavior and the most complete archive of nonsensuous similarity."⁶ The spoken and written word took over the role ancients ascribed to shamanistic ritual and the compulsion to become and act like something or someone else. For Benjamin, one cannot avoid the primitive impulses shared with ancient cultures. Today, the eye, compulsive habit, and technology have surpassed language as the bearers and domains of mimetic desire. No longer are we dancing with the ancients, listening to the storyteller, or reading the books of authors; the eye—as "the organ of tactility"—now merges the object world and the visual copy, as Australian anthropologist Michael Tausig writes in *Mimesis and Alterity*.[7]

The mimetic act seeks completion—it has *telos*—that does not remember the original catalyst for the action. Marching toward its goal, mimesis is a powerful connecting agent, whether one is connected to repressed memories or tied to a scapegoat. Likewise, it connects one to a childhood that may have been good enough, but a life that has wounds and is in need of reparation and relationships. Mimesis is an attempt to control the original situation and all involved. When lived into, it has magical qualities. "The wonder of mimesis," Tausig writes, "lies in the copy drawing on the character and power of the original, to the point whereby the representation may even assume that character and power."[8] When we bring Taussig's argument to our relationships with technology, we have to admit that technology, in an uncanny way, is the creator of a holding environment few can escape. Technology invents "mimetically capacious [image-making] machines" that affect what is replicated in life and the holding environment while connecting a person to this special setting. Between copy and connection, the mimetic faculty thrives.

Technology mimicking the holding environment humans need confirms its intimate knowledge of human nature. Our communications technologies create spaces where expression of self and identity formation can occur, where deep connections can be made, where transitional imagination can infuse vitality, where the promise of reparation resides, where one can play and discover. With its mimetic power, technology brings a new holding environment into being, one where individual need is removed and then assimilated into a greater whole. Between imitation and control, the holding environment established by technology fails because it cannot replace the human face and the symbolism of love, relationship, and more. Technology, always at hand, can facilitate how one navigates life. That may be technology's biggest contribution. As the mimetic acts of shamans protected against angry spirit worlds, fingering and handling a phone protects against a breakdown of a holding environment experienced before. It protects against the confused, isolated, and often lonely self longing for relationship and vitality. The holding environment created by parents and caregivers through love and concern is thus challenged by the holding environment that technology creates through acquisition and imitation.

The mimetic act, Girard warns, "requires a certain degree of *misunderstanding*. The celebrants do not and must not comprehend the true role of sacrifice."⁹ Technology is attractive as we hope for the reestablishment of a life-giving environment, long for the reparation of wounds received, and seek a creative life. The multinational corporations behind the technologies and apps we use perpetuate the *misunderstanding* that technology is exclusively about progress and a requirement to be a successful self in a neoliberal market economy. They effectively promise that the latest upgrade to a phone, a wearable, game or app will transform oneself while remaining silent that holding environments are replaced. Grown-downs, however, know better: the experiences of similarity that technology's holding environments bring do not fool them. They guard friendships where mutuality, support, and sacrifice are found. As Twitter or Instagram turns friends into followers, our understanding of what it means to be a friend is challenged anew.

Mimesis, tied as it is to memory, discloses that when one does not remember anymore, one is most likely to reenact mimetically. Contemporary mimesis thus introduces a significant paradox: as one's physical memory of a life-giving holding environment is depleted because of an overreliance on technology, one's unconscious memory of what was lost increases! With schedules and reminders that alert, push notifications, searchable data, and apps that know one's location, technology reduces memory to searching online and transforms activity into reactivity. This kind of memory does not remove the unconscious remembering we always engage in.

French psychoanalyst Jacques Lacan discusses the importance of dreaming and having access to one's dreams, both personally and in conversation with an analyst or counselor: "One does not get better because one remembers. One remembers because one gets better."[10] It is common for someone starting a counseling journey rarely to remember dreams or core childhood experiences. The person, after all, is there to address a concern in the here and now. In therapy, dreams, relationships, and experiences are not only remembered, they have meaning to be discerned. Grown-downs remember their lives, especially their childhoods, and resist fleeing to a future filled with promises but possibly wrapped in uncertainty, anxiety, or fear. To be curious about one's personal history is a strength. *Growing Down* extends an invitation to remember the formative relationships and moments of childhood, as they remain foundational to being a person, regardless of one's age. It seeks to awaken memory of the first holding environment and empowers mindfulness in how one shapes one's current environment. As such, *Growing Down* is the invitation to be a storyteller, to tell about one's life, but also to be curious and interested in the stories others bring. Many, we are reminded, never receive the chance to tell their stories.[11]

On Hope

One's longing for a holding environment speaks not only of mimesis and memory, but also of hope. Hope is waiting for a benign future that is not yet present to unfold. As such, it informs the present and is not focused on the future. Specifically, we hope for a restored holding environment, one that is good enough, one where past experiences that could not be integrated into the self can be remembered. In the essay "Fear of Breakdown," Winnicott asks, "Why does a [person] go on being worried by [what] belongs to the past? The answer must be that the original experience of primitive agony cannot get into the past tense unless the ego can first gather it into its own present time experience and into omnipotent control now. . . . In other words, the [person] must go on looking for the past details which is not yet experienced."[12] Winnicott identifies two failures: the failure of the past and current holding environment to keep impingements at bay and the failure of any defense mechanisms called upon to protect the self. Defenses failed because the infant and childhood selves were not developed enough when the failure of the holding environment occurred. The wounded self of childhood becomes the foundation upon which one's adulthood is built.

Persons who know the fear of breakdown compulsively look into the future as they continue to long to be an integrated self living a creative life. Restoration lies in remembering one's past while living into the present.[13] The trust and safety in a counseling relationship, between a parent and a child, or in an intimate relationship make this kind of remembering possible. So too can engaging in acts of creativity bring closure. "Through artistic expression one can hope to keep in touch with primitive selves whence the most intense feelings and even fearfully acute sensations derive, and we are poor indeed if we are only sane."[14] The primitive self is not to be understood in evolutionary or sociological terms, but in psychodynamic terms, where it refers to the experiences and travails of infancy and childhood. Chasing the grown-up life, perceived as independence, wealth, power, and prestige as W. E. B. Du Bois warned, and living a reactive and compliant life are some of the defenses used against returning to the place of breakdown. The holding environment established by technology provides effective ways to ward off the disillusionment of a holding environment and an outer world that failed or continues to fail. Such a defensive approach to life, however, affirms and strengthens the false self, the caretaker self, that is ever compliant to outside demands but also keeps the spontaneity of the true self at bay. The mimetic replication of our childhood holding environments is bound to fail, as we have experienced before. Seeing oneself as a unique person with vitality, as one relates to persons and things, is central to being able to say, "I am here, I exist here and now, and on this basis I can enter the lives of others, and without a sense of threat to my own basis for being myself."[15] Being open to life—being real—is central to Winnicott's psychodynamic theory. He envisions persons who have affection for others, who have an exuberance about life, and who can experience serenity. Grown-downs can stick with things, are compassionate, and are convinced that persons and things are sacred. They find themselves involved in loyal commitments with no need to force their way in life. Grown-downs can marshal and direct their energies wisely and know that a rigid or a reactive life rarely promotes creative living.[16] Becoming a grown-down takes intentionality and grace.

Evolutionary psychologists and neuroscientists remind us that human *nature* is rather stagnant.[17] To argue that human nature has changed through our engagement with technology, however, would mean that the psychodynamic theory of the past 120 years will have to be rewritten.[18] Even if it is likely that the human brain will mature in less than twenty-five years in a few hundred years or that the need for a holding environment that welcomes newborns into life will diminish, human *behavior* does change. We no longer sacrifice persons on hilltops or attack bordering villages to widen the gene pool. Technology's rapid progress with the new behaviors it brings creates the dangerous illusion that human nature is changing at the same pace. The questions about how humans should engage technology will certainly multiply in the face of technological advances. The foundational question, however, is not one about technology or even of theology, but one that invites the exploration of human nature.

Toward a . . .

The "Toward a . . ." subtitle of each chapter argues that just as there are many anthropologies describing human nature, so too one finds many theologies of technology. *Growing Down* offers insights into human nature that can inform the study of humans and the tools we use and rely on. This study is important because human nature, with its tendency to change little over time, needs to reckon with human behaviors and societal trends, which do change often. When our behaviors contradict the needs our human nature portrays, selves languish, relationships fail, psyches rebel, and our bodies become shelters to the anxiety experienced. *Growing Down,* in exploring elements of human nature, seeks to inform ethical or moral frameworks guiding our interactions with technology. It also seeks to conduct a critical analysis of *La Technique,* which is how philosopher and theologian Jacques Ellul describes technology's power to force humans to adapt to technology's efficiency, rationality, automatism, and universality and to accept total change.[19] "[W]hat is at issue here is evaluating the danger of what might happen to our humanity in the present half-century, and distinguishing between what we want to keep and what we are ready to lose, between what we can welcome as legitimate human development and what we should reject with our last ounce of strength as dehumanization. I cannot think that choices of this kind are unimportant," Ellul warns.[20] The task to reflect on human nature and to draft new anthropologies and theologies of technology remains.

Home Is Where It Starts From[21]

Technology is not the first force challenging human nature. Political theorist Hannah Arendt reflects on the impact the birth of the city had on the self. She identifies humans as "social animals" and writes, "No human life, not even the life of the hermit in nature's wilderness, is possible without a world which directly or indirectly testifies to the presence of other human beings."[22] The Latin word *societas*, she writes, originally indicated an alliance between people for a specific purpose. The ancient Greeks, frowning on the social nature of humanity, argued for the political nature of humanity. The *polis* (city) with its freedoms replaced the *oikos* (home), for the two were never equal. The political was the first second life humans lived. In three thousand years the *polis* could not eradicate the importance of the *oikos* or the social nature of humans. Rather, the social became more important because the city's health depends on what happens at home. Digital and virtual spaces are replacing the city as a third era of human history. We moved from home to city and are moving to the virtual. Just as the *polis* could not eradicate the *oikos*, so too the virtual will not be able to eradicate human nature, even if artificial intelligence might develop in threatening ways.

The importance of selves born into homes and relationships will remain, even if one's future may be virtual. The rise of technology has not diminished the need for personal and societal holding environments. Rather, technology reiterates the importance of being human. "Wanting to be understood, as adults, can be, among many other things, our most violent form of nostalgia."[23] As we live *with* our communications technologies and handle our phones, we know that "human nature is *almost* all we have."[24]

NOTES

Introduction

1 D. W. Winnicott, *Deprivation and Delinquency*, ed. Clare Winnicott, Ray Shepard, and Madeleine Davis (London: Tavistock Publications, 1997), 220.

2 In Lesley Caldwell, ed., *Sex and Sexuality: Winnicottian Perspectives*, Winnicott Studies Monograph Series (London: Karnac Books, 2005), 12.

3 Jean Laplanche and J. B. Pontalis, *The Language of Psycho-Analysis* (New York: Norton, 1974), 277.

4 Jay R. Greenberg and Stephen A. Mitchell, *Object Relations in Psychoanalytic Theory* (Cambridge, Mass.: Harvard University Press, 1983), 3.

5 In Gerard Fromm and Bruce L. Smith, *The Facilitating Environment: Clinical Applications of Winnicott's Theory* (Madison, Conn.: International Universities Press, 1989), 130.

6 See Annette Kuhn, *Little Madnesses: Winnicott, Transitional Phenomena and Cultural Experience* (London: I. B. Tauris, 2013).

7 See Jessica Benjamin, "Recognition and Destruction: An Outline of Intersubjectivity," in *Relational Perspectives in Psychoanalysis*, ed. Neil J. Skolnick and Susan C. Warshaw (Hillsdale, N.J.: Analytic Press, 1992), 46.

8 Janice L. Doane and Devon L. Hodges, *From Klein to Kristeva: Psychoanalytic Feminism and the Search for the "Good Enough" Mother*, Critical Perspectives on Women and Gender (Ann Arbor: University of Michigan Press, 1992), 1.

9 See Diane Jonte-Pace, "Object Relations Theory, Mothering, and Religion: Toward a Feminist Psychology of Religion," *Horizons* 14, no. 2 (1987): 311. Jonte-Pace identifies three themes object relations theory and feminism share: "First, its theory of human motivation relies upon interpersonal relatedness rather than drives; second, its normative vision of human nature acknowledges and values dependence as well as autonomy; and third, in bringing attention to the earliest human relationships, it makes the pre-oedipal, maternal-infant relationship foundational to its understanding of personality." Each wave of feminism engaged Winnicott differently. Quoting Juliet Mitchell, Jonte-Pace identifies first-wave feminism as aiming to "put right the wrongs of women." The second wave of feminism revalued motherhood and domesticity—peace, caring, nurturance—but had its opponents, such as first-wave feminist Simone de Beauvoir, who saw motherhood as a patriarchal institution. The third wave of feminism questions cultural norms of gender and sexuality, affirming intersectionality and the empowerment of women. This wave remains critical of Winnicott.

10 Nancy Chodorow, *The Reproduction of Mothering: Psychoanalysis and the Sociology of Gender* (Berkeley: University of California Press, 1978), 39. For feminist critiques of Winnicott, see Rozsika Parker, *Mother Love/Mother Hate: The Power of Maternal Ambivalence* (New York: Basic Books, 1995); Nancy Chodorow, *Feminism and Psychoanalytic Theory* (New Haven: Yale University Press, 1989); Wendy Hollway, *The Capacity to Care: Gender and Ethical Subjectivity*, Women and Psychology (New York: Routledge, 2006); Jessica Benjamin, *The Bonds of Love: Psychoanalysis, Feminism, and the Problem of Domination* (New York: Pantheon Books, 1988); Joyce Anne Slochower, *Holding and Psychoanalysis: A Relational Perspective* (Hillsdale, N.J.: Analytic Press, 1996); Carol Gilligan, *In a Different Voice: Psychological Theory and Women's Development* (Cambridge, Mass.: Harvard University Press, 1993).

11 For Winnicott and religion, see Stephen E. Parker, *Winnicott and Religion* (Lanham, Md.: Jason Aronson, 2011).

12 Dittes writes about ministry: "I think of ministry as the art of making space for others to grow." Dittes' view of ministry informs this author's view of being a pastoral theologian. See James E. Dittes, *Re-Calling Ministry*, ed. Donald Capps (St. Louis: Chalice Press, 1999), 9.

13 For a practical theological reflection on technology, see Elaine Graham, "Being, Making and Imagining: Toward a Practical Theology of Technology," *Culture and Religion* 10, no. 2 (2009): 221–36. As the title suggests, Graham sees the tasks of "being, making and imagining" as fundamental to humanity 'knowing our place' in the world" (235).

14 For an explicit Christian evaluation of our relationship with technology, see Derek C. Schuurman, *Shaping a Digital World: Faith, Culture and Computer Technology* (Downers Grove, Ill.: InterVarsity, 2013). For theological anthropologies built on the contribution of Winnicott and object relations theory, see Ann Belford Ulanov, *Finding Space: Winnicott, God, and Psychic Reality* (Louisville, Ky.: Westminster John Knox, 2001); David Ford, *Self and Salvation: Being Transformed*, Cambridge Studies in Christian Doctrine (Cambridge: Cambridge University Press, 1999); Parker, *Winnicott and Religion*.

15 D. W. Winnicott, "String: A Technique in Communication," in Winnicott, *The Maturational Processes and the Facilitating Environment: Studies in the Theory of Emotional Development* (Madison, Conn.: International Universities Press, 1994), 155. In adolescence, the boy became addicted to drugs as he again tied himself to something.

16 Winnicott, *Deprivation and Delinquency*, 220.

17 W. E. B. Du Bois, "The Field and Function of the Negro College," in *The Education of Black People: Ten Critiques 1906–1960*, ed. Herbert Aptheker (Amherst: University of Massachusetts Press, 1973), 114. For a similar argument to Du Bois', see Archie Smith, *The Relational Self: Ethics & Therapy from a Black Church Perspective* (Nashville: Abingdon, 1982), 18: "Many black Americans who have recently become middle class and upper income earners appear to have lost touch with [the] historical mission of liberating the oppressed." Smith calls for "anamnestic solidarity," anamnesis being the opposite of amnesia, the forgetting of the past.

18 Du Bois, "The Field and Function of the Negro College," in Aptheker, *The Education of Black People*, 127–28.

19 For the packaged self, see Howard Gardner and Katie Davis, *The App Generation: How Today's Youth Navigate Identity, Intimacy, and Imagination in a Digital World* (New Haven: Yale University Press, 2013).

20 James Hillman, *The Soul's Code: In Search of Character and Calling* (New York: Random House, 1996), 42.

21 Hillman, *Soul's Code*, 43.

22 C. G. Jung, *The Collected Works of C. G. Jung*, Bollingen Series (New York: Pantheon Books, 1954), 17:169–70.

23 Melvin Kranzberg, "Technology and History: 'Kranzberg's Laws,'" *Technology and Culture* 27, no. 3 (1986): 544. For a discussion of Kranzberg's aphorism, see chapter 6.

Chapter 1

1 Gil Bailie, *Violence Unveiled: Humanity at the Crossroads* (New York: Crossroad, 1995), xv.

2 Michael Willett Newheart, *Word and Soul: A Psychological, Literary, and Cultural Reading of the Fourth Gospel* (Collegeville, Minn.: Liturgical Press, 2001), 63.

3 Howard Gardner, *Frames of Mind: The Theory of Multiple Intelligences* (New York: Basic Books, 1983), 295. Gardner refers to "intrapersonal intelligence" as being self-smart.

4 Daniel Goleman, *Emotional Intelligence* (New York: Bantam Books, 1995), 42–43. Drawing on the works of Peter Salovey and John Mayer, Goleman defines emotional intelligence as knowing about emotions, managing emotions, motivating oneself, recognizing emotions in others, and handling relationships.

5 William James, *The Principles of Psychology*, vol. 1, *The Works of William James*, ed. Frederick Burkhardt and Fredson Bowers (Cambridge, Mass.: Harvard University Press, 1981), 279–80 (emphasis added to first quotation). James identifies the material self, the social self, the spiritual self, and the pure ego as components of "the empirical self."

6 C. G. Jung, *Memories, Dreams, Reflections* (New York: Pantheon Books, 1963), 158–59.

7 D. W. Winnicott et al., *Babies and Their Mothers* (Reading, Mass.: Addison-Wesley, 1987), 96–97.

8 D. W. Winnicott, *Through Paediatrics to Psycho-Analysis: Collected Papers* (New York: Brunner/Mazel, 1992), 201. Mothers hating their infants reflects the nature of mutuality between a mother or parent and an infant. Reasons mothers hate their babies include the following: the baby is not the mother's mental conception; the baby is a danger to the mother's body in pregnancy and at birth; the baby interferes and disrupts the mother's private life; the baby is ruthless, always demanding and treating mother like an unpaid servant; the baby is suspicious of mother, refuses her good food, and makes her doubt herself; and the baby excites and frustrates mother, also sexually.

9 Slochower, *Holding and Psychoanalysis*, 4–5.

10 D. W. Winnicott, "Birth Memories, Birth Trauma, and Anxiety," in Winnicott, *Through Paediatrics to Psycho-Analysis*, 183.

11 D. W. Winnicott, "Mind in Relation to Psyche-Soma," in Winnicott, *Through Paediatrics to Psycho-Analysis*, 244.

12 D. W. Winnicott, "Psycho-Somatic Illness in Its Positive and Negative Aspects," in C. Winnicott, Shepherd, and Davis, *Psycho-Analytic Explorations*, 106.

13 D. W. Winnicott, "Appetite and Emotional Disorder (1936)," in Winnicott, *Through Paediatrics to Psycho-Analysis*, 36.

14 Nitza Yarom, *Psychic Threats and Somatic Shelters: Attuning to the Body in Contemporary Psychoanalytic Dialogue* (New York: Routledge, 2015), viii.

15 Yarom, *Psychic Threats and Somatic Shelters*, 65.

16 Yarom, *Psychic Threats and Somatic Shelters*, 25.

17 Yarom, *Psychic Threats and Somatic Shelters*, 23.

18 Yarom, *Psychic Threats and Somatic Shelters*, 41–42.

19 C. G. Jung, *The Archetypes and the Collective Unconscious*, Bollingen Series (New York: Pantheon Books, 1959), 28.

20 D. W. Winnicott, "Creativity and Its Origins," in Winnicott, *Playing and Reality* (London: Tavistock, 1993), 77.

21 See the chapter "Male and Female," in Ulanov, *Finding Space*, 68.

22 "Male and Female," in Ulanov, *Finding Space*, 70.

23 See D. W. Winnicott, "The Concept of False Self," in D. W. Winnicott, *Home Is Where We Start From: Essays by a Psychoanalyst*, ed. Clare Winnicott, Ray Shepherd, and Madeleine Davis (New York: Norton, 1986), 65, 66.

24 D. W. Winnicott, "Ego Distortion in Terms of True Self and False Self," in Winnicott, *Maturational Processes and the Facilitating Environment*, 142–43.

25 Winnicott and the British School of Object Relations, possibly due to their Victorian morality, engaged with sexuality as "both there and not there, assumed and demonstrated, displaced and concealed." Winnicott rarely analyzed sexual content with his patients, especially in the transference relationship. See Caldwell, *Sex and Sexuality*, 4.

26 Helen Taylor Robinson, "Adult Eros in D.W. Winnicott," in Caldwell, *Sex and Sexuality*, 84.

27 D. W. Winnicott, *Human Nature* (New York: Schocken Books, 1988), 59.

28 Robinson, "Adult Eros in D.W. Winnicott," in Caldwell, *Sex and Sexuality*, 95.

29 Winnicott, *Playing and Reality*, 26. It is no coincidence that pornography often focuses on oral and anal sex and external, visual orgasms.

30 Mario Bertolini and Francesca Neri, "Sex as a Defence against Sexuality," in Caldwell, *Sex and Sexuality*, 114.

31 Bertolini and Neri, "Sex as a Defence against Sexuality," in Caldwell, *Sex and Sexuality*, 110–11.

32 Bertolini and Neri, "Sex as a Defence against Sexuality," in Caldwell, *Sex and Sexuality*, 111.

33 Winnicott, *Home Is Where We Start From*, 149.

34 Christopher Bollas, *The Shadow of the Object: Psychoanalysis of the Unthought Known* (London: Free Association Books, 1987), 14.

35 Bollas' psychoanalytic foundations place primacy on the unconscious seeking ways to actualize inner tensions stemming from early trauma. Therapeutic work and mindfulness can minimize and even break the power the unconscious has over our actions.

36 Newheart, *Word and Soul*, 63–64.

37 Winnicott, *Human Nature*, 12.

38 Winnicott, *Maturational Processes and the Facilitating Environment*, 158.

Chapter 2

1 Seyla Benhabib, *Situating the Self: Gender, Community, and Postmodernism in Contemporary Ethics* (New York: Routledge, 1992), 52.

2 Desmond Tutu, *No Future without Forgiveness* (New York: Doubleday, 1999), 34–35.

3 Sherry Turkle, *Alone Together: Why We Expect More from Technology and Less from Each Other* (New York: Basic Books, 2011), 157.

4 See Numbers 6:24-26: "The Lord bless you and keep you; the Lord make his face shine on you and be gracious to you; the Lord turn his face toward you and give you peace." See also 2 Corinthians 4:6: "For God, who said, 'Let light shine out of darkness,' made his light shine in our hearts to give us the light of the knowledge of God's glory displayed in the face of Christ."

5 Ford, *Self and Salvation*, 24–25.

6 Benjamin, *Bonds of Love*, 13. In writing on the importance of mirroring in relationships, Benjamin builds her theory on Winnicott, who in turn relied on French psychoanalyst Jacques Lacan, each theorist spanning a gap of about twenty years.

7 Benjamin, *Bonds of Love*, 15–16.

8 Benjamin, *Bonds of Love*, 21.

9 D. W. Winnicott, "Mirror-role of Other and Family in Child Development," in Winnicott, *Playing and Reality*, 112.

10 Winnicott, "Mirror-role of Other and Family in Child Development," in Winnicott, *Playing and Reality*, 114.

11 Clive Thompson, *Smarter Than You Think: How Technology Is Changing Our Minds for the Better* (New York: Penguin, 2013), 221.

12 Ionela-Maria Răcătău, "Adolescents and Identity Formation in a Risky Online Environment: The Role of Negative User-Generated and Xenophobic Websites," *Journal of Media Research* 3, no. 17 (2013): 16. For a similar study, see Chorng-Shyong Ong, Shu-Chen Chang, and Chih-Chien Wang, "Comparative Loneliness of Users Versus Nonusers of Online Chatting," *Cyberpsychology, Behavior, and Social Networking* 14, nos. 1–2 (2011): 35. Also Joshua Lewandowski et al., "The Effect of Informal Social Support: Face-to-Face Versus Computer-Mediated Communication," *Computers in Human Behavior* 27 (2011): 1806–14; Valerie Priscilla Goby, "Psychological Underpinnings of Intrafamilial Computer-Mediated Communication: A Preliminary Exploration of CMC Uptake with Parents and Siblings," *Cyberpsychology, Behavior, and Social Networking* 14, no. 6 (2011): 368.

13 Levinas and Winnicott both ask: "How can one relate without imposing on the other?" They both find an infinite distance between the self and a self that stays incommunicative (Winnicott) or an other that remains

a stranger (Levinas). Both also see violence as imposing on others, and there is little distinction between the contradictions of Levinas and the paradoxes of Winnicott.

14 Emmanuel Levinas, *Totality and Infinity: An Essay on Exteriority*, trans. Alphonso Lingis, Duquesne Studies Philosophical Series (Pittsburgh: Duquesne University Press, 1969), 183.

15 Levinas, *Totality and Infinity*, 188.

16 Pauline Hope Cheong and Kishonna Gray, "Mediated Intercultural Dialectics: Identity Perceptions and Performances in Virtual Worlds," *Journal of International and Intercultural Communication* 4, no. 4 (2011): 268.

17 Martin Buber and Walter A. Kaufmann, *I and Thou* (New York: Scribner's, 1970).

18 Martin Buber, *Tales of the Hasidim*, 2 vols. (New York: Schocken Books, 1991), 2: 283.

19 D. W. Winnicott, "The Use of an Object and Relating through Identifications," in C. Winnicott, Shepherd, and Davis, *Psycho-Analytic Explorations*, 219.

20 Barbara Johnson, *Persons and Things* (Cambridge, Mass.: Harvard University Press, 2008), 6. Johnson states our use of the *apostrophe* (addressing a dead entity as if alive), *prosopopeia* (the voice that speaks from the grave, the epitaph), *anthropomorphism* (assigning human-like characteristics to objects), and *personification* or *prosopopeia* (seeing an abstract idea as a person or object) enlivens objects.

21 D. W. Winnicott et al., "Communication between Infant and Mother, Mother and Infant, Compared and Contrasted," in Winnicott et al., *Babies and Their Mothers*, 103. "Use" here carries connotations of being discovered.

22 Johnson, *Persons and Things*, 105.

23 Paul Ekman and Richard J. Davidson, *The Nature of Emotion: Fundamental Questions* (New York: Oxford University Press, 1994), 32–33.

24 Katrin Döveling, Christian von Scheve, and Elly Konijn, *The Routledge Handbook of Emotions and Mass Media*, Routledge International Handbooks (New York: Routledge, 2011), 16, 60, 75 (emphasis added).

25 D. W. Winnicott, "The Capacity to Be Alone," in Winnicott, *Maturational Processes and the Facilitating Environment*, 29.

26 Winnicott, "The Capacity to Be Alone," in Winnicott, *Maturational Processes and the Facilitating Environment*, 34.

27 Michael Eigen, *Feeling Matters: From the Yosemite God to the Annihilated Self* (London: Karnac Books, 2007), v.

28 Eigen, *Feelings Matter*, 141–42. Eigen uses "destruction" differently from the destruction Winnicott uses in the context of fantasies.

29 Eigen, *Feelings Matter*, 2.

30 Harry Guntrip, *Mental Pain and the Cure of Souls* (London: Independent Press, 1956), 49.

31 Guntrip, *Mental Pain and the Cure of Souls*, 43.

32 Guntrip's threefold understanding of internalized relationships is based on the work of Fairbairn. See W. Ronald D. Fairbairn, "Endopsychic Structure Considered in Terms of Object-Relationships," in W. Ronald D. Fairbairn, *Psychoanalytic Studies of the Personality* (New York: Routledge, 1996), 82ff.

33 Adam Phillips, *On Flirtation* (Cambridge, Mass.: Harvard University Press, 1994), xxiii. Phillips draws on Freudian thought and object relations theory, but his expansive mind also takes him to literature, history, and culture.

34 Phillips, *On Flirtation*, 19.

35 David Harris Smith and Deborah Fels, "The Disintegrated Erotics of Second Life," *The International Journal of the Image* 2, no. 3 (2012): 129.

36 Benhabib, *Situating the Self*, 162. Benhabib identifies "stronger" and "weaker" postmodern theories. With stronger theories, the self is completely socially constructed "all the way down," a view held by Judith Butler. Benhabib, holding a "weaker" position, states the self is only partially constructed by society and is not a mere product of an ideology or ideologies. Her self is thus situated and able to author personal narratives, whereas Butler's self is displaced. For Butler, see Judith Butler, *Bodies That Matter: On the Discursive Limits of "Sex"* (New York: Routledge, 1993); idem, *The Psychic Life of Power: Theories in Subjection* (Stanford, Calif.: Stanford University Press, 1997).

37 Benhabib, *Situating the Self*, 159.

38 Benhabib, *Situating the Self*, 52.

39 Sherry Turkle, *Reclaiming Conversation: The Power of Talk in a Digital Age* (London: Penguin, 2015), 16–17 (emphasis in original).

Chapter 3

1 D. W. Winnicott, "Transitional Objects and Transitional Phenomena," in Winnicott, *Playing and Reality*, 2 (emphasis in original).

2 I discuss this narrative, found in 2 Kings 6, in Jaco J. Hamman, *A Play-Full Life: Slowing Down and Seeking Peace* (Cleveland: Pilgrim Press, 2011), 48. Old Testament scholar Walter Brueggemann, using a Winnicottian lens, discusses the narrative in *Interpretation and Obedience: From Faithful Reading to Faithful Living* (Minneapolis: Fortress, 1991), 31–35.

3 Winnicott, "Transitional Objects and Transitional Phenomena," in Winnicott, *Playing and Reality*, 2. Transitional objects in Winnicott's theory corresponds with *object a* in Lacan. For Lacan, *object a* is the object that brings satisfaction, that causes desire.

4 The transitional object can develop into a fetish object that may persist as a characteristic of an adult's sexual life. In such a situation, control over the object is never surrendered.

5 Paul W. Pruyser, *The Play of the Imagination: Towards a Psychoanalysis of Culture* (New York: International Universities Press, 1983), 166.

6 Quoted in Pruyser, *Play of the Imagination*, 152.

7 Reworked diagram first described by Pruyser. See Pruyser, *Play of the Imagination*, 65.

8 Thomas Ogden, quoted in Kuhn, *Little Madnesses*, 4.

9 Ana-Maria Rizzuto, *The Birth of the Living God: A Psychoanalytic Study* (Chicago: University of Chicago Press, 1979), 177–78.

10 Rizzuto, *Birth of the Living God*, 176.

11 Rizzuto, *Birth of the Living God*, 179.

12 Rizzuto, *Birth of the Living God*, 90.

13 Rizzuto, *Birth of the Living God*, 149ff.

14 Rizzuto, *Birth of the Living God*, 171.

15 D. W. Winnicott, *Winnicott on the Child* (Cambridge, Mass.: Perseus, 2002), 78.

16 D. W. Winnicott, "The Concept of a Healthy Individual," in Winnicott, *Home Is Where We Start From*, 36. Analyst Michael Eigen describes the place where God and Spirit resides, the intermediate area of experiencing in culture, as an "area of faith." See Eigen, "The Area of Faith in Winnicott, Lacan and Bion," *International Journal of Psycho-Analysis* 62 (1981): 413–33.

17 Elizabeth Presa, "Ways of Being: Transitional Objects and the Work of Art," in *The Winnicott Tradition: Lines of Development (Evolution of Theory and Practice over the Decades)*, ed. Margaret Boyle Spelman and Frances Thomson-Salo (London: Karnac Books, 2015), 322.

18 Eric Schmidt and Jared Cohen, *The New Digital Age: Reshaping the Future of People, Nations and Business* (London: Hodder & Stoughton, 2014), 253.

19 Cédric Courtois, Peter Mechant, and Lieven De Marez, "Communicating Creativity on Youtube: What and for Whom?" *CyberPsychology, Behavior & Social Networking* 15, no. 2 (2012): 129.

20 Adam Phillips, *On Kissing, Tickling, and Being Bored: Psychoanalytic Essays on the Unexamined Life* (Cambridge, Mass.: Harvard University Press, 1993), 68.

21 Martin Heidegger, *The Fundamental Concepts of Metaphysics: World, Finitude, Solitude*, Studies in Continental Thought (Bloomington: Indiana University Press, 1995), 74ff. Heidegger's 1929–1930 lectures address boredom as a primary subject in more than one hundred pages of discussion. In Heidegger's essay "The Question Regarding Technology," he describes technology as a way of thinking, a way of being in and a means to disclose the world. Heidegger calls this way of being "enframing." Enframing keeps us in the realm of technology, which keeps us from evaluating

technology with clarity. Heidegger saw reflecting on art as a way to criticize technology. See idem, *The Question Concerning Technology and Other
Essays* (New York: Harper & Row, 1977), 4.

22 Heidegger, *Fundamental Concepts of Metaphysics*, 80, 90, 140.

23 Stephen J. Vodanovich et al., "Culture and Gender Differences in Boredom Proneness," *North American Journal of Psychology* 13, no. 2 (2011): 221.
Some studies suggest the gender gap on boredom is closing.

24 Phillips, *On Kissing, Tickling, and Being Bored*, 69.

25 Phillips, *On Kissing, Tickling, and Being Bored*, 70, 71.

26 Gray Graffam, "Avatar: A Posthuman Perspective on Virtual Worlds," in
*Human No More: Digital Subjectivities, Unhuman Subjects, and the End of Anthro-
pology*, ed. Neil L. Whitehead and Michael Wesch (Boulder: University
Press of Colorado, 2012), 139.

27 Phillips, *On Kissing, Tickling, and Being Bored*, 78.

28 Søren Kierkegaard et al., *The Essential Kierkegaard* (Princeton, N.J.: Princeton University Press, 2000), 51.

29 Dietrich Bonhoeffer, *Letters and Papers from Prison* (New York: Macmillan,
1972), 303.

30 Kenneth Earl Morris, *Bonhoeffer's Ethic of Discipleship: A Study in Social Psy-
chology, Political Thought, and Religion* (University Park: Pennsylvania State
University Press, 1986), 65. For Bonhoeffer on polyphony, see also Ford,
Self and Salvation, 254–57.

31 Bonhoeffer, *Letters and Papers from Prison*, 305.

32 D. W. Winnicott, *The Family and Individual Development* (London: Tavistock
Publications, 1995), 61.

Chapter 4

1 Turkle, *Reclaiming Conversation*, 33.

2 Sara H. Konrath, Edward H. O'Brien, and Courtney Hsing, "Changes
in Dispositional Empathy in American College Students over Time: A
Meta-Analysis," *Personality and Social Psychology Review* 15, no. 2 (2011): 182.

3 Konrath, O'Brien, and Hsing, "Changes in Dispositional Empathy," 189.

4 Hollway, *Capacity to Care*, 3.

5 Hollway, *Capacity to Care*, 42.

6 Alice Miller, *The Drama of the Gifted Child: The Search for the True Self* (New
York: Basic Books, 1997), 1.

7 Miller, *Drama of the Gifted Child*, 9.

8 Miller, *Drama of the Gifted Child*, 2; emphasis added.

9 See 2 Corinthians 1:3b-4; Joel 2:25.

10 Donald Kalsched, *Trauma and the Soul: A Psycho-Spiritual Approach to Human
Development and Its Interruption* (New York: Routledge, 2013), 13.

11 Joseph Michael Reagle, *Reading the Comments: Likers, Haters, and Manipulators at the Bottom of the Web* (Cambridge, Mass.: MIT Press, 2015), 180.

12 Ian D. Suttie, *The Origins of Love and Hate* (London: Free Association Books, 1988), 211. Winnicott did not give credit to Suttie, but Suttie wrote on infant development from the "self" to the "not-self" and portrays "gratuitous, spontaneous" "tiny acts" twenty years prior to Winnicott's writing about the "Me" and the "Not-me" and "spontaneous gestures." By placing loving and hating together, Suttie is also the master of paradox and ambivalence (see Suttie, *Origins of Love and Hate*, 59).

13 Suttie, *Origins of Love and Hate*, 23.

14 Suttie, *Origins of Love and Hate*, 14, 19. "Germ plasma" is Suttie's early way to refer to neuroscience and evolutionary psychology.

15 Suttie, *Origins of Love and Hate*, 19.

16 Rebecca M. Chory and Alan K. Goodboy, "Is Basic Personality Related to Violent and Non-Violent Video Game Play and Preferences?" *Cyberpsychology, Behavior, and Social Networking* 14, no. 4 (2011): 191.

17 For a discussion of this case, see Allison Cerra and Christina James, *Identity Shift: Where Identity Meets Technology in the Networked-Community Age* (Indianapolis: John Wiley & Sons, 2012), 96.

18 Suttie, *Origins of Love and Hate*, 60. See also pages 50–51 on hate as a "*reflex response* like fear, which (theoretically) need never have been evoked at all as it is contingent upon environmental stimuli" (emphasis in original).

19 Winnicott, *Maturational Processes and the Facilitating Environment*, 73.

20 Psychoanalyst Melanie Klein, a pivotal figure who bridged Freudian psychoanalysis and object relations theory, described concern in terms of "the depressive position." Depression here refers to the sense of guilt that sets in when an infant recognizes that she has hurt her caregiver. Winnicott moved away from Klein's term, as the sense of guilt is normal and healthy rather than pathological. See Melanie Klein, *Love, Guilt, and Reparation, and Other Works, 1921–1945*, The Writings of Melanie Klein (New York: Free Press, 1984).

21 Reagle, *Reading the Comments*, 180.

22 Turkle, *Alone Together*, 234–35.

23 Hollway, *Capacity to Care*, 43.

24 D. W. Winnicott, "The Development of the Capacity for Concern," in Winnicott, *Maturational Processes and the Facilitating Environment*, 75–76.

25 Winnicott, "The Development of the Capacity for Concern," in Winnicott, *Maturational Processes and the Facilitating Environment*, 73.

26 Guntrip, *Mental Pain and the Cure of Souls*, 135.

27 D. W. Winnicott, "Metapsychological and Clinical Aspects of Regression within the Psycho-Analytical Set-Up," in Winnicott, *Through Paediatrics to Psycho-Analysis*, 281.

28 Winnicott, "Metapsychological and Clinical Aspects of Regression," in Winnicott, *Through Paediatrics to Psycho-Analysis*, 284.

29 Miller, *Drama of the Gifted Child*, 49.

30 Miller, *Drama of the Gifted Child*, 50.

31 Miller compares Johanna's story with Ann, a woman with a similar history but whose frozen moments never thawed. Feeling abandoned by others, she chased relationships that never gave her the love and reparation she longed for. In despair, she committed suicide.

32 Kalsched, *Trauma and the Soul*, 24. Kalsched's project draws primarily on Jung, but also Winnicott, Fairbairn, Kohut, and other object relations and self psychology theorists.

33 Kalsched, *Trauma and the Soul*, 11.

34 Kalsched also draws on Jungian depth psychology.

35 Kalsched, *Trauma and the Soul*, 9.

36 Kalsched, *Trauma and the Soul*, 31.

37 Kalsched, *Trauma and the Soul*, 33.

38 Kalsched, *Trauma and the Soul*, 58.

39 Turkle, *Reclaiming Conversation*, 33.

40 D. W. Winnicott, "Reparation in Respect of Mother's Organized Defence against Depression," in Winnicott, *Through Paediatrics to Psycho-Analysis*, 91. On guilt and reparation, Winnicott drew extensively on the work of Melanie Klein. See Klein, *Love, Guilt, and Reparation*.

41 See Jaco J. Hamman, "Revisiting Forgiveness as a Pastoral-Theological Problem," *Pastoral Psychology* 61, no. 4 (2012): 435–50.

42 C. Fred Alford, *Trauma and Forgiveness: Consequences and Communities* (Cambridge: Cambridge University Press, 2013), 83.

43 Alford, *Trauma and Forgiveness*, 134.

44 Alford, *Trauma and Forgiveness*, 135 (emphasis in original).

45 Jacques Derrida, *The Work of Mourning*, ed. Pascale-Anne Brault and Michael Naas, trans. Pascale-Anne Brault (Chicago: University of Chicago Press, 2001), 2.

46 Alford, *Trauma and Forgiveness*, 86.

47 Alford, *Trauma and Forgiveness*, 91.

48 Alford, *Trauma and Forgiveness*, 97. Here Alford draws on an essay by Robert C. Roberts entitled "Forgivingness." See Robert C. Roberts, "Forgivingness," *American Philosophical Quarterly* 32, no. 4 (1995): 289–306. Forgiveness, of course, is not the only path to reparation. There is clemency ("the moderation or suspension of punishment without forgiveness"), mercy ("suspension of punishment due to feelings of pity and common humanity"), reconciliation (continuing in relationship without forgiveness present), pardon (tolerance and a release from punishment) and "just accepting what happened" (Alford, *Trauma and Forgiveness*, 105).

49 Quoted in Alford, *Trauma and Forgiveness*, 109.

50 Alford, *Trauma and Forgiveness*, 154.

51 Jaron Lanier, *You Are Not a Gadget: A Manifesto* (New York: Vintage Books, 2011), 87.

52 Abraham Joshua Heschel, *The Prophets* (New York: HarperPerennial, 2001), 4.

53 Adam Phillips and Barbara Taylor, *On Kindness* (New York: Farrar, Straus & Giroux, 2009), 8–9.

54 Phillips and Taylor, *On Kindness*, 17.

55 Phillips and Taylor, *On Kindness*, 8.

56 Jessica Benjamin, *Shadow of the Other: Intersubjectivity and Gender in Psychoanalysis* (New York: Routledge, 1998), 86.

57 Winnicott, *Home Is Where We Start From*, 117.

Chapter 5

1 Debrah Aaron, *Jokes and the Linguistic Mind* (New York: Routledge, 2012), 156.

2 Turkle, *Reclaiming Conversation*, 21.

3 Plato wrote, "Then, I said, let us begin and create in idea a State; and yet the true creator is necessity, who is the mother of our invention." See Plato, *Republic*, book II (http://classics.mit.edu/Plato/republic.3.ii.html).

4 Johan Huizinga, *Homo Ludens: A Study of the Play-Element in Culture* (London: Routledge & Kegan Paul, 1949), 158.

5 Diane Ackerman, *Deep Play* (New York: Random House, 1999), 26.

6 Miguel Sicart, *Play Matters* (Cambridge, Mass.: MIT Press, 2014), 2–3.

7 See Psalms 137:4.

8 Hugo Rahner, *Man at Play* (New York: Herder & Herder, 1967), 92; Jürgen Moltmann et al., *Theology of Play* (New York: Harper & Row, 1972), 2.

9 See Isaiah 11:6-8 and Zechariah 8:4-5. "The wolf will live with the lamb, the leopard will lie down with the goat, the calf and the lion and the yearling together; and a little child will lead them. . . . The infant will play near the hole of the cobra, and the young child put his hand into the viper's nest" (Isaiah 11:6-8). "This is what the LORD Almighty says: Once again men and women of ripe old age will sit in the streets of Jerusalem, each with cane in hand because of his age. The city streets will be filled with boys and girls playing there" (Zechariah 8:4-5). For contemporary theologians exploring play, see Hamman, *A Play-Full Life*; Bonnie J. Miller-McLemore, *Also a Mother: Work and Family as Theological Dilemma* (Nashville: Abingdon, 1994); James H. Evans, *Playing*, Christian Explorations of Daily Living (Minneapolis: Fortress, 2010); Michael Sherwood Koppel, *Open-Hearted Ministry: Play as Key to Pastoral Leadership* (Minneapolis: Fortress, 2008).

10 Jerome Berryman, *Godly Play: An Imaginative Approach to Religious Education* (Minneapolis: Augsburg, 1991).

11 See D. W. Winnicott, "The Observation of Children in a Set Situation (1941)," in Winnicott, *Through Paediatrics to Psycho-Analysis*, 52–69.

12 Winnicott, "Appetite and Emotional Disorder (1936)," in Winnicott, *Through Paediatrics to Psycho-Analysis*, 47.

13 D. W. Winnicott, "Why Children Play," in *The Child, the Family, and the Outside World* (New York: Addison-Wesley, 1987), 144.

14 Winnicott, "Why Children Play," in Winnicott, *The Child, the Family, and the Outside World*, 145.

15 Winnicott, "Why Children Play," in Winnicott, *The Child, the Family, and the Outside World*, 145.

16 D. W. Winnicott, "What Do You Mean by a Normal Child?" in Winnicott, *The Child, the Family, and the Outside World*, 130.

17 William Cheng, *Sound Play: Video Games and the Musical Imagination* (Oxford: Oxford University Press, 2014), 5, quoting Anthony Julius, *Transgressions: The Offences of Art* (Chicago: University of Chicago Press, 2002).

18 William Cheng, *Sound Play: Video Games and the Musical Imagination*, 5.

19 Winnicott famously writes, "Psychotherapy takes place in the overlap of two areas of playing, that of the patient and that of the therapist. It has to do with two people playing together. The corollary of this is that where playing is not possible then the work done by the therapist is directed in bringing the patient from a state of not being able to play to a state of being able to play." See D. W. Winnicott, "Playing: A Theoretical Statement," in Winnicott, *Playing and Reality*, 36.

20 For a discussion on corrupted forms of play, see Hamman, *Play-Full Life*, 21–58.

21 Al Gini, *Importance of Being Lazy: In Praise of Play, Leisure, and Vacations* (New York: Routledge, 2003), 86–87.

22 Donald Capps, *The Depleted Self: Sin in a Narcissistic Age* (Minneapolis: Fortress, 1993), 22.

23 Peter Gray, *Free to Learn: Why Unleashing the Instinct to Play Will Make Our Children Happier, More Self-Reliant, and Better Students for Life* (New York: Basic Books, 2013), 221.

24 Lawrence J. Cohen, *Playful Parenting: A Bold New Way to Nurture Close Connections, Solve Behavior Problems, and Encourage Children's Confidence* (New York: Ballantine Books, 2001), 197.

25 Dorothy W. Martyn, *Beyond Deserving: Children, Parents, and Responsibility Revisited* (Grand Rapids: Eerdmans, 2007), 122–23.

26 See John Mordechai Gottman and Nan Silver, *The Seven Principles for Making Marriage Work* (New York: Crown Publishers, 1999). The other three horsemen are contempt, stonewalling, and defensiveness. With criticism these attitudes can indicate the extent to which a relationship is under threat.

27 Brian W. Grant, *A Theology for Pastoral Psychotherapy: God's Play in Sacred Spaces* (New York: Haworth Pastoral Press, 2001), 91–92.

28 Plato quoted in Al Gini, *Importance of Being Lazy: In Praise of Play, Leisure, and Vacation* (New York: Routledge, 2003), 112.

29 See James P. Carse, *Finite and Infinite Games: A Vision of Life as Play and Possibility* (New York: Free Press, 1986).

30 Joe L. Frost, *A History of Children's Play and Play Environments: Toward a Contemporary Child-Saving Movement* (New York: Routledge, 2010), 120.

31 Frost, *History of Children's Play*, xv.

32 Frost, *History of Children's Play*, 2.

33 Frost, *History of Children's Play*, 226.

34 Frost, *History of Children's Play*, 87. Sixty percent of the children were boys. The sample covered 28 percent of New York's population.

35 Frost, *History of Children's Play*, 204–8.

36 Victor Burgin, "The Location of Virtual Experience," in Kuhn, *Little Madnesses: Winnicott, Transitional Phenomena and Cultural Experience*, 33. Digital virtuality became available in the late 1950s when Morton Heilig created the Sensorama. Isolating the senses of the user, Heilig introduced sound, vibration, wind, and odor to film, creating an immersive experience.

37 Frost, *History of Children's Play*, 219.

38 John Woods, "Seeing and Being Seen: The Psychodynamics of Pornography through the Lens of Winnicott's Thought," in Spelman and Thomson-Salo, *Winnicott Tradition*, 164. Research indicates that one-third of men in the US Military experience erectile dysfunction. See Sherrie L. Wilcox, Sarah Redmond, and Teaniese L. Davis, "Genital Image, Sexual Anxiety, and Erectile Dysfunction among Young Male Military Personnel," *The Journal of Sexual Medicine* 12, no. 6 (2015): 1389–97.

39 See also Smith and Fels, "The Disintegrated Erotics of Second Life."

40 Susan Edwards, "Post-Industrial Play: Understanding the Relationship between Traditional and Converged Forms of Play in the Early Years," in *Children's Virtual Play Worlds: Culture, Learning, and Participation*, ed. Anne M. Burke and Jackie Marsh (New York: Peter Lang, 2013), 11.

41 Adapted from Edwards, "Post-Industrial Play," in Burke and Marsh, *Children's Virtual Play Worlds*, 15–16.

42 Reagle, *Reading the Comments*, 180.

43 D. W. Winnicott, "The Squiggle Game," in C. Winnicott, Shepherd, and Davis, *Psycho-Analytic Explorations*, 301.

44 The case is discussed in Michael Jacobs, *D. W. Winnicott*, Key Figures in Counselling and Psychotherapy (London: Sage Publications, 1995), 69–70.

45 Matthew D. Selekman and Mark Beyebach, *Changing Self-Destructive Habits: Pathways to Solutions with Couples and Families* (New York: Brunner-Routledge, 2013), 124.

46 Selekman and Beyebach, *Changing Self-Destructive Habits*, 125.

47 Ackerman, *Deep Play*, 38.

48 Erik H. Erikson, *Toys and Reasons: Stages in the Ritualization of Experience* (New York: W. W. Norton, 1977), 99–100.

49 Winnicott, *Playing and Reality*, 47.

50 On the ludic century, See Sicart, *Play Matters*, 99.

51 Lawrence Pearsall Jacks, *Education through Recreation* (New York: Harper & Brothers, 1932), 155. Edited to reflect gender neutrality.

Chapter 6

1 Audre Lorde, *Sister Outsider: Essays and Speeches* (Berkeley: Crossing Press, 2007), 110. From her 1984 essay with the same title.

2 Kranzberg, "Technology and History," 544. This aphorism became one of six "laws" historian of technology Kranzberg named in his presidential address at the 1986 Society for the History of Technology Meeting. The first law is "Technology is neither good nor bad; nor is it neutral." The second law is "Invention is the mother of necessity" (548). Kranzberg's third law is "Technology comes in packages, big and small" (549). The fourth law is "Although technology might be a prime element in many public issues, nontechnical factors take precedence in technology-policy decisions" (550). This law sees that "many complicated sociocultural factors, especially human elements," are involved in our technology, in how it is conceived, manufactured, and used (551). Here Kranzberg also highlights environmental concerns. Kranzberg's fifth law states, "All history is relevant, but the history of technology is the most relevant" (554). The sixth and final law states, "Technology is a very human activity—and so is the history of technology" (557).

3 Kranzberg, "Technology and History," 557.

4 Theologian Allan Padgett argues that we are evolving into "*homo technicus, or techno sapiens.*" See Padgett, "God Versus Technology? Science, Secularity, and the Theology of Technology," *Zygon* 40, no. 3 (2005): 578.

5 Kranzberg, "Technology and History," 558.

6 Adam Phillips, *Winnicott*, Modern Masters (London: Fontana, 1988), 129.

7 danah boyd, quoted in Eli Pariser, *The Filter Bubble: What the Internet Is Hiding from You* (New York: Penguin, 2011), 14.

8 Ben Spencer, "Mobile Users Can't Leave Their Phone Alone for Six Minutes and Check It Up to 150 Times a Day," *Daily Mail*, February 10, 2013.

9 Larry D. Rosen, *iDisorder: Understanding Our Obsession with Technology and Overcoming Its Hold on Us* (New York: Palgrave Macmillan, 2012), 13.

10 Rosen, iDisorder, 14.

11 For a theology of technology structured around classic Christian themes such as "Reflection," "Rebellion," "Redemption," and "Restoration," see John Dyer, *From the Garden to the City: The Redeeming and Corrupting Power of Technology* (Grand Rapids: Kregel Publications, 2011). See also Albert Borgmann, *Power Failure: Christianity in the Culture of Technology* (Grand Rapids: Brazos Press, 2003); Jacques Ellul, *The Technological Bluff* (Grand Rapids: Eerdmans, 1990); idem, *The Technological Society* (New York: Alfred A. Knopf, 1964); Philip J. Hefner, *Technology and Human Becoming*, Facets (Minneapolis: Fortress, 2003); Stephen V. Monsma, *Responsible Technology: A Christian Perspective* (Grand Rapids: Eerdmans, 1986); Carl Mitcham and Jim Grote, *Theology and Technology: Essays in Christian Analysis and Exegesis* (Lanham, Md.: University Press of America, 1984).

12 Michael Stadter, "The Influence of Social Media and Communications Technology on Self and Relationships," in *Psychoanalysis Online: Mental Health, Teletherapy and Training*, ed. Jill Savege Scharff (London: Karnac Books, 2013), 3.

13 Winnicott, *Maturational Processes and the Facilitating Environment*, 27.

14 Winnicott, *Deprivation and Delinquency*, 121–22.

15 See American Psychiatric Association, *Diagnostic and Statistical Manual of Mental Disorders: DSM-5*, 5th ed. (Washington, D.C.: American Psychiatric Association, 2013), 480.

16 danah boyd, *It's Complicated: The Social Lives of Networked Teens* (New Haven: Yale University Press, 2014), 102.

17 danah boyd, *It's Complicated*, 86, 91.

18 Winnicott, "String: A Technique in Communication," in Winnicott, *Maturational Processes and the Facilitating Environment*, 155.

19 Turkle, *Reclaiming Conversation*, 104.

20 Turkle, *Reclaiming Conversation*, 26.

21 Turkle, *Reclaiming Conversation*, 108.

22 For a fetish object as replacement for the face, see Gilles Deleuze and Félix Guattari, *A Thousand Plateaus: Capitalism and Schizophrenia*, trans. Brian Massumi (Minneapolis: University of Minnesota Press, 1987), 170. The authors write, "Hand, breast, stomach, penis, vagina, thigh, leg, and foot, all come to be facialized. Fetishism, erotomania, etc., are inseparable from the processes of facialization."

23 Nir Eyal, *Hooked: How to Build Habit-Forming Products* (New York: Penguin, 2014), 39.

24 Eyal, *Hooked*, 7–10. Eyal's book is behavior-oriented. External triggers can be paid, earned, relationship based, or owned (44–46). Internal triggers are emotions, especially negative ones such as fear or loneliness, as well as pain, stress, frustration, or depression (47–51).

25 Eyal, *Hooked*, 62. Eyal draws on the work of Professor B. J. Fogg of Stanford University. Fogg's behavioral model states that behavior will occur when motivation, ability, and a trigger are present (B = MAT). Eyal also draws on neuroscience, showing how apps and games activate "basal ganglia, an area of the brain associated with involuntary actions" (16).

26 Eyal, *Hooked*, 92.

27 Eyal, *Hooked*, 100.

28 Eyal, *Hooked*, 118. The gamification of non-game areas of life, such as education and healthcare, is increasing.

29 Eyal, *Hooked*, 135.

30 Burgin, "Location of Virtual Experience," in Kuhn, *Little Madnesses: Winnicott, Transitional Phenomena and Cultural Experience*, 32.

31 Bruce Damer and Randy Hinrichs, "The Virtuality and Reality of Avatar Cyberspace," in *The Oxford Handbook of Virtuality*, ed. Mark Grimshaw (Oxford: Oxford University Press, 2014), 18.

32 Karen E. Dill, *How Fantasy Becomes Reality: Seeing through Media Influence* (Oxford: Oxford University Press, 2009), 10. Dill uses "fantasy" in a popular sense and not in the psychodynamic sense used in *Growing Down*. Dill is a vocal critic of the game *Grand Theft Auto*. The game's developers named a car in the fourth edition: "Karin Dilettante."

33 Dill, *How Fantasy Becomes Reality*, 78 (emphasis in original).

34 Dill, *How Fantasy Becomes Reality*, 70.

35 Dave Grossman and Gloria DeGautano, *Stop Teaching Our Kids to Kill: A Call to Action against TV, Movie & Video Game Violence* (New York: Harmony, 2014), 7–9. The games played ranged from *Doom* to *Combat Arms* and *Grand Theft Auto*.

36 Michael Labossiere, *Sexbots, Killbots & Virtual Dogs: Essays on Ethics & Technology* (Lexington, Ky.: self published, 2014), 17.

37 Dill, *How Fantasy Becomes Reality*, 67.

38 Konrath, O'Brien, and Hsing, "Changes in Dispositional Empathy," 182.

39 Jane McGonigal, *Reality Is Broken: Why Games Make Us Better and How They Can Change the World* (New York: Penguin, 2011), 4.

40 McGonigal, *Reality Is Broken*, 21.

41 McGonigal, *Reality Is Broken*, 120.

42 McGonigal, *Reality Is Broken*, 354.

43 D. W. Winnicott, "Primary Maternal Preoccupation," in Winnicott, *Through Paediatrics to Psycho-Analysis*, 300.

44 Winnicott, "Primary Maternal Preoccupation," in Winnicott, *Through Paediatrics to Psycho-Analysis*, 302.

45 Winnicott, *Playing and Reality*, 51.

46 Mihály Csíkszentmihályi, *Flow: The Psychology of Optimal Experience* (New York: Harper & Row, 1990).

47 Howard Rheingold, *Net Smart: How to Thrive Online* (Cambridge, Mass.: MIT Press, 2012), 36.
48 Rheingold, *Net Smart*, 38.
49 Rheingold, *Net Smart*, 15.
50 Rheingold, *Net Smart*, 39.
51 Rheingold, *Net Smart*, 45.
52 Rheingold, *Net Smart*, 58. Rheingold is quoting technologist Linda Stone. Stone identified e-mail apnea in persons reading e-mail.
53 Rheingold, *Net Smart*, 1. Rheingold invites us to pay attention to the ways we attend to the various screens we look at and to detect the "crap" we find online, encouraging us to participate and collaborate in cyberspace while exercising net smarts.
54 Winnicott, "The Development of the Capacity for Concern," in Winnicott, *Maturational Processes and the Facilitating Environment*, 75.
55 Haim Weinberg, *The Paradox of Internet Groups: Alone in the Presence of Virtual Others* (London: Karnac Books, 2014), 71.
56 Weinberg, *The Paradox of Internet Groups*, 72.
57 Quoted in Gillian Isaacs Russell, *Screen Relations: The Limits of Computer-Mediated Psychoanalysis and Psychotherapy*, Library of Technology and Mental Health (London: Karnac Books, 2015), 140.
58 Russell, *Screen Relations*, 138.
59 Russell, *Screen Relations*, 26.
60 Russell, *Screen Relations*, 75.
61 Weinberg, *Paradox of Internet Groups*, 85 (emphasis original).
62 Russell references Giuseppe Riva and John Waterworth, who draw on the work of Antonio Damasio, distinguishing between proto presence, core presence, and extended presence. *Proto presence* speaks to "an embodied presence related to the level of perception-action coupling." Here, perception needs to correctly interpret action. In *core presence*, the self, changed by a proto presence experience, connects with the external object. That object becomes the focus of selective attention, and the self recognizes the importance of the present moment. In *extended presence*, the emphasis is more than the here and now, as it includes the past and the future. The experience becomes part of a much larger personal narrative. See Russell, *Screen Relations*, 140–43.
63 Jonathan Miller, *On Reflection* (London: National Gallery Publications, 1998), 2.
64 Anita Colloms, "Reflections on Mirrors," in *Winnicott's Children: Independent Psychoanalytic Approaches with Children and Adolescents*, ed. Ann Horne and Monica Lanyado (New York: Routledge, 2012), 61.
65 Colloms, "Reflections on Mirrors," in Horne and Lanyado, *Winnicott's Children*, 68.

66 Catherine Steiner-Adair and Teresa Barker, *The Big Disconnect: Protecting Childhood and Family Relationships in the Digital Age* (New York: HarperCollins, 2013), 13. Sherry Turkle reports research describing similar experiences to the ones mentioned by Steiner-Adair. See Turkle, *Reclaiming Conversation*, 107–9.

67 Steiner-Adair and Barker, *Big Disconnect*, 17 (emphasis original).

68 Turkle, *Reclaiming Conversation*, 157.

69 Jeffrey I. Cole, "Surveying the Digital Future, Year Eleven," in *The 2013 Digital Future Report* (Los Angeles: University of Southern California, 2013), 105. "Compared to respondents who said they are ignored by a member of the household who spends too much time online or on television (see the previous question), a much higher percentage (92 percent) said they were ignored because a household member spends too much time on a mobile device—either talking, texting, or Web browsing."

70 Steiner-Adair and Barker, *Big Disconnect*, 262.

71 Winnicott, "Notes on Play," in C. Winnicott, Shepherd, and Davis, *Psycho-Analytic Explorations*, 61.

72 D. W. Winnicott, "Use of an Object and Relating through Identifications," in C. Winnicott, Shepherd, and Davis, *Psycho-Analytic Explorations*, 219.

73 Kishonna Gray, ed., *Race, Gender, and Deviance in Xbox Live: Theoretical Perspectives from the Virtual Margins the Theoretical Criminology Series* (New York: Elsevier, 2014), x.

74 Gray, *Race, Gender, and Deviance in Xbox Live*, xvii.

75 Gray, *Race, Gender, and Deviance in Xbox Live*, xxii.

76 Gray, *Race, Gender, and Deviance in Xbox Live*, 5.

77 Gray, *Race, Gender, and Deviance in Xbox Live*, 5–6.

78 Gray, *Race, Gender, and Deviance in Xbox Live*, 75. Gray is quoting the Caribbean-American womanist Audre Lorde. See Lorde, *Sister Outsider*.

79 Pariser, *Filter Bubble*, 12.

80 Pariser, *Filter Bubble*, 15.

81 Pariser, *Filter Bubble*, 44.

82 Pariser, *Filter Bubble*, 16.

83 Pariser, *Filter Bubble*, 94.

84 Psalm 115:4-8: "But their idols are silver and gold, made by human hands. They have mouths, but cannot speak, eyes, but cannot see. They have ears, but cannot hear, noses, but cannot smell. They have hands, but cannot feel, feet, but cannot walk, nor can they utter a sound with their throats. Those who make them will be like them, and so will all who trust in them."

85 For digiphrenia, see Douglas Rushkoff, *Present Shock: When Everything Happens Now* (New York: Current, 2013), 73, 74.

86 Winnicott, "Capacity to Be Alone," in Winnicott, *Maturational Processes and the Facilitating Environment*, 34–35. Philosopher Jacques Lacan writes about similar moments as *jouissance*.

Conclusion

1 Winnicott, *Human Nature*, 1.

2 Sigmund Freud and C. J. M. Hubback, *Beyond the Pleasure Principle*, The International Psycho-Analytical Library, authorized translation from the second German edition (London: International Psycho-analytical Press, 1922), 18. Freud saw repression and forgetting as serving the death drive.

3 This is the argument of cultural theorist René Girard and his theory of societal scapegoating. See René Girard, "Mimesis and Violence: Perspectives in Cultural Criticism," in *The Girard Reader*, ed. James G. Williams (New York: Crossroad, 1979). Also, idem, *Violence and the Sacred*, trans. Patrick Gregory (Baltimore: Johns Hopkins University Press, 1979). For a discussion around mimesis and aggression in René Girard and D. W. Winnicott, see Martha J. Reineke, "Transforming Space: Creativity, Destruction, and Mimesis in Winnicott and Girard," *Contagion: Journal of Violence, Mimesis, and Culture* 14 (2007).

4 Michael T. Taussig, *Mimesis and Alterity: A Particular History of the Senses* (New York: Routlege, 1993), xiii.

5 Benjamin, *Walter Benjamin: Selected Writings, Volume 2, Part 2, 1931–1934*, ed. Michael W. Jennings, Howard Eiland, and Gary Smith (Cambridge, Mass.: Harvard University Press, 2005), 720.

6 Benjamin, *Walter Benjamin*, 722.

7 Taussig, *Mimesis and Alterity*, 20, 35. Taussig builds his argument on Walter Benjamin's essay "The Work of Art in the Age of Mechanical Reproduction." In this essay, Benjamin saw a relationship between mimetic desire and a child's relationship with mother. Taussig refers to Miriam Hansen's work on Benjamin. She quotes Benjamin's notes in his "Arcades Project": "What the child (and weakly remembering, the man) finds in the old folds of the mother's skirt that he held on to—that's what these pages should contain" (37). Benjamin's thought validates the argument that persons mimetically desire a holding environment.

8 See Taussig, *Mimesis and Alterity*, xiii–xiv, 105–8. Taussig, drawing on ethnographic studies, describes how the mimetic act of chanting during healing rituals brings the spirit world into existence for the indigenous Cuna people of Colombia and Panama's San Blas Islands. The Cuna worship wooden figurines (*nuchukana* or *nuchus*) that look remarkably similar to European colonists clothed in what looks like seventeenth-century garb. Their traditional art, *molas*, mimics popular culture. We are social

constructionists, Taussig argues as he wonders why the Canu chose the Colonial Other as an object of worship.

9   Girard, *Violence and the Sacred*, 7 (emphasis added).

10 Jacques Lacan and Bruce Fink, *Écrits: The First Complete Edition in English* (New York: W. W. Norton, 2006), 521 (emphasis added).

11 See Phillips' essay, "The Telling of Selves," in Phillips, *On Flirtation*, 65.

12 D. W. Winnicott, "The Fear of Breakdown," in C. Winnicott, Shepherd, and Davis, *Psycho-Analytic Explorations*, 91.

13 Winnicott, "Fear of Breakdown," in C. Winnicott, Shepherd, and Davis, *Psycho-Analytic Explorations*, 92.

14 Winnicott, "Primitive Emotional Development," in Winnicott, *Through Paediatrics to Psycho-Analysis*, 150.

15 Madeleine Davis and David Wallbridge, *Boundary and Space: An Introduction to the Work of D.W. Winnicott* (London: Karnac Books, 1990), 83. The authors quote an unpublished paper by Winnicott.

16 This image of personhood comes from Galatians 5:22-23. See Eugene H. Peterson, *The Message: The Bible in Contemporary Language* (Colorado Springs: NavPress, 2005).

17 Roy F. Baumeister, *The Cultural Animal: Human Nature, Meaning, and Social Life* (Oxford: Oxford University Press, 2005), 49: "Sexual manuals written thousands of years ago in ancient China covered almost all the same techniques one would find in a sex manual today, with only one major exception (sadomasochism)."

18 Winnicott wrote, "[I want to] develop the theme not so much of society that changes as of human nature that does not change. Human nature does not change. This is an idea that could be challenged. Nevertheless, I shall assume its truth, and build on its foundation. It is true that human nature evolved, just as human bodies and being evolved, in the course of hundreds of thousands of years. But there is very little evidence that human nature has altered in the short span of recorded history." See Winnicott, "Morals and Education," in Winnicott, *Maturational Processes and the Facilitating Environment*, 93.

19 Jacques Ellul, *What I Believe* (Grand Rapids: Eerdmans, 1989), 136.

20 Ellul, *What I Believe*, 140.

21 Heading taken from Winnicott, *Home Is Where We Start From*.

22 Hannah Arendt, *The Human Condition*, Charles R. Walgreen Foundation Lectures (Chicago: University of Chicago Press, 1958), 22.

23 Adam Phillips, *Missing Out: In Praise of the Unlived Life* (London: Hamish Hamilton, 2012), 59.

24 Winnicott famously said, "There is no such thing as an infant," by which he meant one only has an infant *with* primary caregivers, *with* a family, and *with* a society. See Winnicott, "Morals and Education," in Winnicott, *Maturational Processes and the Facilitating Environment*, 39. See also Winnicott, *Human Nature*, 1.

WORKS CITED

Aaron, Debrah. *Jokes and the Linguistic Mind.* New York: Routledge, 2012.

Ackerman, Diane. *Deep Play.* New York: Random House, 1999.

Alford, C. Fred. *Trauma and Forgiveness: Consequences and Communities.* Cambridge: Cambridge University Press, 2013.

American Psychiatric Association. *Diagnostic and Statistical Manual of Mental Disorders: DSM-5.* 5th ed. Washington, D.C.: American Psychiatric Association, 2013.

Arendt, Hannah. *The Human Condition.* Charles R. Walgreen Foundation Lectures. Chicago: University of Chicago Press, 1958.

Bailie, Gil. *Violence Unveiled: Humanity at the Crossroads.* New York: Crossroad, 1995.

Baumeister, Roy F. *The Cultural Animal: Human Nature, Meaning, and Social Life.* Oxford: Oxford University Press, 2005.

Benhabib, Seyla. *Situating the Self: Gender, Community, and Postmodernism in Contemporary Ethics.* New York: Routledge, 1992.

Benjamin, Jessica. *The Bonds of Love: Psychoanalysis, Feminism, and the Problem of Domination.* New York: Pantheon Books, 1988.

— — —. *Shadow of the Other: Intersubjectivity and Gender in Psychoanalysis.* New York: Routledge, 1998.

Benjamin, Walter. *Walter Benjamin: Selected Writings, Volume 2, Part 2, 1931–1934.* Edited by Michael W. Jennings, Howard Eiland, and Gary Smith. Cambridge, Mass.: Harvard University Press, 2005.

Berryman, Jerome. *Godly Play: An Imaginative Approach to Religious Education.* Minneapolis: Augsburg, 1991.

Bertolini, Mario, and Francesca Neri. "Sex as a Defence against Sexuality." In Caldwell, *Sex and Sexuality: Winnicottian Perspectives,* 83–103.

Bollas, Christopher. *The Shadow of the Object: Psychoanalysis of the Unthought Known.* London: Free Association Books, 1987.

Bonhoeffer, Dietrich. *Letters and Papers from Prison.* New York: Macmillan, 1972.

Borgmann, Albert. *Power Failure: Christianity in the Culture of Technology.* Grand Rapids: Brazos Press, 2003.

boyd, danah. *It's Complicated: The Social Lives of Networked Teens.* New Haven: Yale University Press, 2014.

Brueggemann, Walter. *Interpretation and Obedience: From Faithful Reading to Faithful Living.* Minneapolis: Fortress, 1991.

Buber, Martin. *Tales of the Hasidim.* 2 vols. New York: Schocken Books, 1991.

Buber, Martin, and Walter A. Kaufmann. *I and Thou.* New York: Scribner's, 1970.

Burgin, Victor. "The Location of Virtual Experience." In Kuhn, *Little Madnesses: Winnicott, Transitional Phenomena and Cultural Experience,* 23–38.

Butler, Judith. *Bodies That Matter: On the Discursive Limits of "Sex."* New York: Routledge, 1993.

— — —. *The Psychic Life of Power: Theories in Subjection.* Stanford, Calif.: Stanford University Press, 1997.

Caldwell, Lesley, ed. *Sex and Sexuality: Winnicottian Perspectives.* Winnicott Studies Monograph Series. London: Karnac Books, 2005.

Capps, Donald. *The Depleted Self: Sin in a Narcissistic Age.* Minneapolis: Fortress, 1993.

Carse, James P. *Finite and Infinite Games: A Vision of Life as Play and Possibility.* New York: Free Press, 1986.

Cerra, Allison, and Christina James. *Identity Shift: Where Identity Meets Technology in the Networked-Community Age.* Indianapolis: Wiley & Sons, 2012.

Cheng, William. *Sound Play: Video Games and the Musical Imagination.* Oxford: Oxford University Press, 2014.

Cheong, Pauline Hope, and Kishonna Gray. "Mediated Intercultural Dialectics: Identity Perceptions and Performances in Virtual Worlds." *Journal of International and Intercultural Communication* 4, no. 4 (2011): 265–71.

Chodorow, Nancy. *Feminism and Psychoanalytic Theory.* New Haven: Yale University Press, 1989.

— — —. *The Reproduction of Mothering: Psychoanalysis and the Sociology of Gender.* Berkeley: University of California Press, 1978.

Chory, Rebecca M., and Alan K. Goodboy. "Is Basic Personality Related to Violent and Non-Violent Video Game Play and Preferences?" *Cyberpsychology, Behavior, and Social Networking* 14, no. 4 (2011): 191–98.

Cohen, Lawrence J. *Playful Parenting: A Bold New Way to Nurture Close Connections, Solve Behavior Problems, and Encourage Children's Confidence.* New York: Ballantine Books, 2001.

Cole, Jeffrey I. "Surveying the Digital Future, Year Eleven." In *The 2013 Digital Future Report.* Los Angeles: University of Southern California, 2013.

Colloms, Anita. "Reflections on Mirrors." In Horne and Lanyado, *Winnicott's Children*, 60–76.

Courtois, Cédric, Peter Mechant, and Lieven De Marez. "Communicating Creativity on Youtube: What and for Whom?" *Cyberpsychology, Behavior & Social Networking* 15, no. 3 (2012): 129–34.

Csíkszentmihályi, Mihály. *Flow: The Psychology of Optimal Experience.* New York: Harper & Row, 1990.

Damer, Bruce, and Randy Hinrichs. "The Virtuality and Reality of Avatar Cyberspace." In *The Oxford Handbook of Virtuality*, edited by Mark Grimshaw, 17–41. Oxford: Oxford University Press, 2014.

Davis, Madeleine, and David Wallbridge. *Boundary and Space: An Introduction to the Work of D. W. Winnicott.* London: Karnac Books, 1990.

Deleuze, Gilles, and Félix Guattari. *A Thousand Plateaus: Capitalism and Schizophrenia.* Translated by Brian Massumi. Minneapolis: University of Minnesota Press, 1987.

Derrida, Jacques. *The Work of Mourning.* Edited by Pascale-Anne Brault and Michael Naas. Translated by Pascale-Anne Brault. Chicago: University of Chicago Press, 2001.

Dill, Karen E. *How Fantasy Becomes Reality: Seeing through Media Influence.* Oxford: Oxford University Press, 2009.

Dittes, James E. *Re-Calling Ministry.* Edited by Donald Capps. St. Louis: Chalice Press, 1999.

Doane, Janice L., and Devon L. Hodges. *From Klein to Kristeva: Psychoanalytic Feminism and the Search for the "Good Enough" Mother. Critical Perspectives on Women and Gender.* Ann Arbor: University of Michigan Press, 1992.

Döveling, Katrin, Christian von Scheve, and Elly Konijn. *The Routledge Handbook of Emotions and Mass Media.* Routledge International Handbooks. New York: Routledge, 2011.

Du Bois, W. E. B. "The Field and Function of the Negro College." In *The Education of Black People: Ten Critiques 1906–1960,* edited by Herbert Aptheker, 83–102. Amherst: University of Massachusetts Press, 1973.

Dyer, John. *From the Garden to the City: The Redeeming and Corrupting Power of Technology.* Grand Rapids: Kregel Publications, 2011.

Edwards, Susan. "Post-Industrial Play: Understanding the Relationship between Traditional and Converged Forms of Play in the Early Years." In *Children's Virtual Play Worlds: Culture, Learning, and Participation,* edited by Anne M. Burke and Jackie Marsh, 10–25. New York: Peter Lang, 2013.

Eigen, Michael. "The Area of Faith in Winnicott, Lacan and Bion." *International Journal of Psycho-Analysis* 62 (1981): 413–33.

— — —. *Feeling Matters: From the Yosemite God to the Annihilated Self.* London: Karnac Books, 2007.

Ekman, Paul, and Richard J. Davidson. *The Nature of Emotion: Fundamental Questions.* New York: Oxford University Press, 1994.

Ellul, Jacques. *The Technological Bluff.* Grand Rapids: Eerdmans, 1990.

— — —. *The Technological Society.* New York: Alfred A. Knopf, 1964.

— — —. *What I Believe.* Grand Rapids: Eerdmans, 1989.

Erikson, Erik H. *Toys and Reasons: Stages in the Ritualization of Experience.* New York: W. W. Norton, 1977.

Evans, James H. *Playing. Christian Explorations of Daily Living.* Minneapolis: Fortress, 2010.

Eyal, Nir. *Hooked: How to Build Habit-Forming Products.* New York: Penguin, 2014.

Fairbairn, W. Ronald D. "Endopsychic Structure Considered in Terms of Object-Relationships." In idem, *Psychoanalytic Studies of the Personality*, 82–136. New York: Routledge, 1996.

Ford, David. *Self and Salvation: Being Transformed*. Cambridge Studies in Christian Doctrine. Cambridge: Cambridge University Press, 1999.

Freud, Sigmund, and C. J. M. Hubback. *Beyond the Pleasure Principle*. The International Psycho-Analytical Library. Authorized translation from the second German edition. London: International Psycho-analytical Press, 1922.

Fromm, Gerard, and Bruce L. Smith. *The Facilitating Environment: Clinical Applications of Winnicott's Theory*. Madison, Conn.: International Universities Press, 1989.

Frost, Joe L. *A History of Children's Play and Play Environments: Toward a Contemporary Child-Saving Movement*. New York: Routledge, 2010.

Gardner, Howard. *Frames of Mind: The Theory of Multiple Intelligences*. New York: Basic Books, 1983.

Gardner, Howard, and Katie Davis. *The App Generation: How Today's Youth Navigate Identity, Intimacy, and Imagination in a Digital World*. New Haven: Yale University Press, 2013.

Gilligan, Carol. *In a Different Voice: Psychological Theory and Women's Development*. Cambridge, Mass.: Harvard University Press, 1993.

Gini, Al. *The Importance of Being Lazy: In Praise of Play, Leisure, and Vacations*. London: Routledge, 2003.

Girard, René. "Mimesis and Violence: Perspectives in Cultural Criticism." In *The Girard Reader*, edited by James G. Williams, 9–19. New York: Crossroad, 1979.

— — —. *Violence and the Sacred*. Translated by Patrick Gregory. Baltimore: Johns Hopkins University Press, 1979.

Goby, Valerie Priscilla. "Psychological Underpinnings of Intrafamilial Computer-Mediated Communication: A Preliminary Exploration of CMC Uptake with Parents and Siblings." *Cyberpsychology, Behavior, and Social Networking* 14, no. 6 (2011): 365–70.

Goleman, Daniel. *Emotional Intelligence*. New York: Bantam Books, 1995.

Gottman, John Mordechai, and Nan Silver. *The Seven Principles for Making Marriage Work*. New York: Crown Publishers, 1999.

Graffam, Gray. "Avatar: A Posthuman Perspective on Virtual Worlds." In *Human No More: Digital Subjectivities, Unhuman Subjects, and the End of Anthropology*, edited by Neil L. Whitehead and Michael Wesch, 131–46. Boulder: University Press of Colorado, 2012.

Graham, Elaine. "Being, Making and Imagining: Toward a Practical Theology of Technology." *Culture and Religion* 10, no. 2 (2009): 221–36.

Grant, Brian W. *A Theology for Pastoral Psychotherapy: God's Play in Sacred Spaces*. New York: Haworth Pastoral Press, 2001.

Gray, Kishonna, ed. *Race, Gender, and Deviance in Xbox Live: Theoretical Perspectives from the Virtual Margins Theoretical Criminology Series*. New York: Elsevier, 2014.

Gray, Peter. *Free to Learn: Why Unleashing the Instinct to Play Will Make Our Children Happier, More Self-Reliant, and Better Students for Life*. New York: Basic Books, 2013.

Greenberg, Jay R., and Stephen A. Mitchell. *Object Relations in Psychoanalytic Theory*. Cambridge, Mass.: Harvard University Press, 1983.

Grossman, Dave, and Gloria DeGautano. *Stop Teaching Our Kids to Kill: A Call to Action against TV, Movie & Video Game Violence*. New York: Harmony, 2014.

Guntrip, Harry. *Mental Pain and the Cure of Souls*. London: Independent Press, 1956.

Hamman, Jaco J. *A Play-Full Life: Slowing Down and Seeking Peace*. Cleveland: Pilgrim Press, 2011.

— — —. "Revisiting Forgiveness as a Pastoral-Theological Problem." *Pastoral Psychology* 61, no. 4 (2012): 435–50.

Hefner, Philip J. *Technology and Human Becoming*. Facets. Minneapolis: Fortress, 2003.

Heidegger, Martin. *The Fundamental Concepts of Metaphysics: World, Finitude, Solitude*. Studies in Continental Thought. Bloomington: Indiana University Press, 1995.

— — —. *The Question Concerning Technology and Other Essays*. New York: Harper & Row, 1977.

Heschel, Abraham Joshua. *The Prophets*. New York: Harper-Perennial, 2001.

Hillman, James. *The Soul's Code: In Search of Character and Calling*. New York: Random House, 1996.

Hollway, Wendy. *The Capacity to Care: Gender and Ethical Subjectivity*. Women and Psychology. New York: Routledge, 2006.

Horne, Ann, and Monica Lanyado, eds. *Winnicott's Children: Independent Psychoanalytic Approaches with Children and Adolescents.* New York: Routledge, 2012.

Huizinga, Johan. *Homo Ludens: A Study of the Play-Element in Culture.* London: Routledge & Kegan Paul, 1949.

Jacks, Lawrence Pearsall. *Education through Recreation.* New York: Harper & Brothers, 1932.

Jacobs, Michael. *D.W. Winnicott.* Key Figures in Counselling and Psychotherapy. London: Sage Publications, 1995.

James, William. *The Principles of Psychology.* Vol. 1, *The Works of William James.* Cambridge, Mass.: Harvard University Press, 1981.

Johnson, Barbara. *Persons and Things.* Cambridge, Mass.: Harvard University Press, 2008.

Jonte-Pace, Diane. "Object Relations Theory, Mothering, and Religion: Toward a Feminist Psychology of Religion." *Horizons* 14, no. 2 (1987): 310–27.

Jung, C. G. *The Archetypes and the Collective Unconscious.* Bollingen Series. New York: Pantheon Books, 1959.

— — —. *Memories, Dreams, Reflections.* New York: Pantheon Books, 1963.

— — —. *The Collected Works of C. G. Jung.* Bollingen Series. New York: Pantheon Books, 1954.

Kalsched, Donald. *Trauma and the Soul: A Psycho-Spiritual Approach to Human Development and Its Interruption.* New York: Routledge, 2013.

Kierkegaard, Søren. *The Essential Kierkegaard.* Edited by Howard V. Hong and Edna H. Hong. Princeton, N.J.: Princeton University Press, 2000.

Klein, Melanie. *Love, Guilt, and Reparation, and Other Works, 1921–1945.* The Writings of Melanie Klein. New York: Free Press, 1984.

Konrath, Sara H., Edward H. O'Brien, and Courtney Hsing. "Changes in Dispositional Empathy in American College Students over Time: A Meta-Analysis." *Personality and Social Psychology Review* 15, no. 2 (2011): 180–98.

Koppel, Michael Sherwood. *Open-Hearted Ministry: Play as Key to Pastoral Leadership.* Minneapolis: Fortress, 2008.

Kranzberg, Melvin. "Technology and History: 'Kranzberg's Laws.'" *Technology and Culture* 27, no. 3 (1986): 544–60.

Kuhn, Annette. *Little Madnesses: Winnicott, Transitional Phenomena and Cultural Experience.* London: I. B. Tauris, 2013.

Labossiere, Michael. *Sexbots, Killbots & Virtual Dogs: Essays on Ethics & Technology*. Lexington, Ky.: self published, 2014.

Lacan, Jacques, and Bruce Fink. *Écrits: The First Complete Edition in English*. New York: W. W. Norton, 2006.

Lanier, Jaron. *You Are Not a Gadget: A Manifesto*. New York: Vintage Books, 2011.

Laplanche, Jean, and J. B. Pontalis. *The Language of Psycho-Analysis*. New York: Norton, 1974.

Levinas, Emmanuel. *Totality and Infinity: An Essay on Exteriority*. Translated by Alphonso Lingis. Duquesne Studies Philosophical Series. Pittsburgh: Duquesne University Press, 1969.

Lewandowski, Joshua, Benjamin D. Rosenberg, M. Jordan Parks, and Jason T. Siegel. "The Effect of Informal Social Support: Face-to-Face Versus Computer-Mediated Communication." *Computers in Human Behavior* 27 (2011): 1806–14.

Lorde, Audre. *Sister Outsider: Essays and Speeches*. Berkeley: Crossing Press, 2007.

Martyn, Dorothy W. *Beyond Deserving: Children, Parents, and Responsibility Revisited*. Grand Rapids: Eerdmans, 2007.

McGonigal, Jane. *Reality Is Broken: Why Games Make Us Better and How They Can Change the World*. New York: Penguin, 2011.

Miller, Alice. *The Drama of the Gifted Child: The Search for the True Self*. New York: Basic Books, 1997.

Miller, Jonathan. *On Reflection*. London: National Gallery Publications; distributed by Yale University Press, 1998.

Miller-McLemore, Bonnie J. *Also a Mother: Work and Family as Theological Dilemma*. Nashville: Abingdon, 1994.

Mitcham, Carl, and Jim Grote. *Theology and Technology: Essays in Christian Analysis and Exegesis*. Lanham, Md.: University Press of America, 1984.

Moltmann, Jürgen, Robert E. Neale, Sam Keen, and David LeRoy Miller. *Theology of Play*. New York: Harper & Row, 1972.

Monsma, Stephen V. *Responsible Technology: A Christian Perspective*. Grand Rapids: Eerdmans, 1986.

Morris, Kenneth Earl. *Bonhoeffer's Ethic of Discipleship: A Study in Social Psychology, Political Thought, and Religion*. University Park: Pennsylvania State University Press, 1986.

Newheart, Michael Willett. *Word and Soul: A Psychological, Literary, and Cultural Reading of the Fourth Gospel.* Collegeville, Minn.: Liturgical Press, 2001.

Ong, Chorng-Shyong, Shu-Chen Chang, and Chih-Chien Wang. "Comparative Loneliness of Users Versus Nonusers of Online Chatting." *Cyberpsychology, Behavior, and Social Networking* 14, nos. 1–2 (2011): 35–40.

Padgett, Allan. "God Versus Technology? Science, Secularity, and the Theology of Technology." *Zygon* 40, no. 3 (2005): 577–84.

Pariser, Eli. *The Filter Bubble: What the Internet Is Hiding from You.* New York: Penguin, 2011.

Parker, Rozsika. *Mother Love/Mother Hate: The Power of Maternal Ambivalence.* New York: Basic Books, 1995.

Parker, Stephen E. *Winnicott and Religion.* Lanham, Md.: Jason Aronson, 2011.

Peterson, Eugene H. *The Message: The Bible in Contemporary Language.* Colorado Springs: NavPress, 2005.

Phillips, Adam. *Missing Out: In Praise of the Unlived Life.* London: Hamish Hamilton, 2012.

— — —. *On Flirtation.* Cambridge, Mass.: Harvard University Press, 1994.

— — —. *On Kissing, Tickling, and Being Bored: Psychoanalytic Essays on the Unexamined Life.* Cambridge, Mass.: Harvard University Press, 1993.

— — —. *Winnicott.* Modern Masters. London: Fontana, 1988.

Phillips, Adam, and Barbara Taylor. *On Kindness.* New York: Farrar, Straus & Giroux, 2009.

Presa, Elizabeth. "Ways of Being: Transitional Objects and the Work of Art." In Spelman and Thomson-Salo, *Winnicott Tradition,* 315–26.

Pruyser, Paul W. *The Play of the Imagination: Towards a Psychoanalysis of Culture.* New York: International Universities Press, 1983.

Răcătău, Ionela-Maria. "Adolescents and Identity Formation in a Risky Online Environment: The Role of Negative User-Generated and Xenophobic Websites." *Journal of Media Research* 3, no. 17 (2013): 16–36.

Rahner, Hugo. *Man at Play.* New York: Herder & Herder, 1967.

Reagle, Joseph Michael. *Reading the Comments: Likers, Haters, and Manipulators at the Bottom of the Web.* Cambridge, Mass.: MIT Press, 2015.

Reineke, Martha J. "Transforming Space: Creativity, Destruction, and Mimesis in Winnicott and Girard." *Contagion: Journal of Violence, Mimesis, and Culture* 14 (2007): 79–95.

Rheingold, Howard. *Net Smart: How to Thrive Online.* Cambridge, Mass.: MIT Press, 2012.

Rizzuto, Ana-Maria. *The Birth of the Living God: A Psychoanalytic Study.* Chicago: University of Chicago Press, 1979.

Roberts, Robert C. "Forgivingness." *American Philosophical Quarterly* 32, no. 4 (1995): 289–306.

Robinson, Helen Taylor. "Adult Eros in D.W. Winnicott." In Caldwell, *Sex and Sexuality*, 83–103.

Rosen, Larry D. *iDisorder: Understanding Our Obsession with Technology and Overcoming Its Hold on Us.* New York: Palgrave Macmillan, 2012.

Rushkoff, Douglas. *Present Shock: When Everything Happens Now.* New York: Current, 2013.

Russell, Gillian Isaacs. *Screen Relations: The Limits of Computer-Mediated Psychoanalysis and Psychotherapy.* Library of Technology and Mental Health. London: Karnac Books, 2015.

Schmidt, Eric, and Jared Cohen. *The New Digital Age: Reshaping the Future of People, Nations and Business.* London: Hodder & Stoughton, 2014.

Schuurman, Derek C. *Shaping a Digital World: Faith, Culture and Computer Technology.* Downers Grove, Ill.: InterVarsity, 2013.

Selekman, Matthew D., and Mark Beyebach. *Changing Self-Destructive Habits: Pathways to Solutions with Couples and Families.* New York: Brunner-Routledge, 2013.

Sicart, Miguel. *Play Matters.* Cambridge, Mass.: MIT Press, 2014.

Skolnick, Neil J., and Susan C. Warshaw, eds. *Relational Perspectives in Psychoanalysis.* Hillsdale, N.J.: Analytic Press, 1992.

Slochower, Joyce Anne. *Holding and Psychoanalysis: A Relational Perspective.* Hillsdale, N.J.: Analytic Press, 1996.

Smith, Archie. *The Relational Self: Ethics & Therapy from a Black Church Perspective.* Nashville: Abingdon, 1982.

Smith, David Harris, and Deborah Fels. "The Disintegrated Erotics of Second Life." *The International Journal of the Image* 2, no. 3 (2012): 125–35.

Spelman, Margaret Boyle, and Frances Thomson-Salo, eds. *The Winnicott Tradition: Lines of Development (Evolution of Theory and Practice over the Decades).* London: Karnac Books, 2015.

Spencer, Ben. "Mobile Users Can't Leave Their Phone Alone for Six Minutes and Check It Up to 150 Times a Day." *Daily Mail*, February 10, 2013.

Stadter, Michael. "The Influence of Social Media and Communications Technology on Self and Relationships." In *Psychoanalysis Online: Mental Health, Teletherapy and Training*, edited by Jill Savege Scharff, 3–14. London: Karnac Books, 2013.

Steiner-Adair, Catherine, and Teresa Barker. *The Big Disconnect: Protecting Childhood and Family Relationships in the Digital Age*. New York: HarperCollins, 2013.

Suttie, Ian D. *The Origins of Love and Hate*. London: Free Association Books, 1988.

Taussig, Michael T. *Mimesis and Alterity: A Particular History of the Senses*. New York: Routledge, 1993.

Thompson, Clive. *Smarter Than You Think: How Technology Is Changing Our Minds for the Better*. New York: Penguin, 2013.

Turkle, Sherry. *Alone Together: Why We Expect More from Technology and Less from Each Other*. New York: Basic Books, 2011.

— — —. *Reclaiming Conversation: The Power of Talk in a Digital Age*. London: Penguin, 2015.

Tutu, Desmond. *No Future without Forgiveness*. New York: Doubleday, 1999.

Ulanov, Ann Belford. *Finding Space: Winnicott, God, and Psychic Reality*. Louisville, Ky.: Westminster John Knox, 2001.

Vodanovich, Stephen J., Steven J. Kass, Frank Andrasik, Wolf-Dieter Gerber, Uwe Niederberger, and Cassie Breaux. "Culture and Gender Differences in Boredom Proneness." *North American Journal of Psychology* 13, no. 2 (2011): 221–30.

Weinberg, Haim. *The Paradox of Internet Groups: Alone in the Presence of Virtual Others*. London: Karnac Books, 2014.

Wilcox, Sherrie L., Sarah Redmond, and Teaniese L. Davis. "Genital Image, Sexual Anxiety, and Erectile Dysfunction among Young Male Military Personnel." *Journal of Sexual Medicine* 12, no. 6 (2015): 1389–97.

Winnicott, Clare, Ray Shepherd, and Madeleine Davis, eds. *Psycho-Analytic Explorations*. Cambridge, Mass.: Harvard University Press, 1994.

Winnicott, D. W. "Appetite and Emotional Disorder (1936)." In Winnicott, *Through Paediatrics to Psycho-Analysis: Collected Papers*.

— — —. "Birth Memories, Birth Trauma, and Anxiety." In Winnicott, *Through Paediatrics to Psycho-Analysis: Collected Papers*, 174–93.

— — —. "The Capacity to Be Alone." In Winnicott, *Maturational Processes and the Facilitating Environment*, 29–36.

— — —. *The Child, the Family, and the Outside World*. New York: Addison-Wesley, 1987.

— — —. "The Concept of a Healthy Individual." In Winnicott, *Home Is Where We Start From*, 21–38.

— — —. "The Concept of False Self." In Winnicott, *Home Is Where We Start From*, 65–71.

— — —. "Creativity and Its Origins." In Winnicott, *Playing and Reality*, 65–85.

— — —. "The Development of the Capacity for Concern." In Winnicott, *Maturational Processes and the Facilitating Environment*, 73–82.

— — —. "Ego Distortion in Terms of True Self and False Self." In Winnicott, *Maturational Processes and the Facilitating Environment*, 140–52.

— — —. *The Family and Individual Development*. London: Tavistock Publications, 1995.

— — —. "The Fear of Breakdown." In C. Winnicott, Shepherd, and Davis, *Psycho-Analytic Explorations*, 87–95.

— — —. *Home Is Where We Start From: Essays by a Psychoanalyst*. Edited by Clare Winnicott, Ray Shepherd and Madeleine Davis. New York: Norton, 1986.

— — —. *Human Nature*. New York: Schocken Books, 1988.

— — —. *The Maturational Processes and the Facilitating Environment: Studies in the Theory of Emotional Development*. Madison, Conn.: International Universities Press, 1994.

— — —. "Metapsychological and Clinical Aspects of Regression within the Psycho-Analytical Set-Up." In Winnicott, *Through Paediatrics to Psycho-Analysis*, 278–94.

— — —. "Mind in Relation to Psyche-Soma." In Winnicott, *Through Paediatrics to Psycho-Analysis: Collected Papers*, 243–54.

— — —. "Mirror-role of Other and Family in Child Development." In Winnicott, *Playing and Reality*, 111–18.

— — —. "Morals and Education." In Winnicott, *Maturational Processes and the Facilitating Environment*, 93–105.

— — —. "Notes on Play." In C. Winnicott, Shepherd, and Davis, *Psycho-Analytic Explorations*, 59–63.

— — —. "The Observation of Children in a Set Situation (1941)." In Winnicott, *Through Paediatrics to Psycho-Analysiss*, 52–69.

— — —. "Playing: A Theoretical Statement." In Winnicott, *Playing and Reality*, 36–52.

— — —. *Playing and Reality*. London: Tavistock, 1993.

— — —. "Primary Maternal Preoccupation." In Winnicott, *Through Paediatrics to Psycho-Analysis*, 300–306.

— — —. "Primitive Emotional Development." In Winnicott, *Through Paediatrics to Psycho-Analysis*, 145–56.

— — —. "Psycho-Somatic Illness in Its Positive and Negative Aspects." In C. Winnicott, Shepherd, and Davis, *Psycho-Analytic Explorations*, 103–14.

— — —. "Reparation in Respect of Mother's Organized Defence against Depression." In Winnicott, *Through Paediatrics to Psycho-Analysis*, 91–96.

— — —. "The Squiggle Game." In C. Winnicott, Shepherd, and Davis, *Psycho-Analytic Explorations*, 299–317.

— — —. "String: A Technique in Communication." In Winnicott, *Maturational Processes and the Facilitating Environment*, 152–57.

— — —. *Through Paediatrics to Psycho-Analysis: Collected Papers*. New York: Brunner/Mazel, 1992.

— — —. "Transitional Objects and Transitional Phenomena." In Winnicott, *Playing and Reality*, 1–25. Reprinted in Winnicott, *Through Paediatrics to Psycho-Analysis: Collected Papers*, 229–42. New York: Brunner/Mazel, 1992.

— — —. "The Use of an Object and Relating through Identifications." In C. Winnicott, Shepherd, and Davis, *Psycho-Analytic Explorations*, 218–27.

— — —. "What Do You Mean by a Normal Child?" In Winnicott, *The Child, the Family, and the Outside World*, 124–30.

— — —. "Why Children Play." In Winnicott, *The Child, the Family, and the Outside World*, 143–46.

— — —. *Winnicott on the Child*. Cambridge, Mass.: Perseus, 2002.

Winnicott, D. W., Clare Winnicott, Ray Shepherd, and Madeleine Davis. *Babies and Their Mothers*. Reading, Mass.: Addison-Wesley, 1987.

— — —. "Communication between Infant and Mother, Mother and Infant, Compared and Contrasted." In Winnicott et al., *Babies and Their Mothers*, 89–103.

———. *Deprivation and Delinquency*. Edited by Clare Winnicott, Ray Shepard, and Madeleine Davis. London: Tavistock Publications, 1997.

Woods, John. "Seeing and Being Seen: The Psychodynamics of Pornography through the Lens of Winnicott's Thought." In Spelman and Thomson-Salo, *Winnicott Tradition*, 163–74.

Yarom, Nitza. *Psychic Threats and Somatic Shelters: Attuning to the Body in Contemporary Psychoanalytic Dialogue*. New York: Routledge, 2015.

INDEX